BEHOLD THE
LAMB

A TREATISE ON
THE CHARACTER
OF
GOD

INTENDED TO FACILITATE A BETTER UNDERSTANDING OF THE DIVINE NATURE, AND OF THE SCRIPTURES IN GENERAL

BY

PATRICK IRVING

"AND THIS IS LIFE ETERNAL, THAT THEY MIGHT KNOW THEE THE ONLY TRUE GOD, AND JESUS CHRIST, WHOM THOU HAST SENT." JOHN 17:3

Please note that the author has highlighted sections of certain Bible verses with bold to emphasize a specific point gathered from those texts. In other cases, brackets have been used to indicate the author's own additions to various quotations, excluding times when the Amplified Bible (AMPC) is referenced.

Unless otherwise identified, scripture quotations are taken from the King James Version (KJV).

This book and all other publications are available for free at maranathamedia.com. To order additional copies, please contact us at fatheroflovefellowship@gmail.com.

Library of Congress Control Number: 2024904928

ISBN: 979-8-218-38544-6

Published in Lexington, Kentucky

Edited by Danutasn Brown

This book is dedicated to my loving wife,

Elizabeth-Anne

"God is Love. There is, indeed, no greater knowledge, no greater source of healing than what is contained in these three words. Yet Timothy tells us that no one has ever seen God and no one can ever see Him (I Timothy 6:16). If this is true, how can we humans ever truly know and trust God?

"The boundless Creator of the universe, infinite in power and knowledge, condescended into the womb of one of his own creatures, lived the life of a servant, and died the death of a criminal. But how is this love, you may ask? God became a human being, so that we could see and understand His character, trust His Person, and learn to love and appreciate His ways and eventually be healed from all our brokenness through the power of His unspeakable love... Two thousand years after the life and death of Jesus, far too many are still afraid of God, shackled with the belief that God needs to be appeased and that He requires blood in order to forgive us. The pagan belief that Jesus died to create love for us in the heart of the Father and to shield us from His wrath, is beautifully replaced by the Good News that Jesus came to reveal the Father's heart of love, so that the Father might hold us tightly in His arms of love.

"No truth is as paramount in significance as the truth about the character of God Almighty. This is the truth that has the power to set free imprisoned hearts and minds to a living faith that God is indeed Love personified."

(George Fifield, God is Love, Preface)

BEHOLD THE LAMB

A TREATISE ON THE CHARACTER OF GOD

CONTENTS

Acknowledgement

The ideas presented herein are not my own but have been revealed to me by prayerful study and fellowship with other brothers and sisters in Christ. I hope this special truth touches your heart as it has mine. Blessed be our God of love and His Son who "hath declared Him." (John 1:18)

"Unless men shall know God as Christ has revealed him, they will never form a character after the divine similitude, and will therefore never see God."

(Ellen G. White, *Review and Herald,* March 9, 1897)

All quotes from scripture are supplied from the KJV unless otherwise noted.

Introduction

What does it mean to *know* God? The idea of "knowing," in the context of the Ancient Hebrews, denotes a more personal understanding—it carries with it a deep relational aspect that our modern definition of the term cannot bestow. We may say that we "know" someone, but simply mean we only "know" of his or her existence. However, in Hebrew thought, one can only say they "know" someone if they have a deeply personal and intimate relationship with them. The Hebrew term, יָדַע (yāḏa‘), "to know" (Strong's H3045), appears nearly 950 times in the Old Testament. In the context of Genesis 4:1, the term is used to denote a sexual intimacy between Adam and Eve. The very same Hebrew term is also used in Exodus 33:17 by God when He says to Moses: "I know thee by name," expressing how close they are, as the Lord speaks to Moses face to face "as a man speaketh unto his friend." (Exodus 33:11). Thus, biblically, to know God is not to know about Him in a mere abstract or impersonal manner, but rather to know Him *intimately*. Certainly, we may be assured that God knows us:

> "But even the very hairs of your head are all numbered..." (Luke 12:7)

But sadly, many of us do not know God. Many today profess love and obedience to God merely out of fear of punishment or loss—as a servant would, rather than a friend. But God knows that true love and obedience can never come by way of fear.

> "There is no fear in love; but **perfect love casteth out fear...**" (I John 4:18)

Love can only stem from love, and true love by a correct understanding, and a correct understanding by intimacy. But many fear coming close to God and, therefore, do not correctly understand Him. Many view Him in the wrong light; many misconstrue His true intentions; many pervert His true character.

Familiarity with our heavenly Father is evaded and substituted for erroneous assumptions of who He is and how He operates. Trust is placed in one's own understanding of God rather than the understanding that Christ came to bestow. This misplaced trust is cherished and defended to the uttermost—even to the point of rejecting God as He truly is. Fear and distrust are mingled together by confusion, and folly is surely the result. To be afraid of God is to misunderstand—even to deny—that which He paid such a price to reveal.

He also knows, as He sought to explain to us at such a cost, that when individuals obey Him out of fear, it ultimately leads to their own rebelliousness against Him. Rebelliousness, being the very essence of sin, poses a significant obstacle in God's divine plan. Hence, God, in His benevolence, sent His Son to address and eradicate sin, as Romans chapter 8 aptly reminds us. However, in order to effectively mitigate rebelliousness and build trust, it becomes necessary for Him to eliminate the root cause for His children's rebellion—fear. The pervasive power of fear has unfortunately steered multitudes away from God and has even instigated defiance in the hearts of those who ardently seek to comply with His commands but do not know Him well. Even genuine Christians lack a profound understanding of His true nature as it is revealed in Christ. The result is, as Paul warned, that they practice "a form of godliness," but deny "the power thereof..." (2 Timothy 3:5). This, or they utterly reject God; they claim, as did Lucifer, that He is a tyrant to be disregarded—a primeval taskmaster to be put away. All of these difficulties arise simply by how one views God's character.

Fundamentally, God offered up His own life, as a testament, to quell any fears His children may harbor toward Him.

> "...God was in Christ, **reconciling the world unto himself...**" (2 Corinthians 5:19)

The prevailing message unveiled through this self-sacrificial act is one that unequivocally declares there exists no justification for trepidation in our relationship with Him. Undoubtedly, a Being who suffers such extraordinary measures to convey that, despite His omnipotence, there remains no rationale for us to fear Him, is profoundly deserving of our love, veneration, devotion, receptiveness, and reliance upon Him.

If God really were the type of ruler that His enemies make Him out to be—arbitrary, vengeful, exacting, and severe—then consequently there would exist no freedom under such a government, and any confession of love or reverence on our part would be tarnished and made vain through our own fear and distrust of Him; and how could God be satisfied with expressions of love from children who are afraid? But no wonder so many millions have turned away from God when you consider Satan's perversion of the truth in this matter. Satan has placed God in such a light that mankind sees Him in the same way our adversary does—as One that is without love, mercy, or forgiveness; as One that finds pleasure in executing arbitrary punishments; as One to be feared rather than relied upon. But the pen of inspiration declares otherwise:

"...God is love." (I John 4:8)

As Adventist minister George Fifield once said, love stands as the central attribute of God, the wellspring from which all other attributes emanate. "God is love," according to John (1 John 4:8), and in this statement are contained depths of philosophy. Yet many are jaded about love, its importance profaned by how loosely the world talks about it. But beyond the unspeakable joy agape-love brings, the entire potency of Christ's mission to transform the soul and instill in us the works of righteousness depends upon it, for the foundation of righteousness is love itself. And the entirety of God's righteousness, His character of love, finds its embodiment in the Ten Commandments, as David affirms, "The law of the Lord is perfect," (Psalm 19:7) and "all thy commandments are righteousness" (Psalm 119:172). Moreover, God says, "Hearken unto me, ye that know righteousness, the people in whose heart is my law" (Isaiah 51:7).

Thus, it is seen that to have the righteousness of God in the heart is simply to have the law of God written there. Jesus succinctly sums up all the law, and consequently the whole moral duty of man, in the two principles of love to God and love to man (Matthew 22:37-40). John reduces these principles to the one principle of love to God, by showing that if we love God, the Father, we will love man, His child, our brother (1 John 4:20). So Paul encapsulates the whole duty of man and the entirety of God's righteousness in a single statement: "love is the fulfilling of the law" (Romans 13:10), a sentiment John corroborates by asserting, "whoso keepeth his word, in him verily is the love of God perfected" (1 John 2:5). Thus, love dwelling in the heart of man is the fulfilling of all righteousness, and hatred dwelling there is the fulfilling of all iniquity, and the entire sum of the great controversy between Christ and Satan is simply the conflict of these two principles in the hearts of God's creatures.

But what is to change our hearts, that are so saturated with hatred, into hearts brimming solely with love? What is man's hope, that he may foster love for God and for his fellow man, being that love cannot originate from within himself but only hate? What is the source of this selfless, unbiased love? John provides the answer, stating, "love is of God; and every one that loveth is born of God, and knoweth God" and "We love him, because he first loved us" (1 John 4:7,19). Ah, that is it; like begets like—and this principle underscores the mighty, constant, and all-encompassing love of God that, by upholding, guiding, and reconciling us to Himself, begets a similar love in our own hearts. This love leads us to extend the very same to all His creatures, no matter their state or position in life. And this is righteousness, the righteousness of God, and nothing else is righteousness.

Suppose it were possible for a man to do right simply that he might gain heaven. Such a desire, persistently and thoughtlessly nurtured, when so many others are going down to death, would itself be selfishness and sin. Jesus Christ relinquished heaven, accounting it not a thing to be held fast when man was lost. Moses, too, demonstrated a similar sentiment towards those which he loved so dearly (Exodus 32:32). Now consider it were possible that one should do right merely for fear of hell. That at best would be a species of cowardice, determining not to go where it is believed so many others are going. All this would be but an external righteousness; a making "clean the outside of the cup and the platter" but the inward part would remain "full of ravening and wickedness" (Luke 11:39). This external righteousness would lack the genuine principle of righteousness, which is love itself, rendering it self-righteousness, which is as filthy rags in God's sight.

If, then, the love of God constitutes the very substance of all righteousness, the pertinent question becomes not merely *how do we love Him?*—but rather, *why*, when He is the epitome of all loveliness, *do we love Him so sparingly*? Why have we come to think that the very word "love," when applied to God, means a different thing from that which we feel toward a dear friend? Perhaps, when applied to Him, our dull senses misconstrue it as a mixture of awe and reverence more nearly approaching to fear and terror than to love. But how could this be? Could it be that we have adopted false and pagan notions of God?—failing to recognize that God *truly is* love? Many today perceive God as a Being who delights in the punishment of His children, thereby casting Him not as a figure of love, but of fear and torment. Owing to the misinterpretation of scripture, it is widely maintained that our God requires the shedding of blood in order to be appeased; that He delights in the spectacle of sacrifice, effectively making Him the source of death instead of life. This is the pagan conception of God.

The Christian conception of God should be markedly distinct from this notion. The God of the Bible, correctly understood, upholds the attributes of selfless love and nonviolence, for He Himself is love and, therefore, does no harm to others (Romans 13:10). When this realization dawns, and His true character of love is rightly discerned, then "perfect love" will cast "out fear: because fear hath torment" and he "that feareth is not made perfect in love" (1 John 4:18).

Many at the current moment, however, are unable to adequately comprehend God's boundless love. The people of ancient Israel had difficulty comprehending its depth; they could not extend God's love to the Gentiles, nor could they see how the law was meant to be applied. This precise dilemma is one of the reasons why Christ was sent to minister unto men. Yet have we as a Church truly learned what Jesus was trying to teach us? If we had, then the light would have extended all over the world and Jesus would have come back by now. Contemplating this question prompts us to consider the depth of our understanding regarding Jesus' message and its implication for humanity. What was He attempting to reveal to us? Better yet—*Who* was He attempting to reveal to us? The Bible tells us that "neither knoweth any man the Father, save the Son, and he to whomsoever the Son will *reveal* him." (Matthew 11:27, emphasis added). Ah, so Christ came to reveal to us the Father. And yet, many today use the spectacle of mystery in order to avoid any further discussion on topics regarding God's character. But what is the point of revelation, and of the Bible itself, if we are ultimately unable to come to a right knowledge of the God we worship?

There must be more for us to grasp. Having a better understanding of Christ's purpose for being sent to this earth will enable us to more clearly comprehend the height of the Father's loving character, that we may be filled with all the fullness of God. Yes, to know the love of God is to be filled with His fullness, for God *is* love. All goodness, all righteousness, is love, and love is born of love; thus, the crux of the matter lies in understanding that God is love, and this is the understanding which Christ came to impart. To know this is life eternal (John 17:3).

Dear reader, are you skeptical about there being a problem in our theological understanding? Why else is love so often twisted and broken, and the worship of God so full of rancor and strife? Why then are we, the body of Christ, not able to experience victory over sin? The theology of the day is unable to deal with these questions satisfactorily. So, if there is a problem, how does one reconcile this matter? How may we attempt to sort out the confusion? Who is God, and what is He truly like? How can we be sure?

One thing is certain—God is *not* like us. We so easily misunderstand each other, misinterpret what others want from us, twist obvious truths to satisfy our lusts, and are selfish in our goals and motivations. All these have contributed to the one true religion of mankind being broken up into innumerable jarring creeds. The custom of mankind has been, for thousands of years, to project our own nature onto the God of the Bible—to interpret His ways based upon our own ways. But He proclaims:

> **"For my thoughts are not your thoughts, neither are your ways my ways, saith the Lord.** For as the heavens are higher than the earth, so are my ways higher than your ways, and my thoughts than your thoughts." (Isaiah 55:8-9)

> "And [we] changed the glory of the uncorruptible God **into an image made like to corruptible man...**" (Romans 1:23)

> "...thou thoughtest that I was altogether **such an one as thyself...**" (Psalm 50:21)

Many supplant the character of God with their own ideas of justice, love, and mercy. We imagine harsh and vengeful purposes behind His actions, misread the Bible, and thrust our own evil tendencies onto Jehovah.

> "Because of the imperfections of human understanding of language, or the perversity of the human mind, ingenious in evading truth, **many read and understand the Bible to please themselves...**" (Ellen G. White, *Selected Messages*, vol. I, pg. 19)

While this causes God anguish of spirit, He permits us to do this—He allows us to exercise our free will. Our heavenly Father will not interfere with our lives if we do not allow Him to do so; He is not a God of force, but a God of love. Because He accommodates man in order to raise him up, we often blame Him for evil circumstances. However, upon closer examination, the negative consequences that result from sin are never the fault of God; rather, they arise from our own wayward choices and decisions. By rejecting His grace, we place ourselves outside of His hand of protection where "the devil, as a roaring lion, walketh about, seeking whom he may devour..." (1 Peter 5:8). Many today have forgotten this, and, due to the severe depictions of God in the Old Testament and confusion regarding how to understand Biblical language, they envision Him as a Father who seeks pleasure in the destruction of His children rather than in their deliverance. They forget that it is Satan who is the destroyer, not God.

With this in mind, how may we reconcile the portrayals of God in the Old Testament? If God *is* love, as John says, then why are there numerous instances where it seems that He acts contrary to this description? Can God contradict Himself? If every sin must meet its punishment, then how can God extend mercy and still remain just? Is the God of the Old Testament somehow different from the God of the New Testament? These are the questions that led the author to begin a study on the subject of God's character, and this little book is the result. The author is very sensible of its imperfections and limitations. Of the many themes touched, not one is treated exhaustively. Nonetheless, these piercing questions to which we seek answers may all be harmonized by a single truth: the life of Jesus Christ our Lord.

Christ's mission to thc world was to reveal the true character of the Father:

> "No man hath seen God at any time; **the only begotten Son, which is in the bosom of the Father, he hath declared him.**" (John 1:18)

In doing so, Jesus Christ painted a picture of God that challenged the traditional beliefs and customs of the time. Many rejected the idea—and still do—that Christ was the full revelation of the Father. But inspiration declares that He "is the image of the invisible God," and "the brightness of his glory… the express image of his person," (Colossians 1:5; Hebrews 1:3). When Philip asked Him to show them the Father, Jesus said:

> "…Have I been so long time with you, and yet hast thou not known me, Philip? **he that hath seen me hath seen the Father;** and how sayest thou then, Shew us the Father?" (John 14:8)

Christ came to reveal to us *exactly* what the Father is like. Therefore, every act of the Father must be reconciled with the character that Jesus manifested. We must view everything in scripture through the light that Jesus imparted. In doing so, we may come to understand the Father's true disposition.

> "But their minds were blinded: **for until this day remaineth the same vail untaken away in the reading of the old testament; which vail is done away in Christ.**" (2 Corinthians 3:14)

This means that Jesus is the key to understanding the Old Testament passages about God. Through Him, where once we were blinded, we may see; where once we misunderstood, we may understand. Oh, how Satan's deceptions depart as we behold God revealed in Jesus Christ! If we trust that Jesus is the full revelation of the Father, then when we are confronted with a contrary image of the Father's character to that which Jesus Himself displayed, we should suppose that something else is really going on. The adversary has attempted to deceive us in this matter and, for the most part, has been successful in replacing the character of God in the minds of men with his own perception, even going so far as to undermine the true work that Christ came to do—making mankind believe that Christ's mission was for an altogether different purpose.

> "...**the god of this world hath blinded the minds of them which believe not, lest the light of the glorious gospel of Christ, who is the image of God, should shine unto them...** For God, who commanded the light to shine out of darkness, hath shined in our hearts, to give **the light of the knowledge of the glory of God in the face of Jesus Christ.**" (2 Corinthians 4:4,6)

Dear reader, presented herein are subjects of profound importance. In the pages that follow, your perception of God may be challenged. Your preconceptions as to Christ's true mission may be frustrated. However, it is my prayer that seeds are planted and hearts are softened. Amazing peace and assurance has come into the author's life through this investigation, and would that it would be so for the reader also.

Behold the Lamb is the result of a personal study into the all-important subject of God's character. The author is thankful for the prayers offered and counsel given by many others who have helped in this task. As is the case with most books, however, not everyone will agree with all the conclusions drawn. Therefore, "let every man be fully persuaded in his own mind" (Romans 4:15). Having said this, the author does not claim infallibility. This is a study in progress, and there is much more that could be said regarding the character of God. While many of the quotes I share are from fellow brothers and sisters in Christ, I do not necessarily endorse all of their personal beliefs and teachings. I have provided them merely to show that the question of God's character was recognized among certain pioneers of our faith, as well as to highlight the absurdity that lies in the endorsement of God as a vindictive, wrathful, impatient executioner of the harshest of punishments. Many authors' words I have paraphrased, while others are directly supplied. As a well-known sophist once stated:

"To borrow from one author is plagiarism; to borrow from many, is research."

I do not count it robbery to share with you, dear reader, the provoking thoughts of others. Their words and writings have inspired me in this work. In sampling from their texts, I do not seek my own glory—as if the goal of this publication were to impress men with the eloquent words of other men. No. In many of these instances, I simply find that I can do a thought no justice, and so I lean upon the discourse of others to help me along. Nevertheless, I pray that my intentions to glorify Christ, and Christ alone, are clearly seen.

Even so, come, Lord Jesus. Amen.

"Just before us is the closing struggle of the great controversy when, with 'all power and signs and lying wonders, and with all deceivableness of unrighteousness,' **Satan is to work to misrepresent the character of God,** that he may 'seduce, if it were possible, even the elect.' If there was ever a people in need of constantly increasing light from heaven, it is the people that, in this time of peril, **God has called to be the depositaries of His holy law and to vindicate His character before the world.**" (Ellen G. White, *Testimonies for the Church,* vol. 5, pg. 746)

Section 1

God's Character on Trial

Chapter 1

Discerning the Divine Nature: An Analysis of God's True Character According to Inspiration

*"**Beloved, let us love one another: for love is of God;** and every one that loveth is born of God, and knoweth God. He that loveth not knoweth not God; **for God is love.**" (I John 4:7-8)*

Is it possible to love someone without ever knowing them? Can we garner feelings of familiarity or friendship with people whom we've only ever made efforts to avoid? In order to love someone, it follows that we must first come to know them. More importantly, we must know them properly—as they truly are. In misunderstanding a person, we might inadvertently judge them based upon false apprehensions and thereby miss the opportunity to truly connect with them. It is the same with God. Without having a correct understanding of who the Father is, we run the risk of misinterpreting His words; His actions; His intentions toward us; everything about Him!

How can we come to truly love God and have a relationship with Him if we misunderstand who He is? It cannot be done. Our Father sought to reconcile this, and, in His goodwill toward us, He sent His only begotten Son to witness to this fallen world what He was *actually like*. When we look to Christ, we may readily behold the Father. Christ is "the brightness of his [the Father's] glory, and the express image of his person…" (Hebrews 1:3). What exactly does it mean to be the brightness of the Father's glory? Let's allow the Bible to interpret itself in this matter. In Exodus 33:18, Moses asks God to show him His glory. In response to Moses's appeal, scripture tells us that:

"…the Lord descended in the cloud, and stood with him there, **and proclaimed the name of the Lord.** And the Lord passed by

> before him, and proclaimed, **'The Lord, The Lord God, merciful and gracious, longsuffering, and abundant in goodness and truth, Keeping mercy for thousands, forgiving iniquity and transgression and sin...'**" (Exodus 34:5-7)

Notice what's happening here. It is shown that the glory of God is not a mere external glory of rainbows and radiant brightness upon which no eye can look. It is more than this. The Father reveals His glory to Moses by proclaiming His own character! It necessarily follows that the glory of God *is* His character. To be the brightness of His glory, then, must mean to be the visible manifestation of the divine character. We can only discern the sun because of its rays. In the same sense, we can only come to truly understand the Father by the nature of His Son.

> "For God, who commanded the light to shine out of darkness, hath shined in our hearts, **to give the light of the knowledge of the glory of God in the face of Jesus Christ.**" (2 Corinthians 4:6)

We receive the knowledge of the glory—or character—of the Father "in the face of Jesus Christ." (2 Corinthians 4:6). In the life and ministry of Jesus we find the glory of God defined. And yet, we choose to forget the life which Jesus lived, and the character He demonstrated, when contemplating our Father in Heaven and His actions in other eras of human history. Thus, many ascribe a capricious and fickle character to God—perceiving that He is bitter in the Old Testament and endearing in the New. They reason within themselves that God must've had a change of heart and that the Father's nature is different than that of the Son's. God's very word tells us otherwise:

> "For I am the LORD, **I change not...**" (Malachi 3:6)

> "Every good gift and every perfect gift is from above, and cometh down from the Father of lights, **with whom is no variableness, neither shadow of turning.**" (James 1:17)

God's ways *never* change—He is consistent through and through! And regarding His Son:

> "Jesus Christ **the same yesterday, and to day, and for ever.**" (Hebrews 13:8)

If God is love and His ways never change, then the first step in knowing God must be to understand what *kind* of love God is. Inspiration gives us the characteristics of this love:

> "Love is **patient and kind;** love **does not envy or boast;** it is **not arrogant or rude. It does not insist on its own way;** it is **not irritable or resentful...**" (I Corinthians 13:4, *ESV*)

The Greek word for "love" supplied in this passage is ἀγάπη (agapē), (Strong's G0026). This kind of love is defined as unconditional, sacrificial love. This is the kind of love expressed by someone willing to do anything for another—including sacrificing themselves without expecting anything in return. This is the love that God has for each of us. According to Paul, this form of love is patient and kind; it does not impose itself upon others; it's never irritated, nor does it carry grievances. There can be no harsh inclinations cherished by this kind of love, for it cannot be contaminated by evil.

> "For I know the thoughts that I think toward you, saith the LORD, **thoughts of peace, and not of evil...**" (Jeremiah 29:11)

God's love for His children is greater than ever can be imagined by man. It is as infinite as it is unrestricted—all we must do is accept it as a free gift. Once we truly understand this matter, we may begin to see God in His proper context. Confusion and misapprehension will dissipate. We will realize that He never rejects or condemns us—rather, *we* reject Him. The realization of such a circumstance leads the sinner to repentance and reconciliation (Romans 2:4). Love and trust may then begin to be nourished.

> "We love him, **because he first loved us.**" (I John 4:19)

And if these passages weren't enough to cast off all doubt in the matter, then such a compilation of plain and inspired statements as the following should bring hope and joy to any contrite soul…

The Psalmist tells us:

> "But thou, O Lord, art a God **full of compassion, and gracious, longsuffering, and plenteous in mercy and truth.**" (Psalm 86:15)

The comforting words of John declare:

> "Behold, **what manner of love** the Father hath bestowed upon us, **that we should be called the sons of God…**" (I John 3:1)

We are of more value to Him than anything He has made:

> "Are not five sparrows sold for two farthings, and not one of them is forgotten before God? But even the very hairs of your head are all numbered. **Fear not therefore: ye are of more value than many sparrows.**" (Luke 12:6-7)

His love for us is everlasting:

> "The LORD hath appeared of old unto me, saying, Yea, **I have loved thee with an everlasting love: therefore with lovingkindness have I drawn thee.**" (Jeremiah 31:3)

The Lord our God delights in doing good:

> "**But let him that glorieth glory in this, that he understandeth and knoweth me, that I am the LORD which exercise lovingkindness, judgment, and righteousness, in the earth:** for in these things I delight, saith the LORD." (Jeremiah 9:24)

Our Father delights in mercy and forgiveness:

> "Let the wicked forsake his way, and the unrighteous man his thoughts: and let him return unto the LORD, and **he will have mercy upon him;** and to our God, for **he will abundantly pardon.**" (Isaiah 55:7)

The same qualities of character that He aims to bestow upon us are also inherent within Himself. Paul tells us what these characteristics are:

> "But the fruit of the Spirit is **love, joy, peace, longsuffering, gentleness, goodness, faith, Meekness, temperance...**" (Galatians 5:22-23)

The word of God is clear—nothing can separate us from His love. Dear reader, will you take Him at His word?

> "For I am persuaded, that neither death, nor life, nor angels, nor principalities, nor powers, nor things present, nor things to come, Nor height, nor depth, nor any other creature, **shall be able to separate us from the love of God, which is in Christ Jesus our Lord.**" (Romans 8:38-39)

Chapter 2

Divine Distortion: God's Character Misunderstood

*"**By misrepresenting the attributes of God, Satan leads men to conceive of Him in a false character...** Though in a different form, idolatry exists in the Christian world today as verily as it existed among ancient Israel in the days of Elijah. The god of many professedly wise men, of philosophers, poets, politicians, journalists,—the god of polished fashionable circles, of many colleges and universities, even of some theological institutions,—is little better than Baal, the sun-god of Phenicia." (Ellen G. White, The Great Controversy, pg. 583)*

*"It is the darkness of misapprehension of God that is enshrouding the world. **Men are losing their knowledge of His character. It has been misunderstood and misinterpreted.** At this time a message from God is to be proclaimed, a message illuminating in its influence and saving in its power. **His character is to be made known.** Into the darkness of the world is to be shed the light of His glory, the light of His goodness, mercy, and truth." (Ellen G. White, Christ's Object Lessons, pg. 415)*

The character of God has been severely distorted among His children. People of this world believe lies about the Creator; simple hallucinations that have obtained the adhesion of intelligence and become transitory attacks of madness. Because of fear and distrust, humanity casts off His yoke in an inebriated act of spurious liberation. They have been beguiled by the fatal music and have entered into a dance with death. The Lord's Spirit speaks to them, they no more listen; His Spirit warns them, they no longer understand. They slumber in a living grave unawares, believing themselves to be "increased with goods," having "need of nothing;" not knowing that they are "wretched, and miserable, and poor, and blind, and naked..." (Revelation 3:17)—all the while, God is waiting for them with outstretched arms yearning to share with them His blessings.

Even we Christians have a misunderstanding and a distrust of our God—not that we've become irreligious, but that we've allowed ourselves to be deceived by our adversary; and even many who worship, worship a false image of God. The hazards that follow can only be ruinous and depraved, as we tend to become more and more like the one we worship and admire.

> "**Thousands have a false conception of God and his attributes. They are as verily serving a false god as were the servants of Baal. Are we worshiping the true God as he is revealed in his word, in Christ,** in nature, or are we adoring some philosophical idol enshrined in his place? God is a God of truth. Justice and mercy are the attributes of his throne. He is a God of love, of pity, and tender compassion. **Thus he is represented in his Son, our Saviour.** He is a God of patience and long-suffering. **If such is the being whom we adore, and to whose character we are seeking to assimilate, we are worshiping the true God.**" (Ellen G. White, *Signs of the Times*, Feb. 8, 1883)

How is it that we've become so deceived? By transgression, mankind set themselves in stubborn unbelief and rebellion against God's commandments. By professing themselves to be too wise to walk in the Lord's appointed way, they did what men always do when they write out their creed,—they said in their hearts, "He is no higher than our present knowledge of Him;" and so they became fools by changing the glory of the incorruptible God into an image made first like to corruptible man, then to birds, and four-footed beasts, and creeping things, down, down, to that old serpent himself, which is the devil and Satan. Thus, Satan was put in the place of God; and men, by worshipping, instead of being led upward to unity with Him, were led downward into all deformity and strife, hateful and hating one another, till every man's hand was against his neighbor, and the imagination of the thoughts of men's hearts was evil and only evil continually. This was the downward way that led to misery and woe. Fear set in and death became a treasure to be cherished; a spectacle to behold—light and life were made of no value; darkness became familiar. This is the enmity we inherited from Adam. Ever since the fall, humanity's seed has been corrupted, and how may light be described to men born blind? How can God's radiance be discerned by the darkness that *is* man?

> "...God is light, and **in him is no darkness at all.**" (I John 1:5)

> "And the light shineth in darkness; and **the darkness comprehended it not.**" (John 1:5)

> "He was in the world, and the world was made by him, and **the world knew him not.**" (John 1:10)

Sin had brought misery and death, and with these things a misunderstanding of God's character. Man substituted the love of light—the knowledge of God—for the love of darkness.

> "And this is the condemnation, that light is come into the world, and **men loved darkness rather than light, because their deeds were evil.** For every one that doeth evil hateth the light, neither cometh to the light, lest his deeds should be reproved." (John 3:19-20)

The evil that resulted was misattributed to God's own doing. Man was blinded by his own enmity. God became the scapegoat for destruction instead of its true author—sin. The Almighty, in His wrath, was said to be responsible for humanity's fallen state; He was blamed for the circumstances we now find ourselves in. We began to fear our Creator, thinking it was *Him* who needed to be appeased in order to be reconciled to *us*. Our gentle and loving Father became, in the minds of men, the source of disease, decay, and discomfort.

> "'Blame God' is the devil's subterfuge: and **how many thousands of Christians today attribute to God what Satan is doing.** If calamity comes to them, they say 'it is God's hand,' and they either passively yield or else they rebel, with the result that the heart is

heavy and the spirit dulled and oppressed." (Charles H. Usher, *Satan: A Defeated Foe*, pg. 53, published in 1964)

"Satan brings about the actual happenings of accidents, sickness, disease, and calamity, **then causes men to think that God brings these things to pass. Thus He [God] is blamed erroneously for the work of the devil** by millions, even so-called Christians who should know better." (Finis Dake, *Dake's Annotated Reference Bible*, pg. 522)

"**The false theology that God is, in some mysterious way, connected with the sending of sickness and pain and death, blotted out His true character as a God of love many centuries ago,** and this theology has become so imbedded in the system of the Church and her teachings that it requires a strongminded minister or priest to extricate himself from it and practice and teach the simple acts and words of Christ the great healer, who still heals." (Henry B. Wilson, *"Mr. Hickson's Healing Mission" in The Nazarene: Presenting the Message of Healing in Christ*, vol. 4-6, pg. 10, published in 1919)

This distorted theology has obscured the true God from the hearts of humanity. Our fallen state has so infected our minds as to make us believe that God is against us. Men have been led to believe that it is God who punishes the sinner and, therefore, in order to be free from the consequences of sin, men must break free from the hand of God. We regard God in the same way Lucifer did. We have clothed our heavenly Father in the very robes of our adversary.

"**Satan leads men to conceive of God in a false character,** as having attributes which he does not possess." (Ellen G. White, *Spirit of Prophecy*, vol. 4, pg. 399)

"From the beginning it has been Satan's studied plan to cause men to forget God, that he might secure them to himself. **Hence he has sought to misrepresent the character of God, to lead men to cherish a false conception of Him. The Creator has been presented to their minds as clothed with the attributes of the prince of evil himself,—as arbitrary, severe, and unforgiving,—**

that He might be feared, shunned, and even hated by men. Satan hoped to so confuse the minds of those whom he had deceived that they would put God out of their knowledge. Then he would obliterate the divine image in man and impress his own likeness upon the soul; he would imbue men with his own spirit and make them captives according to his will." (Ellen G. White, *Testimonies for the Church,* vol. 5, pg. 738)

"Freedom from sin, or at least from its consequences, is what men have been seeking ever since the fall. Sad to say, however, the great majority have sought it in the wrong way. **It was with a lie against the character of God, that Satan caused the first sin, and he has been vigorously engaged in trying to induce people to believe that lie ever since. So successful has he been, that the mass of mankind regard God as stern and unsympathetic, a being who regards man with a coldly critical eye, and who would much rather destroy than save.** In short, Satan has largely succeeded in putting himself in the place of God, in the minds of men. Thus it is that much of the worship of the heathen is, and always has been, devil-worship." (E. J. Waggoner, *The Present Truth,* vol. 9, September 21, 1893, pg. 387)

Many erroneously presume that God sends pestilence and pain upon the sinner because that is how He remains just—and in order for Him to do this, every sin *must* be severely penalized. It is said that if He were to remit the punishment of sin, He could not be a God of truth and justice. It is said to be the forensic duty of God to chasten the transgressor. He must, in His vengeance, "teach mankind a lesson." Many even use the holy scriptures to defend this devilish doctrine. After all, 2 Thessalonians seems to say that God is the source of strong delusions, which He *sends* to us that we might be damned:

"And for this cause **God shall send them strong delusion, that they should believe a lie:** That they all might be damned who believed not the truth, but had pleasure in unrighteousness." (2 Thessalonians 2:11-12)

In John chapter 12, it appears as if God is the One that blinds our eyes and hardens our hearts:

> "**He [God] hath blinded their eyes, and hardened their heart;** that they should not see with their eyes, nor understand with their heart, and be converted, and I should heal them." (John 12:40)

And Isaiah chapter 44 seems to confirm the notion that it is God's own hand that brings these adverse effects about, and that He even makes it so they can't realize to repent:

> "They have not known nor understood: **for he [God] hath shut their eyes, that they cannot see; and their hearts, that they cannot understand.**" (Isaiah 44:18)

What does one do with such statements? Upon first glance, it appears that God is responsible for these defective reactions in man. It appears to be a direct result of His intervention that we have believed lies, hardened our hearts, and shut our eyes against Him. If so, then what hope can we have against an omnipotent Being that seems to find delight in our downfall?

In order to reconcile these passages, the reader must understand the peculiar use of the Hebrew idiom. In this mode of writing, *the causative verbs of a certain passage may be rendered either as active or passive depending on the context*. Therefore, in every instance where God is said to be actively causing anguish and hardship on account of transgression, His actions are, by an ordinary Hebraism, only permissive in signification though active in sound. And even though the New Testament was written in Greek, its authors were Hebraic in lineage and would necessarily have been acclimated to this mode of writing.

> "In the language of scripture, natural consequences are sometimes spoken of as though they were pre-ordained and irrevocable decrees. **What happens solely through the permission of the Almighty, in the ordinary course of his Providence, is described as though it had taken place through some special and irresistible intervention of his hand. This is a mode of writing peculiar to the Hebrew idiom; an idiom which prevails everywhere throughout the New Testament, as well as the Old.** Thus, when the sacred writers represent God as 'blinding the eyes of men that they

> should not see, and hardening their hearts that they should not understand;' their meaning generally is that **he does not powerfully interfere to prevent those evils which are the natural fruits of our own folly, perverseness, and impenitence.**" (John Goodge Foyster, *Sermons*, pg. 90, published in 1826)

Why does God do this? Why does He *allow* certain instances to take place if He has the power to stop them? For one reason: free will. The Almighty must allow mankind to exercise their own free will. Love cannot be commanded. Therefore, to love Him or not must be a free choice; to obey or not must be ours to decide. If this were not the case, then our love could not be genuine—it would be tarnished by compulsion and vain automation; a strictly mechanical obedience could only appear lackluster. There is no merit in this kind of relationship—there is no love in a forceful arm. This is why God must allow humanity to seek their own desires; but this is not to say that He does not attempt to lead them to a correct knowledge of His divine will. It is only by a constant rejection of His Spirit that we must be left to ourselves—He must give us up to our own inclinations. Upon a closer examination of scripture, we may readily see this principle at work. In Romans chapter 1, we read the following:

> "Wherefore God also **gave them up** to uncleanness **through the lusts of their own hearts...**" (Romans 1:24)

Here we see that, *because of the lusts of their own hearts*, God had to give them up. It was the result of man's own sinful affections that led to His Spirit being withdrawn from them. This was the consequence of humanity's continual estrangement from God's will. They had rejected the Almighty's gentle reproofs and carried on after their own desires. In the very next verse, we read:

> "**Who changed the truth of God into a lie,** and worshipped and served the creature more than the Creator..." (Romans 1:25)

Indeed, it was man that changed the truth of God into a lie! God did not "send them strong delusion, that they should believe a lie..." (2 Thessalonians 2:11). Rather, *mankind did this themselves*—God needed only to *allow* this to take place. By humanity's persistent rejection of the truth, God had no other choice but to permit them to believe deceits and harden their hearts against Him. This was the inward desire of man, not God.

The ability to identify these instances is of the utmost importance when examining scripture if we are to interpret God's character in the proper context. If neglected, God's word becomes ambiguous and contradictory concerning the nature of the Almighty. We will thoroughly examine this principle further in a later section of this work. For now, the author believes that the current understanding of the matter is sufficient.

> "Only like can appreciate like. **Unless you accept in your own life the principle of self-sacrificing love, which is the principle of His character, you cannot know God. The heart that is deceived by Satan, looks upon God as a tyrannical, relentless being; the selfish characteristics of humanity, even of Satan himself, are attributed to the loving Creator.** 'Thou thoughtest,' He says, 'that I was altogether such an one as thyself.' Psalm 50:21. **His providences are interpreted as the expression of an arbitrary, vindictive nature.** So with the Bible, the treasure house of the riches of His grace. The glory of its truths, that are as high as heaven and compass eternity, is undiscerned. To the great mass of mankind, Christ Himself is 'as a root out of a dry ground,' and they see in Him 'no beauty that' they 'should desire Him.' Isaiah 53:2. When Jesus was among men, the revelation of God in humanity, the scribes and Pharisees declared to Him, 'Thou art a Samaritan, and hast a devil.' John 8:48. **Even His disciples were so blinded by the selfishness of their hearts that they were slow to understand Him who had come to manifest to them the Father's love.** This was why Jesus walked in solitude in the midst of men. He was understood fully in heaven alone..." (Ellen G. White, *Thoughts from the Mount of Blessing,* pg. 25)

For the same reason that God allows humanity to face the repercussions of their own choices in their continuous rejection of His Spirit, He naturally must also permit mankind to misunderstand Him—as it is even now.

However, God has promised to make Himself known, so that we might come to experience Him as He truly is.

> "For, behold, the darkness shall cover the earth, and gross darkness the people: **but the LORD shall arise upon thee, and his glory shall be seen upon thee.**" (Isaiah 60:2)

> "And they shall not teach every man his neighbour, and every man his brother, saying, Know the Lord: **for all shall know me,** from the least to the greatest." (Hebrews 8:11)

But how exactly was God to make Himself known to all? This could only be done by the gift of His Son. And so, in the depths of our darkness, God sent forth His Son, Jesus Christ, in order to reconcile humanity to Himself by the revelation of His true character of love. For it is only by the light of Christ that the ambiguity of the Old Testament passages about God may be resolved.

> "But their minds were blinded: **for until this day remaineth the same vail untaken away in the reading of the old testament; which vail is done away in Christ.**" (2 Corinthians 3:14)

Christ's mission to the world was to establish, beyond any reasonable doubt, the true nature of our heavenly Father. The contrast of character between the Almighty God and His accuser, the devil, must be realized. It was Christ who came to resolve this matter, so that we might once again come to see God as the loving and gentle Father that He truly is. It is this course of thought that will be our concept of study in the succeeding chapter.

> "**The earth was dark through misapprehension of God.** That the gloomy shadows might be lightened, that the world might be brought back to God, Satan's deceptive power was to be broken. **This could not be done by force. The exercise of force is contrary to the principles of God's government; He desires only the service of love; and love cannot be commanded; it cannot be won by force or authority. Only by love is love awakened.** To know God is to love Him; His character must be manifested in contrast to the character of Satan. **This work only one Being in all the universe**

could do. Only He who knew the height and depth of the love of God could make it known…" (Ellen G. White, *The Desire of Ages*, pg. 22)

Chapter 3

The Cosmic Commission: Christ's Sacred Mission to the World

"Heaven, looking down and seeing the delusions into which men were led, knew that a divine Instructor must come to the earth. ***Through the misrepresentations of the enemy, many were so deceived that they worshiped a false god, clothed with the attributes of the satanic character.*** *Those in ignorance and moral darkness must have light, spiritual light; for the world knew not God, and He must be revealed to their understanding. Truth looked down from heaven and saw not the reflection of her image; for dense clouds of spiritual darkness and gloom enveloped the world.* ***The Lord Jesus alone was able to roll back the clouds; for He is the light of the world. By His presence He could dissipate the gloomy shadow that Satan had cast between man and God. . .*** *" (Ellen G. White, Counsels to Parents, Teachers, and Students, pg. 28)*

Many today misunderstand the true nature of Christ's first advent. This comes as a result of an insufficient knowledge of the character of God. So many millions worship a god of violence. It is arbitrarily and succinctly taught that the Father's only reason for sending His Son was to condemn Him to death, so that the Father's wrath toward us could be appeased; that His compulsion to kill us could only be quenched by the brutal murder of His own Son. This might be a crude way of stating the matter, but it truly is the core of the issue. And is it any wonder that much of the world isn't interested in *this* gospel? An exacting god of death and punishment does not garner many bona fide followers. But this violent and maleficent picture of the Father is sublimely contradicted by the demonstration of the life of Christ. Christ's mission to this earth was not merely to die, but that through Him it might be saved.

> "'For God so loved the world, that He gave His only begotten Son, that whosoever believeth in Him should not perish, but have everlasting life.' John 3:16. This does not mean to imply that Christ was arbitrarily sent by the Father. **The Father and the Son are one, and therefore the love of God and the love of Christ are the same...** The Father did not send the Son as one would send another on an unpleasant errand; **neither did the Son go of Himself, in order to appease the wrath of God, as if His wounded feelings demanded a sacrifice...**" (E. J. Waggoner, *The Present Truth,* vol. 9, September 7, 1893, pg. 353)

> "For God sent not his Son into the world to condemn the world; **but that the world through him might be saved.**" (John 3:17)

It was because humanity had sorely mistaken the nature of their Creator that Christ was sent. His most precious purpose was to demonstrate to us the true character of the Father.

> "**God is love. This was the great truth that Christ came to the world to reveal.** Satan had so misrepresented the character of God to the world, that man stood remote from God... **The object of Christ's mission to the world was to reveal the Father...**" (Ellen G. White, *Signs of the Times,* April 11, 1895)

> "**But what was Jesus in the world for?—To reveal the Father.** He said, 'I and my Father are one.' 'He that hath seen me hath seen the Father' He revealed a God who is 'our Father,' whose great heart of love ever beats in sympathy with a sorrowing, sin-sick humanity, and who loves us ever, even in our sins, because he made us that he might have some one to love." (George Fifield, *God is Love,* pg. 29)

It may come as a shock for the reader to learn that Christ's very death on the cross was not His sole objective, nor was it within His Father's divine will that anyone—even Christ—

should suffer death as a result of sin.[1] And while the author will promptly supply biblical evidence for this statement in a later section, preparation must be made now if we are to move on any further.

We begin in John chapter 17, immediately before Christ's betrayal and crucifixion. Verse 4 reads as follows:

> "I have glorified thee on the earth: **I have finished the work which thou gavest me to do.**" (John 17:4)

Here we see that Christ, *before ever reaching the cross*, had already finished the work which His Father had given Him. What was the nature of this work? "I have glorified thee on the earth" Christ declares. In the first chapter of this volume, we learned

---

[1] By no means do we, in saying this, reject the idea that Jesus had to die. We merely emphasize the point that it was not the Father who demanded it, but rather ourselves. It was God who *provided* the sacrifice; we are the ones who required it, for without it we would not have believed that God could forgive us for sin. This is why Jesus had to die; for our sake—for our appeasement. Without believing that God could forgive us, we would never have thought it safe to approach Him to receive His regenerative Spirit, and therefore we would have judged ourselves forever unworthy of receiving that life which Jesus seeks to impart to every thirsty soul. We would have steadfastly rejected God, believing Him to be merciless and unforgiving, and believing ourselves to be beyond the point of redemption. So, in His love for us, He stooped down to our level—to our understanding—and died so that we might come to trust Him and believe in His ability to forgive sin. Christ died *for us* (Romans 5:8). Stop for a moment and consider the profound implications of this statement. In it you will see that Christ did not die to appease the wrath of God. Just as in the time of the wilderness with the serpent on the pole, God possessed the capacity to remedy the ailments of the people without resorting to such a measure, had they only exhibited faith. The serpent on the pole served the purpose of man, not God. Similarly, it wasn't God's demand for blood which required Christ to die, as He could have affected our deliverance from sin without anyone having to die. But we refused to believe in His steadfast love, and so, in our misunderstanding of Him, we believed He required sacrifice for the forgiveness of sins. In this way, we demanded Christ's crucifixion; we forced His hand. And it is in this sense that Christ *did* have to die.

what it meant for Christ to glorify the Father. The reader will recall that, in Exodus 33:18, Moses besought the Lord to show him His glory. The Lord answered this plea in Exodus 34:5-7 by proclaiming His character before Moses. Here, the Almighty defines for us what His glory is; it is found in His character. The overwhelming splendor and awe-inspiring attributes of God exemplify a character that is unrivaled, serving as a reminder of His supreme and eternal greatness. Truly, when one encounters a Being such as this, the only words that may readily fall from the lips are "glorious majesty." (Psalm 145:12). And Jesus is the "brightness of his glory," (Hebrews 1:3)—which is to say, that Christ is the visual manifestation—the radiance—of the Father's character. Therefore, to glorify the Father is to demonstrate His character to the world. This was the fulfillment of Christ's earthly mission.

The first half of verse 6 of the same chapter of John advances this idea more:

"I have manifested **thy name...**" (John 17:6)

Here, Jesus is casting further emphasis upon the culmination of His earthly mission. In biblical thought, a name is not merely a label of identification but also an expression of the bearer's essential nature and character. It includes its bearer's reputation, disposition, attributes, and distinctiveness from among others. This is true of many biblical characters, even providing insight into understanding them within the events recorded about them. To illustrate, Jacob—literally meaning, "follower, replacer, supplanter" (Strong's H3290)—supplants his brother Esau twice; firstly for the birthright, and again for the blessing. A supplanter is one who by skill, deceit, or force takes the place of another. When this happens the second time, Esau says, "Is he not rightly named Jacob?" (Genesis 27:36). Regarding the birthright and blessing, Jacob takes Esau's place using the very nature given to us by his name. Thus, Jacob is at first a supplanter, yet when he develops a change in character, God names him more appropriately. Israel is "one who prevails with God" (Strong's H3478).

Similarly, to manifest the name of God is to reveal Him as He truly is—that is, to demonstrate His character. Christ perfectly revealed His Father's glory so that we may, by beholding Him, be partakers of the divine nature, being changed into the same image:

> "But we all, with open face beholding as in a glass the glory of the Lord, **are changed into the same image from glory to glory, even as by the Spirit of the Lord.**" (2 Corinthians 3:18)

This illustrates clearly how Christ's ultimate mission was to unveil His Father's likeness to a darkened and fallen world. Only then could humanity come to know God and be reconciled to Him; only then could humanity begin to be conformed into the same image; and only then could humanity be saved from the perils of their own sin. This is how Christ saves: not through the suffering of death to appease an offended god, but instead through the giving of life to save a fallen humanity.

> "Jesus said unto her, **I am the resurrection, and the life:** he that believeth in me, though he were dead, yet shall he live…" (John 11:25)

To believe in Christ is to believe in His testimony regarding the Father.

> "To this end was I born, and for this cause came I into the world, **that I should bear witness unto the truth.**" (John 18:37)

> "And we know that the Son of God is come, and hath given us an understanding, **that we may know him that is true, and we are in him that is true, even in his Son Jesus Christ. This is the true God, and eternal life.**" (I John 5:20)

And to know Him is to know the Father, for they "are one." (John 10:30). To say that the Son is in some way different than the Father brings glory to neither and only serves to discredit them both. Jesus told His disciple Philip:

> "Philip saith unto him, Lord, shew us the Father, and it sufficeth us. Jesus saith unto him, Have I been so long time with you, and yet hast thou not known me, Philip? **he that hath seen me hath seen the Father;** and how sayest thou then, Shew us the Father?" (John 14:8-9)

Jesus is the *complete* revelation of the Father. He is the true witness to the Almighty's glory and majesty. These verses make no mention of Christ's requirement to be a propitiation in order to fulfill the forensic demands of an angry and vengeful god. Rather, it seems that merely by knowing God as He is revealed in Christ, and thereby opening our hearts to Him and being conformed to the same image, we may inherit eternal life:

> "**And this is life eternal, that they might know thee the only true God,** and Jesus Christ, whom thou hast sent." (John 17:3)

> "And **ye shall know the truth,** and the truth shall make you free." (John 8:32)

This work was finished *before* Jesus died on the cross. By demonstrating the Father's true character, Jesus had completed the work He was given to do. To say that the Son—full of gentleness and benevolence—was ultimately sent to die in order to protect us from the Father—full of wrath and retribution—not only contradicts scripture, but also does injustice to logic. To believe lies about God is to betray the very intellect He gave you. And to instill contrast between the Father and Son is to mar both of their characters. Can love and wrath hold hands? Can the same fountain bring forth water that is both bitter and sweet? To even conceive of such an erroneous doctrine is to cast doubt upon the entire testimony of the Savior. This lie can do nothing but bring obscurity to His true mission.

> "Christ exalted the character of God, attributing to him the praise, and giving to him the credit, of **the whole purpose of his own mission on earth,—to set men right through the revelation of God. In Christ was arrayed before men the paternal grace and the matchless perfections of the Father.** In his prayer just before his

> crucifixion, he declared, 'I have manifested thy name.' 'I have glorified thee on the earth; I have finished the work which thou gavest me to do.' **When the object of his mission was attained,—the revelation of God to the world,—the Son of God announced that his work was accomplished, and that the character of the Father was made manifest to men...**" (Ellen G. White, *Signs of the Times,* January 20, 1890)

The brutal death of Jesus on the cross was not the sole purpose of His being sent to earth, nor did He die to appease by blood the wrath of an angry god. Christ was not killed by the Father. Rather, the enmity hidden amongst mankind was manifested forthwith, and Jesus suffered at the hands of the very ones He was endeavoring to save. God did not demand the death of His Son—*we did.*

> "Ah, yes! There had been gods enough before Jesus came to reveal to a lost world the knowledge of the Father. In Egypt it was said at one time that it was easier to find a god than a man, so numerous were they. **The trouble was, none of them was 'our Father.' They were none of them 'with us.' They were all gods afar off in the distant and in the dim, and none of them loved the human soul.** There were gods of war, and gods of storm, and gods of lust, and theft, and drunken revelings, till every base and angry passion of the lost soul was deified and worshiped, to drag the soul farther down into sin and resultant misery. There was a god in the clouds to shoot forth the arrows of the angry lightnings; a god in the ocean to toss the waves on high, and wreck the ships freighted with human life; a god in the earth to make it tremble with terror, and pour forth the lava from the mountain top, desolating the cities at its base; a god everywhere for wrath and destruction; **a god everywhere whose wrath must be appeased by some bloody sacrifice; a god everywhere, but always too far away to be reached by the prayers of trembling faith, surging up from suffering souls.**" (George Fifield, *God is Love,* pg. 70)

This controversy will be delineated more clearly in a later section of this volume. For now, the current weight of evidence adequately suffices the author's purpose for this chapter. Before moving on, we will further highlight Christ's true mission with excerpts from the biblical record and the spirit of prophecy.

> "**He spoke of God, not as an avenging judge, but as a tender father, and He revealed the image of God as mirrored in Himself.** His words were like balm to the wounded spirit. Both by His words and by His works of mercy He was breaking the oppressive power of the old traditions and man-made commandments, and **presenting the love of God in its exhaustless fullness...**" (Ellen G. White, *The Desire of Ages*, pg. 204)

> "He [Satan] represented God in a false light, clothing him with his own attributes. **Christ came to represent the Father in his true character. He showed that he was not an arbitrary judge, ready to bring judgments upon men, and delighting in condemning and punishing them for their evil deeds...**" (Ellen G. White, *Signs of the Times*, November 18, 1889)

Jesus has the same disposition as the Father. He is "the express image of his person," (Hebrews 1:3). We cannot come to know the Father but by the Son. To even attempt to understand the Father by, at the same time, negating the Son is of the utmost folly. To do so is to make void the truth and strip it of its power, thereby making it of no effect.

> "Jesus saith unto him, I am the way, the truth, and the life: **no man cometh unto the Father, but by me.**" (John 14:6)

It is by the life of Christ, the testimony to the reality of His Father which He bore, that we may come to understand God in His proper context. It is this truth—the truth about our Father's character—that loosens our chains and enables us to accept His regenerative agency into our heart, thereby setting us free from our bondage to sin.

> "And ye shall know the truth, and **the truth shall make you free.**" (John 8:32)

The Pharisees in the time of Christ had deceived themselves. They thought that they knew who God was. Confessing themselves to be free, they became bondmen; claiming to know the truth, they conceded to lies.

> "Professing themselves to be wise, they became fools…" (Romans I:22)

They believed themselves to have eternal life based upon their own merit. Sorely did they misunderstand the nature of heaven. They served a god of violence—an idol of wrath. Punishment and death were due the transgressor instead of love and guidance. By misunderstanding the One whom they sought to worship, they ultimately came to reject Him. The Pharisees had confidence in their own piety and, by searching the scriptures, they believed that they could reason for themselves who God was. This, to them, was eternal life. But if one misinterprets Him, who is the Author of life, as a patron of death, then how are they to seek His reward? They can only go about it the wrong way, thereby forfeiting their eternal gift.

> "**Whosoever denieth the Son, the same hath not the Father:** (but) he that acknowledgeth the Son hath the Father also." (I John 2:23)

> "Search the scriptures; for in them ye think ye have eternal life: **and they are they which testify of me.**" (John 5:39)

Because of their delusion, they could not see God as He truly is. Thus, they could not come into harmony with the Source of life. They were "dead in trespasses and sins…" (Ephesians 2:1). To come into alignment with the Source of life is to have life; all else is death. It was so that humanity could come into cooperation with God—the Source of life—that Christ came into this world. It is only by a knowledge of God as He is revealed in Christ that we may partake of eternal life.

> "No man hath seen God at any time; **the only begotten Son, which is in the bosom of the Father, he hath declared him.**" (John I:18)

> "Jesus, the Lord of life and glory, came to plant the tree of life for the human family, and to invite the members of a fallen race to eat and be satisfied. **He came to reveal to them what was their only hope, their only happiness, both in this world and in that which is to come. 'For this is life eternal, that they might know thee the only true God, and Jesus Christ, whom thou hast sent.'** He would allow nothing to divert his attention from the work which he came to do... **Jesus saw that men needed to have their minds attracted to God, that they might become acquainted with his character, and obtain the righteousness of Christ... He knew that it was necessary that men should have a faithful representation of the divine character, that they might not be deceived by the misrepresentations of Satan,** who had cast his hellish shadow athwart men's pathway, and to their minds clothed God with his own Satanic characteristics." (Ellen G. White, *Signs of the Times*, May 1, 1893)

Mankind had erected prison bars around themselves, that the truth of God's character could not enter into their minds. They became captivated by sin and death. So much was their self-delusion, that they even attributed to God's will their own carnal desires. The world needed a Savior; someone who could demonstrate the reality of the divine nature—someone who could turn back the hearts of men to their heavenly Father. This was Christ's mission alone.

> "The Spirit of the Lord GOD is upon me; because the LORD hath anointed me to preach good tidings unto the meek; **he hath sent me to bind up the brokenhearted, to proclaim liberty to the captives, and the opening of the prison to them that are bound...**" (Isaiah 61:1)

> "**Christ came to represent the character of his Father, to win man back to his allegiance to God, to reconcile man to God.** He proposed to meet the foe and unmask his arts, that man might be able to make choice of whom he would serve..." (Ellen G. White, *The Bible Echo,* November 1, 1892)

This was the true nature of Christ's first advent. The Son of Man came to this earth "with healing in his wings..." (Malachi

4:2), that He might grant remedy to those who were afflicted. His mission was to rectify His Father's character in the minds of all who believe on Him, and thereby bring man back into harmony with the divine will.

Now it may readily be seen by all that learn of Him, that the character of Christ represented the character of the Father. His primary endeavor revolved around showcasing a profound revelation of divine love. By deeply intertwining compassion, mercy, forgiveness, and selflessness, Jesus unveiled a multifaceted portrayal of His Father's nature. This revelation served as a transformative force, urging individuals towards a path of abundant love, ardent discipleship, and an enduring connection with God. Thus, this chapter underscores how Christ, with unsurpassed brilliance, embodied and manifested the essence of love to illuminate humanity's understanding of their heavenly Father. He came to demonstrate the most elevated and glorious of truths: that we serve a God of love.

> **"The work of the good Samaritan represents Christ's mission to the world. Our Saviour came to reveal the character of God, to represent his love for man. He acted just as the Father would have done in all emergencies.** Christ manifested for us a love that the love of man can never equal. He died to save those who were his enemies; he prayed for his murderers. When we were bruised and dying, he had pity upon us. He did not pass us by on the other side, and leave us, helpless, and hopeless, to perish…" (Ellen G. White, *The Home Missionary*, October 1, 1897)

Chapter 4

The Incarnate Image: Jesus as the Embodiment of the Father's True Character

"The Lord Jesus awakens an interest in man by encouraging him to draw nigh and become acquainted with His character. 'This is life eternal, that they might know Thee the only true God, and Jesus Christ, whom Thou hast sent' [John 17:3]. ***We do not contemplate as we should the character of God.*** *'God so loved the world, that He gave His only begotten Son, that whosoever believeth in Him should not perish, but have everlasting life' [John 3:16].* ***Although Satan has misinterpreted God's purposes, falsified His character, and caused man to look upon God in a false light, yet through the ages God's love for man has never ceased. Christ's work was to reveal the Father as merciful, compassionate, full of goodness and truth. The character of Christ represented the character of God.*** *The only begotten Son of God sweeps back the hellish shadow in which Satan has enveloped the Father, and declares, 'I and My Father are one; look on Me and behold God.'" (Ellen G. White, Letters and Manuscripts, vol. 6, Manuscript 25, Jan. 9, 1890)*

All that man needs to know or can know of God has been demonstrated in the life and character of His Son. Gentle, earnest, compassionate, sympathetic, selfless, ever ready to serve others—He fully represented the character of God and was constantly engaged in service for both God and man. He was a healer, the Great Physician, the Prince of Peace. He showed love to a hateful and decrepit world. Without Him we would be lost, and by Him we are saved—saved by the knowledge of the God we serve. Understanding the profound connection between Jesus and His Father is essential in comprehending how Jesus, as the embodiment of His Father's character, exemplifies the divine nature and attributes of God.

> "Christ's Life, then, was a Revelation of what men most wanted to know, of the Character of God. God was in Christ not only 'reconciling the world,' but making Himself known to men: 'He that hath seen Him hath seen the Father.' **As we gaze on Him [Christ] going about with that calm, steadfast mien, doing good, healing the sick, sitting with the despised, at home with little children, counting none too sinful for His help, as we see Him in the Gospels, we gaze on the face of God.**" (Robert Eyton from his sermon, "Christ the Revealer of the Father" in, *The True Life: And Other Sermons,* pg. 155-156, published in 1889)

By looking to Christ, we may readily behold the Father. This fact alone is enough to break the chains of oppression that many are clinging to through their own misperceptions regarding the Father's character. If we perceive the Father in any way contrary to that which Jesus testified of, we are rejecting them both. In doing so, we deny the sacred testimony of Jesus and make Him out to be a liar. John tells us that this is the spirit of antichrist:

> "Who is a liar but he that denieth that Jesus is the Christ? **He is antichrist, that denieth the Father and the Son.**" (I John 2:22)

On the other hand, by coming to a correct understanding of Christ we may also come to understand the Father.

> "**If ye had known me, ye should have known my Father also:** and from henceforth ye know him, and have seen him." (John 14:7)

> "To know God is to understand his character, and to know Christ is to understand his character. **If then to know Christ is to know God, the character of Christ must be the character of God.**" (Otway Caesar, *The Word of God Weighed against the Commandments of Men, in Six Controversial Letters,* pg. 130)

If Christ and His Father truly "are one" (John 10:30), then the words and actions of Christ reflect those of the Father also.

> "Then answered Jesus and said unto them, Verily, verily, I say unto you, **The Son can do nothing of himself, but what he seeth the Father do: for what things soever he doeth, these also doeth the Son likewise.**" (John 5:19)

This is how we may come to know the Almighty as He truly is. We may have a glimpse of His abiding and glorious character in the tender face of His only begotten Son.

Upon an examination of the life and ministry of Jesus Christ, what may we gather about the Father's nature? For one, He does not seek to incite punishment or condemnation upon the sinner, but rather He aims to heal them of their malady and bring them back into harmony with the divine nature. Notice, in Mark chapter 2:

> "And when the scribes and Pharisees saw him eat with publicans and sinners, they said unto his disciples, How is it that he eateth and drinketh with publicans and sinners? When Jesus heard it, he saith unto them, **They that are whole have no need of the physician, but they that are sick: I came not to call the righteous, but sinners to repentance.**" (Mark 2:16-17)

There are two important points of consideration in this passage. Firstly, notice here how Jesus is closely associating sin with sickness or infirmity. Secondly, take close attention of how Jesus addresses the Pharisees in this particular instance. He tells them that He has not come to call the righteous to repentance, but sinners. Was He conceding to the Pharisees' own self-image—that they were righteous of themselves and that, therefore, they had no need of the healing of which He spoke? This cannot be so! The book of Romans tells us that:

> "As it is written, **There is none righteous,** no, not one..." (Romans 3:10)

Jesus was appealing to the very nature of the Pharisees on this occasion. He was allowing them to decide their cases for themselves. Would they sense the magnitude of their inherent sinfulness and seek the very One who could offer them relief? Or, being blinded by a false piety, would they judge themselves honorable and upright—thereby seeking none but themselves? Just as His Father, Jesus too must allow us to exercise our own free will. He cannot help those who refuse to come to Him for aid. By this statement, Christ was knocking on the doors of their hearts—would they let Him in?

If one considers himself to be healthy and in need of nothing, then there is no urgent desire to appear before a physician. A man must feel his need before he will accept help; he must know his disease before he can apply the remedy. Even so, the promise of righteousness would be entirely unheeded by one who does not realize that he is a sinner. On the other hand, if we come to acknowledge that we suffer from a condition which is terminal, being sin, then proper and extensive treatment would be sought at all costs. The Pharisees, being boldly presumptuous, did not consider themselves to be sinful. Pride turned to ignorance, their judgement was disfigured, and they did not sense their rebellious disposition—they were blind to the deep-seated nature of their very souls. They thought themselves to be, by their strict obedience to the letter of the law, closest to God. They also believed, as many do today, that it was God's divine will and duty to punish sinners. Therefore, in many matters, they too sought to inflict swift and furious consequences upon transgressors of the law. Oh how sorely mistaken were these leaders of Israel! Oh how their vengeful deeds reflected the god which they worshipped!

By this story, we see that the Father's most precious desire is to heal His children. Christ associates sinners with "they that are sick..." (Mark 2:17). Those who are in need of the Physician, in this instance, are they that are convicted of sin and have an earnest desire to be made whole. Our heavenly Father, in the same way as Christ, seeks to rehabilitate those who are afflicted.

> "**And you hath he quickened,** who were dead in trespasses and sins..." (Ephesians 2:1)

In the passage under consideration, did Jesus condemn the publicans and sinners whom He was with? Did He threaten them with divine wrath? How about fire and brimstone? No. Rather, He sought to heal them of their afflictions. It is the same with the

Almighty. As the reader will come to realize in the discourse of this volume, God does not arbitrarily punish the sinner. He has no need to. The consequences of sin will naturally come about all on their own. Sin does not need any help from God in the destruction of its victim.

> "For **the wages of sin is death;** but **the gift of God is eternal life** through Jesus Christ our Lord." (Romans 6:23)

> "...sin, when it is finished, **bringeth forth death.**" (James 1:15)

The author will adjourn the discussion of this particular topic until a later section, but it would do the reader well to keep it in mind.

One matter, however, becomes clear from this passage in Mark chapter 2... God's ultimate ambition—His divine will—is to reconcile His children to Himself by restoring the nature that was within them before the fall. He accomplishes this by cleansing the heart of its allegiance to sin.

> "**Create in me a clean heart,** O God; and **renew a right spirit within me.**" (Psalm 51:10)

This is a transcendent and spiritual endeavor that aims to bring the subject back into harmony with the divine nature. And yet, so many misunderstand this work. Many mistakenly attribute the consequences of sin to God Himself, just as the Pharisees did in the time of Christ.

> "**How unwarranted the thought of linking that will [God's will] with anything that makes for physical pain, disease, sorrow and death.** God has not one plan for His will in heaven, and another plan for those of us while we are still on earth. **God's will for man as well as for spiritual beings has behind it always the desire for the expression of a perfect Love-a perfect self-giving.** We shall never fully realize the character of God until we know that He is always giving Himself to each one of us. **This was the revelation Jesus gave of the true character of the Father.**" (Henry B. Wilson, *"Losing the Lord's Prayer" in The Nazarene: A Magazine of*

> *Healing, According to the Methods of Jesus,* vol. 7, pg. 8, published in 1922)

> "With his hosts of fallen beings he [Satan] determined to urge the warfare most vigorously; for **there stood in the world One who was a perfect representative of the Father, One whose character and practices refuted Satan's misrepresentation of God. Satan had charged upon God the attribute[s] he himself possessed. Now in Christ he saw God revealed in His true character—a compassionate, merciful Father, not willing that any should perish, but that all should come to Him in repentance, and have eternal life.**" (Ellen G. White, *Selected Messages,* vol. 1, pg. 254)

We see the benevolent aspect of the Father's will further demonstrated in other aspects of Christ's ministry. Ever was He seeking to edify those around Him; to comfort those who were wronged; to heal those who were sick; and to guide those who were lost. In every instance, He gave of Himself for the sake of others. In every emergency, He armed Himself with love rather than the sword. This was the work which God gave Him to do, that He might properly be revealed among men.

> "How God anointed Jesus of Nazareth with the Holy Ghost and with power: **who went about doing good, and healing all that were oppressed of the devil;** for God was with him." (Acts 10:38)

It is God who heals those that are oppressed. By no means does He act alongside Satan in the devilish work of accusing and inflicting burdensome circumstances upon mankind. This would be contrary to His nature; it would be a betrayal of His glory and majesty. By the demonstration of His character in Christ, humanity may readily see the Father's true intentions and subsequently be reconciled unto Him, thereby commencing the transformative process of restoration.

> "The Lord spoke to the disciples of divers sufferings which they should have to bear, but **when He speaks of sickness, it is always as of an evil caused by sin and Satan, and from which we should be delivered.** Very solemnly He declared that **every disciple of His**

> **would have to bear his cross (Matt. 16:24), but He never taught one sick person to resign himself to be sick. Everywhere Jesus healed the sick, everywhere He dealt with healing as one of the graces belonging to the kingdom of heaven. Sin in the soul and sickness in the body both bear witness to the power of Satan,** and 'the Son of God was manifested that he might destroy the works of the devil' (I John 3:8). **Jesus came to deliver men from sin and sickness that He might make known the love of the Father."** (Andrew Murray, *Divine Healing*, pg. 9)

Christ's behavior, in every instance, exemplified the attributes of the Father. His life and ministry were a perfect transcript of the will and character of God.

> "The highest evidence that He came from God is that **His life revealed the character of God...**" (Ellen G. White, *The Desire of Ages*, pg. 406)

> **"Through Jesus, the Son of God, the Father is more fully revealed to the world.** Jesus said to his disciples: 'If ye had known me, ye should have known my Father also; and from henceforth ye know him, and have seen him. Philip saith unto him, Lord, show us the Father, and it sufficeth us. Jesus saith unto him, Have I been so long time with you, and yet hast thou not known me, Philip? He that hath seen me hath seen the Father.' The souls of thousands are crying out today, 'Show us the Father, and we will be satisfied. We cannot claim God as our Father until we see him.' Jesus says to every such soul, as he said to Philip: 'Have I been so long time with you, and yet hast thou not known me?' Have you seen my works, have you listened to my teachings, have you witnessed the miracles that I have wrought in my Father's name, **and yet have you not understood the nature of God?** I have prayed with you and for you, **and yet can you not comprehend that I am the way, the truth, and the life, and that in my life I have unfolded to you the character of my Father? I am the brightness of my Father's glory, I am the express image of his person.** 'Believest thou not that I am in the Father, and the Father in me? the words that I speak unto you I speak not of myself; but the Father that dwelleth in me, he doeth the works. Believe me that I am in the Father, and the Father in me; or else believe me for the very works' sake.

Verily, verily, I say unto you, He that believeth on me, the works that I do shall he do also; and greater works than these shall he do; because I go unto my Father.'" (Ellen G. White, *Signs of the Times,* June 9, 1890)

Upon a deeper consideration of the Savior's words and actions, the following passage from Luke can reveal to us a broader framework of the Father's true nature.

"But I say unto you which hear, **Love your enemies, do good to them which hate you, Bless them that curse you, and pray for them which despitefully use you.** And unto him that smiteth thee on the one cheek offer also the other; and him that taketh away thy cloke forbid not to take thy coat also." (Luke 6:27-29)

Our Father, just as Christ taught, renders love even to those who hate Him. He aims to pour out His blessings upon whomever allows Him to do so. He never "repays anyone evil for evil, but always seek[s] to do good..." (1 Thessalonians 5:15, *ESV*). He, in His beneficence, imparts grace upon the just *and* the unjust, for He loves all His children regardless of how they feel about Him. He is long-suffering toward us, "not willing that any should perish, but that all should come to repentance." (2 Peter 3:9).

"...he maketh his sun to rise **on the evil and on the good,** and sendeth rain **on the just and on the unjust.**" (Matthew 5:45)

This is the God we serve. This is the God that Jesus declared. He is not a God of condemnation or self-seeking. He is ever merciful and just. He maintains infinite love for each of His children, even though many of us stand in opposition against Him. Many misunderstand the kingdom of heaven and imagine a god that, in order to retain the loyalty of his subjects, must declare war on any who would dare to defy him. This is not our God. A god that inflicts any harm whatsoever is not the God that Jesus came to reveal.

"But love ye your enemies, and do good, and lend, hoping for nothing again; and your reward shall be great, and ye shall be the children of the Highest: **for he is kind unto the unthankful and**

to the evil. Be ye therefore merciful, as your Father also is merciful." (Luke 6:35-36)

"**The principles of kindness, mercy, and love, taught and exemplified by our Saviour, are a transcript of the will and character of God.** Christ declared that He taught nothing except that which He had received from His Father. **The principles of the divine government are in perfect harmony with the Saviour's precept, 'Love your enemies.'**" (Ellen G. White, *The Great Controversy*, pg. 541)

To believe that God comes near the sinner to award him with bitter punishment, as if to say that His love and mercy become desolate in an instant, is to radically misunderstand how His law operates. It is to bring ambiguity and obscenity upon His true reward and upon the innate results of sin. Even worse is to attribute to His Providence the distribution of death to the transgressor. To consider that God can be provoked into slaughtering His children is to disqualify Him entirely as a Father. May His Son correctly be titled the executioner, or the Physician? The irrefutable reality that emerges from carefully examining the entirety of Jesus' earthly existence is that He did not, at any point, engage in the act of killing another human being, nor did He cause harm to anyone.

"...**he had done no violence,** neither was any deceit in his mouth." (Isaiah 53:9)

"...**Christ never killed anyone,** and we may attribute the spirit of persecution... to its origin—Satan. He is a deceiver, a liar, a murderer, and accuser of the brethren..." (Ellen G. White, *Letters and Manuscripts*, vol. 4, Manuscript 62, 1886)

This profound observation serves as a compelling indication that the Father, in all His divine wisdom, does not choose to employ such ruthless methods in His dealings with humanity. To suppose otherwise would be to imply a difference in character between the Father and Son, and to admit any disparity between the two would be to concede heresy.

"Many conceive of the Christian's God as a being whose attribute is stern justice,—one who is a severe judge, a harsh, exacting creditor. The Creator has been pictured as a being who is watching with jealous eye to discern the errors and mistakes of men, that He may visit judgment upon them. **In the minds of thousands, love and sympathy and tenderness are associated with the character of Christ, while God is regarded as the law-giver, inflexible, arbitrary, devoid of sympathy for the beings He has made... Never was there a greater error.**" (Ellen G. White, *Bible Training School*, November 1, 1908)

The vacancy of any violent or harmful actions throughout Jesus' life serves as a definitive testament to the inherent goodness, compassion, and mercy that lie at the core of the Father's divine nature. This noteworthy absence powerfully reinforces the notion that the Father's character and actions align with the principles of selfless love, forgiveness, and a profound respect for human life. So highly does God value our life that He laid down His own, that we might be reconciled unto Him and live.

"**For God so loved the world, that he gave his only begotten Son,** that whosoever believeth in him should not perish, but have everlasting life." (John 3:16)

"**Hereby perceive we the love of God, because he laid down his life for us:** and we ought to lay down our lives for the brethren." (I John 3:16)

In summation, the record of inspiration is clear that Jesus Christ served as the embodiment of the Father's true character, exemplifying qualities such as love, mercy, and compassion. Through His teachings, actions, and ultimate sacrifice, Jesus revealed the depth of God's love toward men, providing a tangible representation of the divine qualities the Father desired to impart upon His creation.

However, in order to gain a comprehensive understanding of this subject, it is crucial to discern the foundational role of God's holy law in elucidating the nature of both God and Jesus, as well as the role of obedience to this law in aligning oneself with the divine purposes of spiritual healing. By exploring the interplay between the character of Christ and the foundation of God's holy law, we can further grasp the glorious manifestation of God's attributes through His Son and ascertain the profound significance of what it means to be obedient to *all* the precepts of God. The subsequent section of this volume will pursue a more exhaustive exploration of this matter.

> "**In the truths of His word, God has given to men a revelation of Himself;** and to all who accept them they are a shield against the deceptions of Satan. It is a neglect of these truths that has opened the door to the evils which are now becoming so widespread in the religious world. **The nature and the importance of the law of God have been, to a great extent, lost sight of… the law is a transcript of the divine perfections… a man who does not love the law does not love the gospel; for the law, as well as the gospel, is a mirror reflecting the true character of God…**" (Ellen. G. White, *The Great Controversy*, pg. 465)

Section 2

The Nature of the Law and its Consequences

Chapter 5

Chronicles of Divinity: The Law as a Transcript of God's Character

*"**God's law is the transcript of His character.** It embodies the principles of His kingdom. **He who refuses to accept these principles is placing himself outside the channel where God's blessings flow…**" (Ellen G. White, Christ's Object Lessons, pg. 305)*

*"The law, which declares men to be sinners, could not justify them except by declaring that sin is not sin. And that would not be justification, but contradiction. Shall we say, 'Then we will do away with the law'? Persistent lawbreakers would gladly do away with the law which declares them guilty. **But the law of God cannot be abolished, for it is the life and character of God.** 'The law is holy, and the commandment holy, and just, and good.' Romans 7:12, KJV. When we read the written law, we find in it our duty made plain. But we have not done it. Therefore we are guilty. Moreover, there is not one who has strength to keep the law, for its requirements are great. **While no one can be justified by the works of the law, the fault is not in the law, but in the individual. Get Christ in the heart by faith, and then the righteousness of the law will be there also.** As the Psalmist says, 'I delight to do Thy will, O My God; Thy law is within My heart.' Psalm 40:8. The one who would throw away the law because it will not call evil good, would also reject God because He 'will by no means clear the guilty.' Exodus 34:7. **But God will remove the guilt, and will thus make the sinner righteous [justified], that is, in harmony with the law… He [Jesus] alone has kept and can keep the law to perfection. Therefore, only by His faith—living faith, that is, His life in us—can we be made righteous.** But this is sufficient… The faith which He gives to us is His own tried and approved faith, and it will not fail us in any contest. We are not exhorted to TRY to do as well as He did, or to TRY to exercise as much faith as He had, but simply to take of His faith,*

and let it work by love, and purify the heart. It will do it!" (E. J. Waggoner, The Glad Tidings, pg. 48-50)

In embarking upon an examination of the profound scriptural composition of the Decalogue, one inevitably encounters a remarkable revelation: these ancient precepts are far *more* than a mere set of arbitrary rules for moral conduct. Instead, they stand as a profound transcription of the divine character, reflecting the essence and nature of God Himself. Through an exhaustive study of the interplay between theology, ethics, and natural phenomena, God's character is more clearly discerned. This section seeks to unravel the profound layers of meaning held within "the perfect law of liberty" (James 1:25), unveiling its intrinsic connection to the attributes and qualities that define the Almighty, and in doing so, illuminate the timeless wisdom encapsulated within this cornerstone of religious thought.

Herein, the reader is embarking upon a tedious subject, and one which the author has gone through much trouble to delineate clearly. Even still, owing to the imperfections of the writer, there might be many instances where the subject addressed is reiterated more than once, or where one item is repeated almost exhaustively throughout. In such cases, dear reader, please bear in mind that an understanding of these things is of the utmost importance if we are to arrive at the conclusions of this publication with a proper framework. Therefore, I pray that you are not troubled by these occurrences, and instead welcome them, as they only act to reinforce these all-important truths.

"It is essential to our eternal well-being to know more of God; for love to God depends on a conception of His goodness, His excellence, and a knowledge of His will. It requires an appreciation of His character. **His law is the transcript of His character, and this law He calls upon us to obey.**" (Ellen G. White, *Signs of the Times*, August 2, 1899)

The Ten Commandments are, for the Christian, the root of all moral conduct. By a knowledge of these precepts, morality matures into an ideology that is absolute and objective. Through the Ten Commandments, morality is no longer a relative construct that conforms to the whims of an ever-changing society, but instead becomes a consistent and unvarying framework of ethics. When one is truly convinced of these principles, embracing them brings forth pure joy, and to deviate from them is to forsake one's own sense of right and wrong, resulting in feelings of shame and guilt. This moral framework, based upon the Decalogue, is grounded in God's very nature and government. Being an expression of His character, if "God is love" (1 John 4:8) then it follows that "love is the fulfilling of the law" (Romans 13:10). The law itself *is* love.

We have always thought of the Ten Commandments as requiring our love to God and to all His creatures, but have we ever thought of them as an expression of His love to us? It would be absolutely foolish to demand our love by arbitrary decree; love cannot be given in that way, for love is born only of love. The State might as well legislate that the sun should not shine or that water should not flow downhill, as for the Lord to make such an arbitrary demand for love. In either case, the law could not affect in the slightest the thing legislated about.

Yet it remains true that all the law of God requires is love, and that, as the apostle says, "love is the fulfilling of the law" (Romans 13:10),—of the *whole* law. How is this?—Simply that the law itself, when we understand it, is a revelation of such infinite love as to beget within us a returning, responsive love that can and will fulfill the law.

"God is love" (1 John 4:8). Every word, every jot and tittle, of that law, coming from love, requires only such service as love dictates. When the same love which that law expresses is begotten in our own hearts, and flows out toward God and all His creatures in loving actions, then the law is fulfilled.

It may be objected that the divine love, in order to beget a returning and responsive love in us, is revealed, not in the law, but only in the life and death of Jesus Christ. In one sense this is true, and in another it is not true. The love that God sought to reveal in His law, and throughout all the administration of that law in His government, has been denied by Satan from the beginning; for he is a liar, "and abode not in the truth" (John 8:44). It has also been so obscured and hidden by sin and sorrow that many have not beheld it. But the love of God as revealed in Jesus Christ is no new love for us. God is the same; with Him is "no variableness, neither shadow of turning" (James 1:17). All this love for us He had from the beginning, and He expressed it in his law; only the devil denied it, and a misunderstanding of the nature of sin obscured it. Christ simply revealed the love that God has ever had for us, and that underlies all His laws and government.

The life of Christ is the law of God in action; His death, but the natural result of perfectly keeping that law, and perfectly proclaiming it to others, in a world that hated truth and righteousness. Look at that life and death of immaculate love. In all this did Christ do more than the law requires?—Impossible, for then He were more than perfect; for the Psalmist says, "The law of the Lord is perfect" (Psalm 19:7). Christ's life, then, reveals no new love, but to hearts that were hardened and to eyes that were blinded by sin He reveals anew the same love which dictated every word of that law. *There can exist no conflict between Sinai and Calvary.*

Nevertheless, many today would argue just the opposite. In modern Christianity, love is not defined by the law but by the individual. To them the law of God has become burdensome. They perceive God as an exacting oppressor and His law as restrictive, subjective, and inconsistently applied by God throughout His dealings with man. For this very reason, some go so far as to say that God's law is no longer in effect, but rather done away with by Christ. It is as if to say that Christ, now, by

His sacrifice, condones idolatry, murder, adultery, theft and all sorts of evil. All of these are inharmonious with love, and only serve to destroy it.

> "Satan declared that mercy destroyed justice, that the death of Christ abrogated the Father's law. **Had it been possible for the law to be changed or abrogated, then Christ need not have died.** But to abrogate the law would be to immortalize transgression, and place the world under Satan's control. **It was because the law was changeless, because man could be saved only through obedience to its precepts, that Jesus was lifted up on the cross. Yet the very means by which Christ established the law Satan represented as destroying it.** Here will come the last conflict of the great controversy between Christ and Satan." (Ellen G. White, *The Desire of Ages*, pg. 762)

Such a misunderstanding of Christ's divine mission can only lead poor souls astray from He who seeks to bless them. He did not come to rid men of their obligation to the law of God, for its precepts can never change because God Himself never changes (Malachi 3:6).

To grasp this reality, the reader need only to contemplate a concise selection of verses and follow them to their logical conclusions, for such will prove sufficient. According to 1 John, sin is the transgression of the law of God:

> "Whosoever committeth sin transgresseth also the law: for **sin is the transgression of the law.**" (I John 3:4)

Sin is characterized as any deed that violates the law of God. In this regard, the Ten Commandments serve as a mirror, revealing the nature of sin to us. We approach the knowledge of sin by coming to a knowledge of the law.

> "...for **by the law is the knowledge of sin.**" (Romans 3:20)

> "**...I had not known sin, but by the law:** for I had not known lust, except the law had said, Thou shalt not covet." (Romans 7:7)

How, then, may we know definitively that the law of God is still abiding today? *Because sin still abounds!* Sin is defined as the transgression of the law. Is it true that we are still able to sin today?—Then there *must be* law. For without the law, we could not rightly call these things sin, for it is only by the law that we gain a knowledge of sin. Furthermore, Paul tells us that the "man of *lawlessness*"—the spirit of antichrist—was already at work in his day:

> "Let no one deceive you in any way. For that day will not come, unless the rebellion comes first, and **the man of lawlessness is revealed, the son of destruction... For the mystery of lawlessness is already at work...**" (2 Thessalonians 2:3,7, *ESV*)

Stripped down to its bare essence, sin is characterized as lawlessness. To be lawless, then, is to rebel against God and cast off His moral standard. According to Paul, this is the spirit of "the son of destruction" (2 Thessalonians 2:3). This antichrist spirit works to abrogate the law of the Almighty. And many Christians, today, have become lawless by their own abuse of God's grace. And while His grace is sufficiently given, we must not use it as an excuse to sin—to do this would be properly termed *dis*grace, a devilish counterfeit. His grace acts to reach us while we are *in* sin (Romans 5:8) and deliver us from it—not to strengthen us further under its influence!

The prophet Daniel, looking forward through the annals of history, prophesies of the antichrist in the following manner:

> "And he [the antichrist] shall speak great words against the most High, and shall wear out the saints of the most High, **and think to change times and laws...**" (Daniel 7:25)

The spirit of antichrist is seeking to blind the minds of men to the perpetual nature of the law of God. The adversary aims to change the very way in which we approach God's holy precepts. The Ten Commandments are under attack. Satan has always said that God's law was arbitrary and unjust, and His government tyrannical. By this means he seeks to justify his secession from that government, and his attempt to exalt his own throne above the stars of God. Dear reader, have you set aside God's holy law? Will you continue in rebellion against the operations of God's government?

"If ye love me, **keep my commandments.**" (John 14:15)

"**God has given us His holy precepts, because He loves mankind. To shield us from the results of transgression, He reveals the principles of righteousness...** God desires us to be happy, and He gave us the precepts of the law that in obeying them we might have joy... **Since 'the law of the Lord is perfect,' every variation from it must be evil... The Saviour's life of obedience maintained the claims of the law; it proved that the law could be kept in humanity, and showed the excellence of character that obedience would develop.** All who obey as He did are likewise declaring that the law is 'holy, and just, and good' (Romans 7:12). On the other hand, all who break God's commandments are sustaining Satan's claim that the law is unjust, and cannot be obeyed. **Thus they second the deceptions of the great adversary, and cast dishonor upon God. They are the children of the wicked one, who was the first rebel against God's law.**" (Ellen G. White, *The Desire of Ages*, pg. 308-309)

"**As that law is God's will and God's character, even he cannot change it without changing himself.** But as he includes all goodness now, he cannot change himself without changing to evil. But for God to become evil would be for him to cease to be God, for the word 'God' means good. **If God himself should change, and command what he has forbidden, and forbid what he has commanded, it would not change the underlying tendencies of those precepts to happiness or misery.** It would change God into the embodiment of all evil, instead of all good. He would then be working for the misery of all his children, as now he is for their happiness and joy. It would then be true that God was hate, as now it is true that God is love.

"The whole argument for the absolute stability and perpetuity of God's law rests on axiomatic truth. As it is utterly inconceivable to the human mind that there ever could be a world

> where, or a time when, two and two would be five instead of four, **so it is unthinkable that there could be a world where, or a time when, these principles, if obeyed, would not lead to unity and happiness, and if disobeyed, to division, discord, misery, and strife. They rest upon love, and love never faileth.**" (George Fifield, *God is Love*, pg. 60-61)

As we've briefly explored a few of the corroboratory claims for the unending relevance of the Ten Commandments, we now pivot our focus back to the central theme of this chapter: the significance of God's law and the mirror it holds to His character.

> "God requires perfection of His children. **His law is a transcript of His own character, and it is the standard of all character.** This infinite standard is presented to all that there may be no mistake in regard to the kind of people whom God will have to compose His kingdom. **The life of Christ on earth was a perfect expression of God's law, and when those who claim to be children of God become Christlike in character, they will be obedient to God's commandments...**" (Ellen G. White, *Christ's Object Lessons*, pg. 315)

With the foundation of the law's enduring effect firmly established, we can come to the realization that Christ did not come to destroy—or bring an end to—the law, but rather to *explain it*.

> "Think not that I am come to destroy the law, or the prophets: **I am not come to destroy, but to fulfil.** For verily I say unto you, **Till heaven and earth pass, one jot or one tittle shall in no wise pass from the law,** till all be fulfilled." (Matthew 5:17-18)

Here, Jesus says that He has come to *fulfill* the law. Many misconstrue the definition of this word to mean "to bring to an end." However, we must take the whole verse as it is rendered and employ context. Just before this, Christ is proclaiming that He has *not* come to destroy the law. To destroy the law would be to bring an end thereof—and Christ tells us that this is not His mission. If it were so, then the verse would read, "I am not come to destroy the law, but to destroy it." Sadly, many prefer this illogical adaptation of the text because it permits them to discard the precepts of God and live a life of promiscuity—free from the guilt brought on by transgression. Dear reader, let us state the matter succinctly: to fulfill *does not* mean to destroy. A true biblical definition of the term is more closely rendered as "to set forth fully,"—to demonstrate; to present; to manifest; to *explain*. Romans chapter 13 illustrates for us what it means to fulfill the law:

> "Owe no man any thing, but to love one another: **for he that loveth another hath fulfilled the law.** For this, Thou shalt not commit adultery, Thou shalt not kill, Thou shalt not steal, Thou shalt not bear false witness, Thou shalt not covet; **and if there be any other commandment, it is briefly comprehended in this saying, namely, Thou shalt love thy neighbour as thyself.** Love worketh no ill to his neighbour: therefore **love is the fulfilling of the law.**" (Romans 13:8-10)

To love one another is to fulfill the law—to demonstrate it in its full and proper glory. *Love is the law explained.* To transgress the law of God is to be in conflict with love—it is to introduce discord, anarchy, and ruin. Therefore, the Ten Commandments are divine guidelines on how we may practice love toward God and one another. Ah, how different this life we are compelled to lead here, because of sin, from that which were possible had these principles always been the rule of human action! This is the truth which Jesus came to manifest to men. This is why He, when answering the lawyer, said:

> "Jesus said unto him, **Thou shalt love the Lord thy God with all thy heart,** and with all thy soul, and with all thy mind. This is the first and great commandment. And the second is like unto it, **Thou shalt love thy neighbour as thyself. On these two commandments hang all the law and the prophets.**" (Matthew 22:37-40)

Here, Christ is not subtracting from the Ten Commandments. Rather, He is summarizing them as thus: "love the Lord thy God" and "love thy neighbour" (Matthew 22:37,39). Upon a closer inspection of the Decalogue, one will notice that the first four commandments are how we may demonstrate our love for God, and the last six are how we may demonstrate love for our fellow man. Hence, all ten of the divine precepts may be summed up into the two which Jesus mentioned in this instance. Upon these two principles of love "hang *all* the law" (Matthew 22:40).

Jesus came to dispel humanity's misunderstanding of the law of God. For so long, man used these ordained tenets of heaven as an excuse to judge and condemn others. For so long, man perceived the Decalogue as restrictive and exacting; an arbitrary and oppressive system of jurisprudence. There can be no love found in such a rudimentary understanding. Christ demonstrated, in every aspect of His life, the love that is innately contained within the precepts of the law of God. Through the extension of this love to others, He was illuminating their darkened minds with the Father's own affection for them, as exemplified by His law. In every matter, Jesus revealed—whether by actions or by words—that the summation of God's law is love. Through the same avenue of expression, He demonstrated the Father's true character. This point is of the utmost importance to our discussion. The Apostle John tells us that:

> "He that loveth not knoweth not God; **for God is love.**" (I John 4:8)

To state the subject abruptly: if the fulfillment of God's law is love, and God *is* love, then His law must be a fulfillment (*a fully set forth demonstration; presentation; manifestation; explanation... a perfect transcript*) of His own character of love. Therefore, to bring understanding to God's law is to also bring understanding to His character. Jesus was the full revelation of both these exemplars of love, thereby bringing them into harmony with one another so that mankind might come to truly know the Father.

To transgress the law of God is to be out of harmony with love—with His very character—and thereby we admit that we "knoweth not God" (1 John 4:8). On the other hand, John also tells us that:

> "God is love; and **he that dwelleth in love dwelleth in God,** and God in him." (I John 4:16)

And how do we dwell in love? By being grounded in the divine precepts—the law of the Almighty! It is by being conformed to the law of God—the Father's moral framework—that we come into harmony with His character.

> "**If ye keep my commandments, ye shall abide in my love;** even as I have kept my Father's commandments, and abide in his love." (John 15:10)

By reflecting upon these two motifs of love that Jesus demonstrated in His life and ministry, our hearts become susceptible to the ministrations of the Holy Spirit and, as a result, a process of transformation is instigated where we begin to be changed into a likeness of the same divine image. We begin to be restored back into the image of God—the nature we had before the fall.

> "But we all, with open face beholding as in a glass the glory of the Lord, **are changed into the same image from glory to glory, even as by the Spirit of the Lord.**" (2 Corinthians 3:18)

> "The Son of God clothed his divinity with humanity, and came to the world without parade or display, that he might be accepted, not because of outward attractions, but because of his heavenly attributes of character, as revealed in his words and works. **He presented to men lessons whereby their souls were brought into comparison with the law of God, not in a legal light, but in the light of the Sun of Righteousness, that man by beholding might be changed into the divine image...**" (Ellen G. White, *Signs of the Times,* November 5, 1894)

It is only by the power of Christ working in us that our sinful condition may be overcome. Christ "was in all points tempted like as we are, yet without sin." (Hebrews 4:15). The Savior revealed to us that the law of God could be faithfully observed—that His character could be manifested among men. Christ perfectly upheld the law in every aspect, never faltering in one point for the sake of convenience or individual aspiration. He kept its precepts, not for mere legal purposes, but because His mission was to reveal the character of His Father.

Due to the innate similitude found among the law of God and the character of God, it logically follows that the Father Himself upholds His own commandments with unwavering commitment. To do otherwise would be to contradict His very nature. In other words, if the law is truly a transcript of the divine character, then the Ten Commandments are not only a moral guide for humanity but also a reflection of the unchanging principles that define God's essence and guide His actions throughout eternity. The life of God, as concerns moral principles, is written in that law, and was demonstrated on earth by Jesus Christ. This idea is evidenced by the words of Jesus in the book of John, where He states that the Son's actions mirror those of the Father. "I have kept my Father's commandments," (John 15:10). Christ upholds the law because His Father does so too.

> "Then answered Jesus and said unto them, Verily, verily, I say unto you, **The Son can do nothing of himself, but what he seeth the Father do: for what things soever he doeth, these also doeth the Son likewise."** (John 5:19)

The inspired evidence for this matter is irrefutably clear and convincing. God has revealed His character to us through the use of two mediums—His Son and His law. For so long mankind misconstrued God's law, which in turn led them to reject the Son and, at the same time, cast ambiguity upon the true character of the Father. As previously outlined, Christ's mission to the world was precisely aimed at rectifying this detrimental miscomprehension. It is here, for the sake of making the author's case even more apparent, that we briefly shift our focus to the sixth commandment:

> "Thou shalt not kill." (Exodus 20:13)

With a thorough grasp of the argument presented above, what this commandment should suggest to the reader is that *God does not kill.* In accordance with His directive to humanity, the same principle is observed by His own actions. To do otherwise would be to betray His own nature; to transgress His very character. This would merely provide an avenue for Satan to level accusations against the Divine, alleging a manifestation of hypocrisy. Oh how misguided we have been in our understanding of God! The God we serve is not an executioner—He is the Great Physician! He is Jehovah Rapha, "the LORD that healeth thee." (Exodus 15:26). Our God does not "render evil for evil" (1 Thessalonians 5:15), no matter the circumstance. Not causing death or harm is an inherent aspect of His natural disposition. Therefore, He *cannot* pay "the wages of sin" (Romans 6:23). The verse reads, "the wages *of* sin is death"—it does *not* say "the wages *for* sin is death." This distinction holds paramount significance! Sin pays its own wages; the natural result of sin is death.

> "Then when lust hath conceived, it bringeth forth sin: **and sin, when it is finished, bringeth forth death.**" (James 1:15)

Death, decay, and destruction are the inherent gifts of sin—but "the gift of God is eternal life through Jesus Christ our Lord." (Romans 6:23). It is Satan, the author of sin, that breeds death and destruction. It was Christ's mission to counteract the works of the devil by revealing the true character of the Father to humanity.

> "He that committeth sin is of the devil; for the devil sinneth from the beginning. **For this purpose the Son of God was manifested, that he might destroy the works of the devil.**" (I John 3:8)

> "Forasmuch then as the children are partakers of flesh and blood, he [Jesus] also himself likewise took part of the same; **that through death he might destroy him that had the power of death, that is, the devil...**" (Hebrews 2:14)

To elaborate upon this idea, let's take a brief look at Revelation chapter 9:

> "And they had a king over them, which is the angel of the bottomless pit, **whose name in the Hebrew tongue is Abaddon, but in the Greek tongue hath his name Apollyon.**" (Revelation 9:11)

The word "angel" here would seem to refer to the chief of the evil angels, viz. Lucifer. The Hebrew name, אֲבַדּוֹן ('Ăḇaddōn), is an indication of "the angel who rules in hell,"—another allusion to Lucifer. This name, Abaddon, is literally translated "destruction." Its Greek equivalent—Ἀπολλύων (Apollyōn)—means "to destroy" (Strong's G0623). The name, Apollyon, properly denotes "a destroyer," and is given to this "angel of the bottomless pit" because this would be his principal characteristic. It is our adversary that may accurately be characterized as "the destroyer,"—not God! God is the Creator; to destroy would conflict with His very nature. The wages of sin is death—and death serves as a form of irreversible destruction. Sin does not need any direct or forceful intervention on behalf of God to result in death and destruction. Rather, these are the natural repercussions of sin—not imposed consequences. To say that God helps in the destruction of the transgressor is unsuitable, anti-biblical, and illogical. God is not the author of sin, and to allege that He is in any way involved in its effects is among the most reprehensible forms of blasphemy.

> "We are to observe carefully every lesson Christ has given throughout His life and teaching. **He does not destroy; He improves whatever He touches...**" (Ellen G. White, *Selected Messages*, vol. 1, pg. 118)

The conclusions drawn from the arguments presented in this chapter, as the author contends, demonstrate a logical consistency and coherence. For the remainder of the current volume, the author intends to employ a contextual interchangeability between the concepts of God's law and His character, as the congruency between the two may be clearly seen. It would, therefore, do the reader well to conceptualize them in this manner: through the act of violating the divine law, and thereby exhibiting conduct contrary to the intrinsic nature of the Divine, which is love, individuals position themselves beyond the conduit through which vitality is upheld, consequently culminating in a state of mortality. It is this line of reasoning which will serve as a segue into the topics addressed in the following chapter.

> "**Satan represents God's law of love as a law of selfishness.** He declares that it is impossible for us to obey its precepts. The fall of our first parents, with all the woe that has resulted, he charges upon the Creator, **leading men to look upon God as the author of sin, and suffering, and death. Jesus was to unveil this deception...**" (Ellen. G. White, *The Desire of Ages,* pg. 24)

> "**He [Jesus] obeyed the law perfectly,** and all who have a right conception of the plan of redemption will see that they cannot be saved while in transgression of God's holy precepts..." (Ellen G. White, *Faith and Works,* pg. 88)

> "**The man who attempts to keep the commandments of God from a sense of obligation merely—because he is required to do so—will never enter into the joy of obedience.** He does not obey. **When the requirements of God are accounted a burden because they cut across human inclination, we may know that the life is not a Christian life. True obedience is the outworking of a principle within. It springs from the love of righteousness, the love of the law of God.** The essence of all righteousness is loyalty to our Redeemer. This will lead us to do right because it is right—because right doing is pleasing to God..." (Ellen G. White, *Christ's Object Lessons,* pg. 97)

Chapter 6

Divine Decree or Cosmic Code: Unraveling the Nature of God's Law

*"**The last great conflict between truth and error is but the final struggle of the long-standing controversy concerning the law of God.** Upon this battle we are now entering—a battle between the laws of men and the precepts of Jehovah, between the religion of the Bible and the religion of fable and tradition." (Ellen G. White, Darkness Before Dawn, pg. 28)*

*"You may have seen something in regard to the righteousness of Christ, but there is truth yet to be seen clearly, and that should be estimated by you as precious as rare jewels. **You will see the law of God and interpret it to the people in an entirely different light from what you have done in the past, for the law of God will be seen by you as revealing a God of mercy and righteousness. The atonement, made by the stupendous sacrifice of Jesus Christ, will be seen by you in an altogether different light.**" (Ellen G. White, Signs of the Times, November 13, 1893)*

The operational dynamic of God's law has, for too long, suffered from gross misunderstanding. Its mode of function—the intended purpose behind it—has been misapplied. Many have erred in assuming that God, vested with His supreme authority, promulgates irrational and capricious decrees, imposing upon humanity a strict judicial obedience that ostensibly comes at the cost of man's own autonomy. This devilish counterfeit has so intoxicated the theology of the Protestant Churches that many today, unbeknownst, find themselves involved in a pagan form of worship. However, this imperial perspective of God's government falls short of capturing the true essence of His law, which transcends mere arbitrary imposition. Accurately understood, His law is intricately woven into the very tapestry of the universe itself, in consonance with its innate structure. Stated another way: sometime in the distant annals of eternity, amidst the course of creation, God ordered the laws of the universe in such a way as to be in direct harmony with His very nature. This would suggest that the law is as eternal and unchanging as God Himself.

> "**For the invisible things of him from the creation of the world are clearly seen, being understood by the things that are made,** even his eternal power and Godhead; so that they are without excuse..." (Romans 1:20)

As established in the prior chapter, a clear alignment emerges between His law and His character. These two aspects are, therefore, effectively interchangeable: His character finds its delineation within His law, while reciprocally, His law serves as a reflective manifestation of His character—both grounded in altruistic love. And it is this coupled principle of love that finds its proper context in the very operations of reality.

> "In presenting the binding claims of the law, many have failed to portray the infinite love of Christ... T**he law is to be presented to its transgressors, not as something apart from God, but rather as an exponent of His mind and character.** As the sunlight cannot be separated from the sun, so God's law cannot be rightly presented to man apart from the divine Author." (Ellen G. White, *Selected Messages*, vol. 1, pg. 371)

Instead of being a system of imposed rules by which existence is governed and enforced, God's law makes up the natural and fundamental protocols upon which reality and life truly function. To deviate from these principles is to be in disharmony with the laws that regulate existence—misery and death are surely the result.

> "**The same power that upholds nature, is working also in man. The same great laws that guide alike the star and the atom control human life.** The laws that govern the heart's action, regulating the flow of the current of life to the body, are the laws of the mighty

Intelligence that has the jurisdiction of the soul. From Him all life proceeds. Only in harmony with Him can be found its true sphere of action. **For all the objects of His creation the condition is the same—a life sustained by receiving the life of God, a life exercised in harmony with the Creator's will. To transgress His law, physical, mental, or moral, is to place one's self out of harmony with the universe, to introduce discord, anarchy, ruin.**" (Ellen G. White, *Education*, pg. 99)

"In some sense, God's wrath is built into the very structure of created reality. In rejecting God's structure and establishing our own, in violating God's intention for the creation and substituting our own intentions, we cause our own disintegration.

"The human condition, which Paul describes in Romans 1:18-32, is not something caused by God. The phrase 'revealed from heaven' (where 'heaven' is a typical Jewish substitute word for 'God') does not depict some kind of divine intervention, but rather **the inevitability of human debasement which results when God's will, built into the created order, is violated.**

"Since the created order has its origin in God, Paul can say that the wrath of God is now (constantly) being revealed 'from heaven.' It is revealed in the fact that the rejection of God's truth (Rom 1:18-20), that is, the truth about God's nature and will, leads to futile thinking (Rom 1:21-22), idolatry (Rom 1:23), perversion of God-intended sexuality (Rom 1:24-27) and relational-moral brokenness (Rom 1:28-32).

"The expression 'God gave them over' (or 'handed them over'), which appears three times in this passage (Rom 1:24, 26, 28), supports the idea that **the sinful perversion of human existence, though resulting from human decisions, is to be understood ultimately as God's punishment which we, in freedom, bring upon ourselves.**

"In light of these reflections, the common notion that God punishes or blesses in direct proportion to our sinful or good deeds cannot be maintained. God's relationship with us is not on a reciprocal basis. God's radical, unconditional love has been demonstrated in that, while we were sinners, Christ died for us.

God loves us with an everlasting love. But the rejection of that love separates us from its life-giving power. The result is disintegration and death.

"Against such a perverted creation, God's wrath is revealed." (Walter C. Kaiser Jr., Peter H. Davids, F.F. Bruce, Manfred T. Brauch, *Hard Sayings of the Bible*, InterVarsity Press, pg. 542-543)

On the correct understanding of these principles of the nature of God's law depends our power to comprehend God's love in all His dealings with His creatures. On this rests the whole philosophy of the purpose of creation and of the plan of redemption. The existence of misery and suffering, the need for an atonement, and how that atonement is accomplished by Christ, can be understood in the light of God's love only as the nature of His law stands revealed. It is for this reason that we purpose to dwell at some length in these pages on the nature of God's law.

For the sake of context, we will refer to God's law as "natural," or design law. We will refer to man's law as "imposed," or imperial law.

Natural law encompasses a collection of unvarying and ethical principles deemed intrinsic to the fabric of nature and the universe. It not only guides the honorable realms of morality and justice, but also extends its influence to encompass the regularities observed in disciplines such as mathematics and physics, underscoring the consistent operation of both physical and moral laws; this is the basis for God's government. Imposed law, on the other hand, refers to legal rules and regulations established by a governing authority, often to maintain the order and control of a society. They may be changed at will in order to conform to varying circumstances; this is the basis for earthly governments. While natural law is seen as universal, immutable, and fundamental, imposed law is artificial, subject to change, and specific to a particular society or jurisdiction.

For example, natural law dictates that when someone jumps into the air, they will inevitably fall back down to earth. This is called the law of gravity. Mankind, of themselves, cannot enact a law that in any way diminishes gravity's effect—this would not only be irrational, but impossible. The immutable character of natural law prohibits its alteration via executive edicts, as it is inherently ingrained within the fundamental fabric of reality. Therefore, the enforcement of natural law is unnecessary, as individuals inevitably experience the ramifications of their own actions in accordance with these intrinsic principles, irrespective of the individual's personal belief system.

If an individual maintains the conviction that they possess the capacity for flight, even ardently, it is imperative to acknowledge that such a mindset does not substantively influence the immutable principles governing gravitational forces. One might, driven by an impassioned faith in their ability to fly, opt to throw themselves from an elevated height; nevertheless, they will meet the inexorable repercussions dictated by the established laws of nature: they will fall. It is the same with the law of God.

Conversely, imposed law remains subject to discretionary enactment or repeal by prevailing authorities or governing entities, depending upon their judgment of specific circumstances. Laws can be added, laws can be changed, and laws can be done away with. Imposed law retains its applicability solely within a defined jurisdiction. For instance, in basketball it is considered just (*right, lawful, etc.*) to handle the ball with your hands, while in a sport like soccer it would be considered unjust (*wrong, illegal, etc.*) to do so. Imposed law needs to be enforced by the compelling arm of an authoritative power, as there is no intrinsic repercussion to their being broken.

Unfortunately, many today perceive God's law as functioning in this very same manner. Just as man's law, God's law is considered to be susceptible to alteration. Many even argue that it was artificially manufactured to suit the selfish desires of an exacting ruler, and that men are either lifted up or cast down according as they help or hinder these narcissistic passions of an egotistical deity. Moreover, it is a prevailing belief that God Himself is obligated to administer punishment to those who transgress His law. All this is to lower the divine down to the human sphere, amalgamating that which is sacred with the secular.

> "But in vain they do worship me, **teaching for doctrines the commandments of men.**" (Matthew 15:9)

> "Jesus answered, **My kingdom is not of this world:** if my kingdom were of this world, then would my servants fight, that I should not be delivered to the Jews: but **now is my kingdom not from hence.**" (John 18:36)

By no means does the author intend to inspire sentiments of rebellion or anarchy in one's attitude toward the civil authority, as we are instructed to render "unto Caesar the things which are Caesar's," and "unto God the things that are God's" (Matthew 22:21). Neither is the author suggesting that the civil government's duty to deal with crime and misconduct should be challenged by God's people. We are called to submit to the authority of our leaders, so much as it does not conflict with our duty to uphold the precepts of Jehovah. The two systems—man's law and God's law—are entirely distinct and should remain so.

As Alonzo T. Jones once brilliantly conveyed, in his work titled, *Civil Government and Religion*, civil statutes define crime, and deal with crime, but not with sin; while the divine statutes define sin, and deal with sin, but not with crime. The moral law pertains to the thoughts and the intents of the heart, and therefore, in the very nature of the case, lies beyond the reach or control of the civil power. To hate, is murder; to covet, is idolatry; to think impurely of a woman, is adultery; these are all equally immoral, and violations of the law of God, but no civil government seeks to punish for them. A man may hate his neighbor all his life; he may covet everything on earth; he may think impurely of every woman that he sees, but so long as these things are confined to his thoughts, the civil power cannot touch him. It does not attempt to punish him. But let us carry this further. Only let that man's hatred lead him, either by word or sign, to attempt an injury to his neighbor, and the State will punish him; only let his covetousness lead him to lay hands on what is not his own, in an attempt to steal, and the State will punish him; only let his impure thoughts lead him to attempt violence to any woman, and the State will punish him. Yet bear in mind that even then the State does not punish him for his *immorality*, but for his *incivility*. The immorality lies in the heart, and can be measured by God only. Therefore it is clear that in fact the State punishes no man because he is immoral, but because he is uncivil. It cannot punish immorality; it must punish incivility.

By all these things it is made clear that the law of God (natural law) and the law of men (imposed law) are entirely disparate in their scope and mode of function. The problem is not necessarily man-made laws. The problem, which the writer seeks to convey in this section, occurs when humanity perceives God's law to work in the *same way* as man's law, which is to say, God must enforce His law in the same manner civil governments enforce their laws, and that, like man's law, His law may be altered. This misunderstanding weakens man's perception of his duty to keep the law of God. Compromises are made; certain precepts are cast down or abrogated for convenience's sake, and the devil wins a decided victory over many souls. What the author suggests is that, by its very method of operation, violations of the moral law carry with them inherent consequences. A man's immoral thoughts work in him a degradation of character and make it so that his heart is hardened, and he is more likely to fall into temptation and sin, thereby reaping the natural repercussions thereof.

To believe that God's law is merely a system of imposed rules that were arbitrarily contrived, and which He chooses to enforce with crude punishments, is to worship a god not conveyed in scripture. It is to liken the kingdom of God to the kingdoms of men. The erroneous idea that God's laws may be changed, or abrogated, is a deceit borrowed from Romanism. His law is as eternal and immutable as Himself, for it is a reflection of the very nature of His Being.

> "There is no such thing as weakening or strengthening the law of Jehovah. **As it has been, so it is. It always has been, and always will be,** holy, just, and good, complete in itself. **It cannot be repealed or changed. To 'honor' or 'dishonor' it is but the speech of men.**" (Ellen G. White, *Prophets and Kings*, pg. 625)

The perception of God's law, as natural or imposed, significantly influences one's understanding of His character. Does one view Him as a benevolent and compassionate Creator, or as an authoritarian and austere dictator? Beneath the distortion of the imposed law view, God's inherent nature becomes perverted. Instead of promoting virtues of affection, sincerity, and tenderness, this doctrine propagates the notion that God's benevolence has been supplanted by severity and inflexibility. He is subject to an obligatory and judicial responsibility of promptly punishing sinners. This imperialistic view has a wrong understanding of divine justice. It proposes that He wields His might to torment and extinguish those who defy Him, thereby casting Him as the Wellspring of death and destruction rather than the Source of life and restoration. Furthermore, this notion contends that true freedom of choice is illusory, for to oppose His will is to invite incendiary annihilation via His own agency, leaving no genuine alternative within this paradigm—as if God were a racketeering and malevolent ruler. Under this ominous ultimatum, individuals are presented with a stark choice: either venerate Him without question, or confront the certainty of their own destruction.

Within this legal framework, God governs through instilling fear in His subjects. But fear and love are inversely proportionate. Is it by fear of punishment that we are brought to kneel before God?—Or is it love?

"**There is no fear in love, but perfect love casts out fear. For fear has to do with punishment,** and whoever fears has not been perfected in love. We love because he first loved us." (I John 4:18-19, *ESV*)

Upon a wide study of the Bible, the governance attributed to God doesn't resemble an imperial rule. Rather than needing to maintain and enforce His laws, they naturally exhibit an unchanging characteristic akin to His own. The core principles of this inherent and timeless law were inscribed and embodied within the Ten Commandments, and it is these ten precepts that guide and direct fallen humanity back into a state of harmony with the divine character of love.

"**Wherefore the law was our schoolmaster to bring us unto Christ, that we might be justified by faith.** But after that faith is come, we are no longer under a schoolmaster." (Galatians 3:24-25)

"**The law of God existed before man was created. The angels were governed by it. Satan fell because he transgressed the principles of God's government. After Adam and Eve were created, God made known to them His law. It was not then written, but was rehearsed to them by Jehovah...** After Adam's sin and fall, nothing was taken from the law of God. **The principles of the Ten Commandments existed before the fall, and were of a character suited to the condition of a holy order of beings. The principles were more explicitly stated to man after the fall, and worded to meet the case of fallen intelligences.** This was necessary in consequence of the minds of men being blinded by transgression." (Ellen G. White, *Christ in His Sanctuary*, pg. 30)

The law's foundation is rooted in His intrinsic quality of love. Nature's operational components are constructed upon the same premise of self-sacrifice and giving, mirroring the essential nature of God, who is selfless; other-centered; love personified.

"Thus every attribute of God is simply the attribute of love. And love includes the all in all of our Father. **His laws are simply the laws of a kind Father, intended to promote the happiness of his children. They are not arbitrary. It is not that God, sitting up on**

> **some high throne, said to mankind, You do thus and so, and I will let you live; but you do otherwise, and I will kill you. God does not kill. He is the Fountain of life. His laws are not so simply because he said so, but even so because they were so.** In infinite wisdom he foreknew the underlying principles of happiness and life, and in infinite love he foretold these principles, saying, This way, my child; here is the joy and peace and life forevermore. Don't go that way. That way is misery and death. Every precept of the decalogue, which is the epitome of his law, directly speaks from this principle…" (George Fifield, *General Conference Daily Bulletin,* February 19, 1897, pg. 90)

Contained within the chronicles of natural law, a common thread may readily be discerned. That thread is selflessness—denying one's self for the sake of another. This is the epitome of love, and this is exactly what Jesus demonstrated for us.

> "Greater love hath no man than this, **that a man lay down his life for his friends.**" (John 15:13)

> "**Hereby perceive we the love of God, because he laid down his life for us:** and we ought to lay down our lives for the brethren." (I John 3:16)

> "Then said Jesus unto his disciples, **If any man will come after me, let him deny himself,** and take up his cross, and follow me." (Matthew 16:24)

Encompassed within the life of Christ, intrinsic to the fundamental nature of the Father, and exemplified through the immutable laws of the natural world, resides an altruistic cycle of charity and generosity—an overarching theme of self-sacrifice. In the same manner that God imparts of His essence to uphold the vitality of His children, so too does the flower disperse its seeds to facilitate the flourishing of new blossoms. These principles of self-sacrificing love and giving are integral to God's creation because they are innate within Himself. If it were not so, life would cease to exist due to the inevitable consequences of greed, self-seeking, and egoism.

"Whosoever shall seek to **save his life shall lose it;** and whosoever shall **lose his life shall preserve it.**" (Luke 17:33)

The Adventist pioneer, Alonzo T. Jones, grasped this concept proficiently. He aptly delineates the attributes of both selfishness and selflessness in the subsequent passage. In this particular context, it's important to note that Jones employs the term "nature" in a manner contrary to the definition put forth in this volume. He substitutes the concepts of greed, self-seeking, and egoism, which we define as unnatural, with his usage of "nature." The author contends that Jones probably uses this expression in the context of a carnal (*sinful*) and animalistic nature, rather than how this volume has employed the term. Additionally, he replaces our conventional use of "natural law"—which is attributed to God—with the term "grace."

"'SELF-PRESERVATION is the first law of nature.' But self-sacrifice is the first law of grace. In order to self-preservation, self-defense is essential. In order to self-sacrifice, self-surrender is essential. In self-defense, the only thing that can be employed is force. In self-surrender, the only thing that can be employed is love. In self-preservation, by self-defense, through the employment of force, force meets force, and this means only war. In self-sacrifice, by self-surrender, through love, force is met by love, and this means only peace. Self-preservation, then, means only war: while self-sacrifice means only peace. But war means only death: Self-preservation, then, meaning only war, means only death. While self-sacrifice, meaning only peace, means only life. Self-preservation being the first law of nature, nature then means only death. While self-sacrifice being the first law of grace, grace means only life. But death is only the wages of sin: nature, then meaning only death, it is so only because nature means sin. While life being only the reward of righteousness: grace meaning only life, it is so only because grace means righteousness. **Sin and righteousness, nature and grace, are directly opposite and antagonistic elements. They occupy realms absolutely distinct. Nature, self-preservation, self-defense, force, war, and death, occupy only the realm of sin. Grace, self-sacrifice, self-surrender, love, peace, and life, occupy only the realm of righteousness. The**

> **realm of sin is the realm of Satan. The realm of grace is the realm of God. All the power of the domain of grace is devoted to saving men from the dominion of sin.** This in order, that 'as sin hath reigned unto death, even so might grace reign, through righteousness, unto eternal life by Jesus Christ our Lord.' On which side do you stand in this great controversy?" (A. T. Jones, *The American Sentinel 12,* March 4, 1897, pg. 129)

This means that selfless love is in utter distinction to the principles maintained by an imperialistic approach to God's law. Love, as an ethos, involves self-sacrifice—a concept which is alien to the force employed through imperialism.

Timothy Jennings, M.D., has been a well-known advocate for the natural model of God's law. Here, he sums up the matter quite nicely:

> "As all Bible students know, Scripture tells us that God is love (I John 4:8), **but what many have not considered is that when God built His universe He built it to operate in harmony with His own nature of love.** The construction protocol on which God built His universe is known as God's law. **And this law is the law of love, an expression of His nature and character [Isaiah 51:6, 7; Romans 13:10]…** Functionally, Paul describes this law as 'love seeks not its own,' or 'love is not self-seeking' (I Corinthians 13:5). This means that love is selfless rather than selfish. **Love is giving rather than taking and life is actually built, by God, to operate on this principle of giving.** A simple example of this law in action is respiration. With every breath we breathe we give away carbon dioxide (CO2) to the plants, and the plants give back oxygen to us (the law of respiration). **This is God's design for life, a perpetual circle of free giving. It is an expression of God's character of love, and life is built to operate on it.** If you break this law, this circle of giving, by tying a plastic bag over your head and selfishly hoarding your body's CO2, you break the design protocol for life, and the result is death. 'The wages [result] of sin is death' (Romans 6:23). This circle of giving is the law that God constructed life to operate on." (Dr. Timothy Jennings, *The Remedy Bible,* Preface)

To, instead, promulgate that God's law is of an imperial framework is to trample upon His true character. It is to misplace His kingdom. It is to disregard the principles of love and selflessness and to idolize fear and covetousness. Imperial kingdoms manifest conspicuous inclinations towards coercion, avarice, and self-seeking pursuits, characteristically driven by a zealous quest for supremacy and subjugation. They make war with those that oppose their purposes; they are swift to chastise and penalize rebellion. In stark contrast, God's kingdom is characterized by principles antithetical to the forceful imposition, rapacious desires, and self-seeking motives observed among imperial dominions. Instead, it embodies virtues of compassion, other-centeredness, and benevolence, reflecting a transcendent paradigm of governance anchored in spiritual and moral values rather than arbitrarily imposed structures of legality.

Within the proper context of natural law, it is understood that God does not come near the sinner to punish or destroy, as to do this is rendered unnecessary by the mere fact that the outworking of the natural course of transgression will manifest inherent consequences. Instead, God's aim is to heal and restore the sinner back to harmony with the divine nature that humanity possessed prior to the fall.

Does the author, by putting forth such a premise as this, in any way diminish God's power? Do we make God out to be weak or idle by the claims presented in this section? Quite the opposite—for the author's position is centered upon edification! While we humans often associate power with coercion and fear, God showcases power through love and truth. Said Napoleon, while languishing in exile on the barren rock of St. Helena:

> "I know man and I tell you, Jesus Christ is no mere man. Between him and every other person in the world there is no possible term of comparison. **Alexander, Caesar, Charlemagne, and I have founded empires, but on what did we rest the creation of our genius? Upon force. Jesus Christ founded his empire upon love;**

> **and at this hour, millions would die for him.**" (Napoleon Bonaparte)

The misperception of the Godhead through the polluted lens of imperial law has led to a situation where individuals exhibit greater fear towards the very One who endeavors to rescue them, as opposed to the sin that is actively causing their demise.

> "**Under imposed law models, there is nothing inherently wrong with breaking the law.** Going 50-mph in a 45-mph zone doesn't naturally result in any injury or harm to the violator of the law. **The violator must be caught by the authorities, have their deeds recorded, their case presented before a judge, and then receive an arbitrarily determined penalty inflicted as punishment. This is human law, not Creator law. This is the way of sinful beings, not a sinless God. This idea of law is the basis of penal substitution theology. It is founded on a lie about God's law and presents a view of God's government that is functionally no different than sinful human governments. In the penal view, God becomes the source of inflicted pain, suffering, and death. It is taught, in the penal view, that God's use of power to torture and kill is 'justice,' because sin must be punished. Such bad theology is the fruit of accepting Satan's lie about God's law and that God, in order to be just, must punish sin. In this view, rather than God working to heal and save the spiritually terminal, God becomes the One from whom we need to be protected,** resulting in theologies that have, as their function, the sole purpose of hiding and protecting us from God, **rather than heal us to be fit to live in His presence.** Consider the many ideas taught in Christianity that have, as their function, the purpose of hiding us from God. Why? Because **people wrongly believe that if God saw their sin and their sinfulness, that He would be required to lash out with wrath and anger to inflict pain and suffering to punish them for their sin. This is exactly what Satan wants people to think, because this idea keeps people hiding themselves from God.** But David of old prayed, 'search me and see the wicked way in me'. **He didn't want to hide his sinfulness from God, because he knew God wouldn't punish him, but was the only One who could heal him,** so he prayed, 'create in me a clean heart and renew a right spirit within

> me.' God's end-time people are to present a message to the world that calls them back to worship the Designer, and to worship 'him who made the heavens, earth, sea and foundations of water.' (Rev. 14:7). **This is a call to reject the dictator-views of God and embrace the Creator,** Designer, and Builder of reality! **This means we must reject imposed law and all the false penal legal theology upon which it is founded.**" (Dr. Timothy Jennings, *Penal Substitution versus Design Law—What's the Difference?*)

At the risk of reiteration, it yet remains imperative for the writer to underscore this assertion anew: God is not the progenitor of malevolent acts, nor does He promulgate the subsequent unfurling of their ramifications. Rather, these phenomena materialize innately and inevitably as a natural result of sin.

> "In rejecting God's structure and establishing our own, in violating God's intention for the creation and substituting our own intentions, **we cause or own disintegration.**" (Kaiser, W., et al., *Hard Sayings of the Bible,* Intervarsity Press, 1996, pg. 542)

> "God gives us the freedom to walk outside the boundaries of His law and **instead of reaping imposed punishments by God, we reap the natural consequences of disobedience.**" (Kevin J. Mullins, *Did God Kill Jesus Instead of Killing Us?,* pg. 8)

Due to its intrinsic function and regularity, natural law may be reliably anticipated. Similar to how one can predict that pushing a glass off the edge of a table will cause it to fall, one may also be equally certain that persisting in a life of sin will sever one's connection to the Wellspring of life, resulting in death. God is love and the Creator of all life—He is the Source by which all life is sustained. To be out of harmony with love—to be disconnected from God—can only mean death.

> "God is love; and **he that dwelleth in love dwelleth in God...**" (I John 4:16)

> "For **in him we live,** and move, and have our being..." (Acts 17:28)

Sin involves breaking the natural law, signifying actions that oppose God's character, resulting in disharmony with love, disconnection from the Wellspring of life, and an embrace of mortality. Sin is expensive—incredibly expensive. But the price isn't paid in cash. Rather, it's paid in mental, emotional, spiritual, and even physical pain.

> "Sin is lawlessness; wrong adjustment to right laws; wrong uses of right things. And this accounts for all the physical and material sorrow, sickness, misery, poverty, bitterness, violence, death in the world... **pain, calamity, sickness, and death are not to be attributed to God as causing them, and as sending them upon us, but that they and all other evils have entered into the world as the fruits and consequences of sin.**" (Charles Cutbert Hall, *Does God Send Trouble?*, pg. 25, 80, published in 1894)

God didn't create an arbitrary list of "DOs" and "DON'Ts" to test our obedience. No, He laid out a set of essential guidelines for living. His grief towards lying, stealing, cheating, coveting, murder, jealousy, and pride is because all these behaviors destroy relationships—they obstruct the cycle of love and giving. Everything that the Bible labels as sin is something that God is trying to protect us from—He wants to heal us of our sinful condition which, if left alone, is terminal. God has no pleasure in the death of the wicked, but instead mourns for every soul that is lost. He yearns for His children to embody the principles of His law and convert life into agreement with itself.

> "**For I have no pleasure in the death of him that dieth,** saith the Lord GOD: **wherefore turn yourselves, and live ye.**" (Ezekiel 18:32)

> "As I live, saith the Lord GOD, **I have no pleasure in the death of the wicked; but that the wicked turn from his way and live: turn ye, turn ye from your evil ways; for why will ye die,** O house of Israel?" (Ezekiel 33:11)

His desire for us is love, peace, grace, and harmony with Him and with all of creation. Sin is our defiant rejection of this in an effort to satisfy our own selfish desires.

> "**Men and women cannot violate natural law by indulging depraved appetite and lustful passions, and not violate the law of God... All our enjoyment or suffering may be traced to obedience or transgression of natural law.** Our gracious heavenly Father sees the deplorable condition of men who, some knowingly but many ignorantly, are living in violation of the laws that He has established. **And in love and pity to the race... He publishes His law and the penalty that will follow the transgression of it, that all may learn and be careful to live in harmony with natural law.** He proclaims His law so distinctly and makes it so prominent that it is like a city set on a hill. All accountable beings can understand it... **To make plain natural law, and urge the obedience of it, is the work that accompanies the third angel's message to prepare a people for the coming of the Lord.**" (Ellen G. White, *Testimonies for the Church*, vol. 3, pg. 161)

> "In Isaiah's day the spiritual understanding of mankind was dark through misapprehension of God. **Long had Satan sought to lead men to look upon their Creator as the author of sin and suffering and death.** Those whom he had thus deceived, imagined that God was hard and exacting. They regarded Him as watching to denounce and condemn, unwilling to receive the sinner so long as there was a legal excuse for not helping him. **The law of love by which heaven is ruled had been misrepresented by the archdeceiver as a restriction upon men's happiness, a burdensome yoke from which they should be glad to escape. He declared that its precepts could not be obeyed and that the penalties of transgression were bestowed arbitrarily...**" (Ellen G. White, *Prophets and Kings*, pg. 311)

Now that we've outlined a clear delineation between natural law (*God's law*) and imposed law (*man's law*), one more observation becomes necessary here. Having already determined the origin of the imperial view of God's kingdom and the change which it caused in the heart of Christianity, we now shift our focus to the events that led to this view being proliferated among the entirety of Christendom. For the sake of the reader's recollection, however, the author will briefly summarize the first two points of contention before delving into that which now becomes our aim.

It must be clearly understood that this imperial perspective of God's kingdom had its roots in Satan's ideology.

> "**Satan is constantly at work, with intense energy and under a thousand disguises, to misrepresent the character and government of God.** With extensive, well-organized plans and marvelous power, he is working to hold the inhabitants of the world under his deceptions." (Ellen, G. White, *Patriarchs and Prophets,* pg. 78)

> "**It is Satan's constant effort to misrepresent the character of God, the nature of sin, and the real issues at stake in the great controversy. His sophistry lessens the obligation of the divine law and gives men license to sin. At the same time he causes them to cherish false conceptions of God so that they regard Him with fear and hate rather than with love.** The cruelty inherent in his own character is attributed to the Creator; it is embodied in systems of religion and expressed in modes of worship." (Ellen G. White, *The Great Controversy,* pg. 569)

The essence of Christianity underwent a transformation when it embraced Satan's interpretation of the heavenly kingdom, along with his malevolent perception of God. Men began to perceive the Father in the same way our adversary does.

> "**The heart in love with sin clothed Him with its own attributes, and this conception strengthened the power of sin. Bent on self-pleasing, men came to regard God as such a one as themselves—** a Being whose aim was self-glory, whose requirements were suited to His own pleasure; a Being by whom men were lifted up or cast down according as they helped or hindered His selfish purpose. **The lower classes regarded the Supreme Being as one scarcely differing from their oppressors, save by exceeding them in power. By these ideas every form of religion was molded.** Each was a system of exaction. **By gifts and ceremonies, the worshipers**

> **sought to propitiate the Deity in order to secure His favor for their own ends...**" (Ellen G. White, *Education*, pg. 75)

Our new objective is to delve into the sequence of events that facilitated the widespread propagation of this viewpoint across the entire Christian world. As it has already been established, the very *idea* of how God's law functions found a new perspective in the minds of mankind. The author places emphasis on the word "idea" here because God's law cannot be changed—not truly. We can only change how we choose to conceive of God's law, but this of itself has no real effect on innate principles that cannot be abrogated or altered. We now inquire as to what that change is and by whom it was ordained and dispersed. For this, we turn our eyes to a prophetic scripture found in the book of Daniel:

> "And he shall speak great words against the most High, and shall wear out the saints of the most High, **and think to change times and laws...**" (Daniel 7:25)

This verse speaks of a little horn power that would arise and seek to place itself above all that is worshipped and obeyed—it would seek to place itself above God Himself. It is well agreed upon by biblical scholars and apologetics that this little horn is, indeed, the antichrist power, as it shares the very same ambition. The question arises: who or what, then, is the manifestation of this antichrist power? The answer to this question alone could fill a series of volumes—for the topic is vast in its scope. Given the constraints of space in the current work, we will refrain from providing an exhaustive examination of the author's process of arriving at the conclusion regarding the identity of the antichrist/little horn power. Instead, we will refer to the prominent insights of the forerunners of our faith: the Protestant reformers. Who did they ardently believe to fill the position of the antichrist power?

> "**Many of the great Christians of Reformation and post-reformation times shared this view of prophetic truth and identified antichrist with the Roman Papacy...** Among the

adherents of this interpretation were the Waldenses, the Hussites, Wyclif, Luther, Calvin, Zwingli, Melanchthon, John Gill, the martyrs—Cranmer, Tyndale, Latimer and Ridley." (*The Blessed Hope*, pg. 33)

"**I know that the pope is antichrist, and that his seat is that of Satan himself...** The papacy is a general chase, by command of the Roman Pontiff, for the purpose of running down and destroying souls." (Martin Luther)

"We call the Roman Pontiff **antichrist.**" (John Calvin)

"**He [the pope] is in an emphatic sense, the 'Man of Sin',** as he increases all manner of sin above measure." (John Wesley)

"The pope should be recognized as the very **antichrist.**" (John Knox)

These statements should awaken the anxiety of all Protestants who prize the pure principles of the gospel. To gain a more comprehensive and biblical understanding into the aspect which we haven't touched upon in this context—namely, the correlation between the Roman papal power and the antichrist/little horn power—the author suggests consulting the following readings:

- *A Woman Rides the Beast*, by Dave Hunt
- *National Sunday Law*, by A. Jan Marcussen
- *Daniel and the Revelation*, by Uriah Smith

In light of the current matter, and for the sake of continuing in our discussion, the author will assume that the reader has a basic understanding of how the Roman Papacy fulfills all the characteristics necessary to be rightly labeled as the antichrist/little horn power.

What is pertinent to our current agenda is the latter part of verse 25 of the seventh chapter of the book of Daniel. Describing that power under the symbol of a little horn, Daniel speaks of it as waging a special warfare against God, wearing out the saints of the Most High, and thinking to change times and laws. The prophet expressly specifies on this point: "He shall... *think* to change times and laws..." (Daniel 7:25). What laws does this authority aim to alter, and whose? Certainly not the laws of other earthly governments; for it is not unusual for a dominant power to modify the laws of another under its rule. Neither can these be the laws of men, as the power represented by the little horn would have power to change these so far as its jurisdiction extended. In order to reason correctly, we must keep in mind that the times and laws in question are those that this authority would merely *think* to change but lack the capability to formally do so. These, therefore, must be the laws of the Supreme Being, the Originator of the unchanging laws of nature—namely, the laws of the Most High. To apply the expression to human laws would be doing evident violence to the language of the prophet. The Papacy has exceeded the realm of mere contemplation and has already succeeded in the alteration of human laws, annulling royal decrees, and asserting dominance over rulers and magistrates. It has intervened in global affairs, even compelling entire nations to submit humbly to its yoke. However, if we interpret the prophet's words in the context of divine laws, the consistency and strength of his message becomes evident, for the prophet beholds greater acts of presumption that surpass the alteration of human imposed laws—something the Papacy has already achieved. Instead, he foresees the Papacy attempting what's beyond its power, a feat that neither individuals nor groups of men can ever achieve: altering the very laws of the Almighty.

The apostle Paul speaks of the same power in 2 Thessalonians chapter 2. He describes it, in the person of the pope, as "that man of sin" "sitting as God in the temple of God" and exalting himself "above all that is called God, or that is worshiped." According to this, the pope sets himself up as the one for all of Christendom to look to for authority, in place of God.

Consider deeply the question of how one could elevate themselves above God. Explore the entire spectrum of human strategy, extend your inquiry to the limits of human endeavor, and contemplate: through what strategy, action, or assertion could this usurper raise himself higher than God? He might establish numerous rituals, prescribe various forms of worship, and wield considerable authority. However, as long as God had innate principles that people felt compelled to regard in preference to his, so long he would not be able to surpass God. Even if he were to institute a law and convince people that they were equally obligated to it as they are to God's law, this would only result in positioning himself as an *equal* to God.

Yet, his ambitions go further; he endeavors to elevate himself even beyond that. This entails issuing a law that contradicts the divine law and demanding that his own law take precedence over God's law. The most potent method for him to assume the role described in the prophecy is by altering the law of the Most High. If he manages to convince the populace to embrace this altered version over the original decree, he, as the modifier of the law, positions himself superior to God, the Originator of the law. This is the very work that Daniel said the power represented by the little horn would *think* to do.

Moreover, the prophecy doesn't suggest that the Papacy, symbolized by the little horn, would completely discard God's law and introduce an entirely new set of edicts. Such an action wouldn't constitute changing the law but rather creating a new one. The prophecy records that he was only to attempt a *change* to the law, so that the laws from God and the laws from the Papacy would appear nearly identical, with the exception of the modification made by the Papacy.

Such a work as this the Papacy will accomplish according to the prophecy, and the prophecy cannot fail. And has the Papacy attempted such a feat? Indeed, it has ventured even into this. The nature of the change which the Papacy has attempted to effect in the law of God is worthy of notice. True to his purpose to exalt himself above God, he undertakes to change the very law of God.

But in what way is an attempt made to change divine law? The answer to this query would naturally be sought among certain distinctive attributes of the papal authority. These attributes may be readily discerned in the Roman Church's adaptation of the Decalogue, as shown in *Figure 1*...

THE LAW OF GOD

AS GIVEN BY JEHOVAH.	AS CHANGED BY MAN.
"I will not alter the thing that is gone out of my lips."	*"He shall think himself able to change times and laws." Daniel 7:25. Douay Bible.*
I. Thou shalt have no other gods before me.	**I.** I am the Lord thy God: thou shalt not have strange gods before me.
II. Thou shalt not make unto thee any graven image, or any likeness of anything that is in heaven above, or that is in the earth beneath, or that is in the water under the earth: thou shalt not bow down thyself to them, nor serve them: for I the Lord thy God am a jealous God, visiting the iniquity of the fathers upon the children unto the third and fourth generation of them that hate me; and showing mercy unto thousands of them that love me, and keep my commandments.	
III. Thou shalt not take the name of the Lord thy God in vain: for the Lord will not hold him guiltless that taketh his name in vain.	**II.** Thou shalt not take the name of the Lord thy God in vain.
IV. Remember the Sabbath day, to keep it holy. Six days shalt thou labor, and do all thy work: but the seventh day is the Sabbath of the Lord thy God: in it thou shalt not do any work, thou, nor thy son, nor thy daughter, thy man-servant, nor thy maid-servant, nor thy cattle, nor thy stranger that is within thy gates: for in six days the Lord made heaven and earth, the sea, and all that in them is, and rested the seventh day: wherefore the Lord blessed the Sabbath day, and hallowed it.	**III.** Remember that thou keep holy the Sabbath day.
V. Honor thy father and thy mother: that thy days may be long upon the land which the Lord thy God giveth thee.	**IV.** Honor thy father and thy mother.
VI. Thou shalt not kill.	**V.** Thou shalt not kill.
VII. Thou shalt not commit adultery.	**VI.** Thou shalt not commit adultery.
VIII. Thou shalt not steal.	**VII.** Thou shalt not steal.
IX. Thou shalt not bear false witness against thy neighbor.	**VIII.** Thou shalt not bear false witness against thy neighbor.
X. Thou shalt not covet thy neighbor's house, thou shalt not covet thy neighbor's wife, nor his man-servant, nor his maid-servant, nor his ox, nor his ass, nor anything that is thy neighbor's.	**IX.** Thou shalt not covet thy neighbor's wife.
	X. Thou shalt not covet thy neighbor's goods.
[*See Ex. 20:3-17.*]	[*See Butler's Catechism, p. 28, edition of 1877, published by Hoffman Bros., Milwaukee, Wis.*]

Figure 1

Figure 1 shows a scanned page from Uriah Smith's work titled, "Daniel and the Revelation." The illustration depicts the Ten Commandments as directly supplied from the scriptures (left), and the Ten Commandments as enshrined by the Catholic Church (right). The reader would do well to note the differences.

> "Let it be borne in mind, that, according to the prophecy [of Daniel 7:25], he was to think to change times and laws. **This plainly conveys the idea of intention and design, and makes these qualities essential to the change in question.** But respecting the omission of the second commandment, Catholics argue that it is included in the first, and hence should not be numbered as a separate commandment; and on the tenth they claim that there is so plain a distinction of ideas as to require two commandments; so they make the coveting of a neighbor's wife the ninth command, and the coveting of his goods the tenth. In all this they claim that they are giving the commandments exactly as God intended to have them understood; so, while we may regard them as errors in their interpretation of the commandments, we cannot set them down as professedly intentional changes. **Not so, however, with the fourth commandment. Respecting this commandment, they do not claim that their version is like that given by God. They expressly claim a change here, and also that the change has been made by the church.**" (Uriah Smith, *Daniel and the Revelation*, pg. 608)

As one may plainly see, the Papacy claims to have changed the fourth commandment. They have muddied the sanctity of the seventh-day Sabbath by replacing it with Sunday sacredness. This change is made without any proof whatsoever from the scriptures, because there is no such proof. All the reasons for the change given are purely of human and ecclesiastical invention.

> "The church **after changing the day of rest from the Jewish Sabbath or seventh-day of the week to the first, made the third commandment refer to Sunday** as the day to be kept holy as the Lord's day." (*Catholic Encyclopedia*, vol. 4, pg. 153)

But by what authority, if not from scripture, have they issued such a change? By their own admission, they claim that the change comes from the innate authority of the Church—the Roman Pontiff. They claim, falsely so, that Church tradition supersedes any scriptural authority, even going so far as to deny the very word of God.

"**Sunday is our Mark of authority...** Church tradition is above the Bible, and this transference of Sabbath observance is proof of that fact." (*Catholic Record,* September 1, 1923)

"**Prove to me from the Bible alone that I am bound to keep Sunday holy. There is no such law in the Bible. It is a law of the holy Catholic Church alone.** The Bible says 'Remember the Sabbath day to keep it holy.' The Catholic Church says 'No. By my divine power I abolish the Sabbath day and command you to keep holy the first day of the week.' **And lo! The entire civilized world bows down in reverent obedience to the command of the Holy Catholic Church.**" (Thomas Enright, CSSR, President, Redemptorist College [Roman Catholic], Kansas City, MO., February 18, 1884)

In An Abridgment of the Christian Doctrine, we find the following testimony:

"Q.— How prove you that the church hath power to command feasts and holy days?

A.— **By the very act of changing the Sabbath into Sunday, which Protestants allow of; and therefore they fondly contradict themselves by keeping Sunday strictly,** and breaking most other feasts commanded by the same church.

Q.— How prove you that?

A.— Because **by keeping Sunday they acknowledge the church's power** to ordain feasts, and **to command them under sin.**" (Henry Tuberville, *An Abridgment of the Christian Doctrine,* pg. 58)

The observance of Sunday is but "the commandments of men." (Matthew 15:9). This is an endeavor by the Roman Church, the little horn power, the antichrist, that subordinate of Satan, to supersede God's majesty—attempting to position itself above all that is worshipped or obeyed.

"But," says one, "I supposed that Christ changed the Sabbath day." A great many suppose so, for they have been so taught. We would remind such persons, however, that according to the prophecy, the only change ever to be made in the law of God was to be made by the little horn of Daniel 7, the man of sin of 2 Thessalonians chapter 2. Now, if Christ made this change, He filled the office of the blasphemous power spoken of by both Daniel and Paul—a conclusion that is repulsive to any honest Christian. One would also do well to remember that God's law of love, which the Ten Commandments point us to, is eternal. By no means are His precepts arbitrarily set in place. The immutable natural law in which we have referred to in this chapter includes the very principles which the Sabbath day embodies. The Sabbath law of rest agrees with the law of nature requiring cessation of labor and a period for refreshment, meditation, and worship—for in such there is a blessing to be received.

The Papacy aims to supplant this holy day with its own imposed day of worship by its unwarranted claim to the throne of the Most High. Indeed, it can be convincingly shown through the Papacy's own writings and deeds that it believes itself to hold all things, in heaven and earth, under its hellish yoke of bondage—even God Himself.

> "All temporal power is his [the pope's]: **the dominion, jurisdiction, and government of the whole earth is his by divine right.** All rulers of earth are his subjects and must submit to him." (The Council of Trent, 1545-1563)

> "**God himself is obliged to abide by the judgement of His priests,** and either not to pardon or to pardon, according as they refuse or give absolution... **The sentence of the priest precedes, and God subscribes to it.**" (*Dignities and Duties of the Priest,* vol 12, pg. 27)

Lucius Ferraris, in his *Prompta Bibliotheca* which the *Catholic Encyclopedia* refers to as "a veritable encyclopedia of religious knowledge" and "a precious mine of information," declares, in its articles on the pope, that:

> "**...the pope is of so great dignity and so exalted that he is not a mere man, but as it were God, and the vicar of God... The pope**

> **is as it were God on earth,** sole sovereign of the faithful of Christ, chief king of kings, having plenitude of power, to whom has been intrusted by the omnipotent God direction not only of the earthly but also of the heavenly kingdom... **The pope is of so great authority and power that he can modify, explain, or interpret even divine laws.**" (Translated from Lucius Ferraris, *Prompta Bibliotheca,* art. "Papa," II, vol. VI, pg. 26-29)

Is there any room left for doubt that the papal power and the antichrist/little horn power are synonymous? When the prophecy states that a specific authority will think to change God's law, and that authority emerges at the expected time, fulfills the predicted actions, and openly acknowledges doing so, what need have we of further evidence?

> "**The pope has power to change times, to abrogate laws,** and to dispense with all things, **even the precepts of Christ.**" (Descretal de Translat. Episcop. Cap.)

It's important for the world to recognize that the significant departure from the true faith, as predicted by Paul, has already occurred; that the man of sin, who controlled Christian teaching for a considerable period during the Dark Ages, works the same evil works even now; that the mystery of iniquity has spread its shadow and erroneous doctrines across nearly all of Christendom; and that from this era of confusion, obscurity, and corruption, the theology of our day has emerged.

Would it, then, be strange if there were yet some relics of popery to still be discarded before the Reformation will be complete?—Before a peculiar people could be set apart? Alexander Campbell, speaking of the different Protestant sects, says:

> "**All of them retain in their bosom, in their ecclesiastical organizations, worship, doctrines, and observances, various relics of popery. They are at best a reformation of popery, and only reformations in part.** The doctrines and traditions of men yet

impair the power and progress of the gospel in their hands." (Alexander Campbell, *Christian Baptism*, pg. 15)

But what, may we inquire, are these leftover relics of popery? Do we still cherish, in any form, the religious ideologies that this papal power holds? How about our view of God? Do we, as Adventists, perceive God in a similar way as does the antichrist power? It is to be wished that such is not the case, but upon uncovering the truth, one might be utterly astonished.

It is here that the author must remind the reader that our perception of God's character, as we have seen, is ultimately based upon our perception of His law—as the two are effectively synonymous. Natural law, or imposed law; Creator, or dictator—the ramifications of one's view becomes profoundly significant!

In what way would this antichrist/little horn power attempt to change divine law? Would it merely be a physical change to the commandments, as is clearly demonstrated with the abrogation of the fourth? Would this be enough to, if it were possible, "deceive the very elect" (Matthew 24:24)? We would do well to remember that this deception is to cause nearly "all the world" to wonder "after the beast." (Revelation 13:3). Is a slight change to one commandment enough for this work?—Or could it be that Satan aims to modify the very manner in which we comprehend the *entirety* of God's law and how it truly functions? The author would contend that it is the latter, and we would do well to separate ourselves from all that this antichrist power seeks to teach and propagate. This includes the imperial perspective of God's kingdom!

So, then, what is the evidence for such a change in the conceptual framework of God's law by Rome? For the sake of analogy: can any assembly be identified which has resolved to amend the law of gravity? The absence of such endeavors is attributed to the inalterable characteristics of natural law. Consequently, were a religious council to deliberate upon modifying God's law, it would imply a shift in perspective—

regarding His law not as intrinsic and natural (fundamental to the operations of life), but rather as imposed law (liable to modification).

It is quite apparent, that the Roman Church perceives God's law as an imposed system, subject to alteration. As a result of this, they worship a god who must enforce his list of arbitrary rules with severe imperial punishments. These he inflicts swiftly, by the might of his own hand, upon transgressors. So too, does the Roman Church seek to imitate their deity in their call for the utter destruction of rebels and heretics.

> "The Catholic Church is a respecter of conscience and of liberty... nevertheless, **when confronted by heresy,... she has recourse to force, to corporal punishment, to torture...** she lit in Italy... the funeral piles of the Inquisition." (Catholic Professor Alfred Baudrillart, *The Catholic Church, Renaissance, and Protestantism,* pg. 182-183)

This devilish deception serves a double purpose. If the law is a transcript of the divine character, then an attempt to produce a change in the law, ultimately, would require an attempt to produce a perceived change in the character of the Almighty. It necessarily follows, that in order for Satan to persuade the populace that the laws of God are subject to change, he must first direct a transformation of God's very character in the minds of men. If God's laws are no longer seen as natural and immutable, then it must mean that they are artificial. If His laws are artificial, and there is no natural consequence to transgression, then it must mean that God Himself is the ultimate enforcer of His law—His kingdom suddenly becomes an imperial treasure-trove of subjugation, fear, and death. Love is cast down and corruption is exalted. The precepts of Christ no longer reign, but instead the toxicities of paganism are cherished and maintained.

By the plague of Romanism, the early church became tainted with the notion that God's law operates in the same manner—and is of the same quality—as human law: a set of regulations devoid of intrinsic repercussions, necessitating an overseer to enforce these rules through the menace of penalties. Consequently, the perception of God began to resemble that of a Roman dictator. Eusebius, the first church historian, wrote:

> "With the Roman Empire **monarchy had come on earth as the image of the monarchy in heaven.**" (S.L. Greenslade, *Church and State from Constantine to Theodosius,* London: SCM Press, 1954)

Christianity embraced the imperial Roman concept of divine law, abandoning the law of love that underpinned God's creation of life. Now, likened to Rome, the purpose of God's law is seen merely as a mechanism to manage conduct, evaluate compliance, and punish rebellion. Within Christianity emerged the belief that God governs His universe in a manner reminiscent of Constantine's governance over Rome. He might be called Creator, but He's worshipped as a dictator.

> "When disputes arose in the church, Constantine believed it was his right and duty as Roman emperor to guide the warring factions toward a resolution... **Once the bishops had arrived at a decision, Constantine accepted it as a divine word and backed up conciliar decisions with legal sanctions,** mainly exile for those found guilty of heresy." (Peter Leithart, *Defending Constantine,* Intervarsity Press 2010, pg. 302-303)

If the author were mistaken in his interpretation of God's law, and God's system of government truly does operate on an imperial basis, then Adventists find themselves between a rock and a hard place. The pope says worship on Sunday or I'll kill you; God says worship on the Sabbath or I'll kill you. This is a dilemma from which there is no deliverance.

Dear reader, this is *not* the God we serve. Our God is a God of love and life, not fear and death. Deep study and prayer should be earnestly sought on this matter.

> "This God who loves us with His great breadth and depth of love is really a good God. Whenever we say God is good, the devil

> feels pain, but glory is given to God. **Today, in so many pulpits, God is misrepresented. Some ministers only present Him as a God who is waiting for sinners to make a mistake so He can judge them with stern and fearful punishment.**" (David Yonggi Cho, *Salvation, Health & Prosperity: Our Threefold Blessings in Christ*, pg. 15)

This outlines the historical narrative of the Roman Church during the Dark Ages; Rome effectuated modifications to the second, fourth, and tenth commandments. And yet, the central concern of the matter transcends the alteration of specific commandments. These adjustments serve as a diversion from the core issue. The true alteration in the law lies in this: Romanism not only modified the commandments, but it also transformed the very essence and function of the law in the minds of men. Consequently, the law ceased to be perceived as a natural order and began to be seen as a dictated imposition—leading to a shift from perceiving God as a benevolent and loving Creator to regarding Him as an authoritative and burdensome ruler. This is the true change that was instigated by the influence of the little horn power of Daniel 7:25.

If God's law is an imposed system, then transgressing it necessitates an imposed death penalty. Consequently, in order to maintain justice, God is compelled to impose death. This results in God, not sin, being the origin of suffering and death. Humanity must appease or propitiate God in order to avert His anger and inflicted retribution. As a result, God's own wrath and condemnation become the barrier, rather than sin, which separates humanity from everlasting life. The focus shifts to the need for God to be reconciled to humanity, rather than the need for humanity to be reconciled to God. This perspective grossly contradicts the gospel as it is conveyed in scripture. It ultimately means that Jesus died to pay our legal debt to an offended God. The cross then becomes perverted to promote Satan's view of God—trust in God is undermined and fear grips the soul; desperation and hopelessness are surely the result.

> **"The same thing that Satan accomplished in paganism he has also accomplished in the papacy. To papists, God is the stern, the distant judge, incapable of human sympathy or love, and Christ the mediator and intercessor, whose duty it is, if possible, to touch the heart of God with a feeling of our needs, and arouse his compassion.** But even Christ is not touched with the feelings of all our infirmities; so he must be approached through the mediation of the Virgin, his mother, and of canonized saint, and living pope, and bishop, and priest. **Thus again God is placed far away, and the beautiful, the living fact of his love is denied.** He is no more 'our Father,' who takes delight in giving good gifts to his children." (George Fifield, *God is Love,* pg. 23)

However, as we have already established, God's law is clearly demonstrated as reflecting a kingdom of love and beneficence—His law is merely the natural order of things. Under this view, it becomes unnecessary for God to punish or condemn us. When we transgress His law, we wantonly place ourselves out of harmony with His design. The consequences of such an undertaking are inherently damaging. When we deviate from God's intended design for us, we undermine our own moral fiber, causing harm to ourselves. This destructive pattern conflicts with our well-being. God's affection for us seeks to foster life within us. Through His displays of love, and His counsel to refrain from sin, He unveils both the true nature of sin as well as His own inherent qualities. By transgressing natural law, we violate the principles of health; death and decay ensue.

> **"In the unbiblical legal model of how God and His law are understood in traditional Christianity, God arbitrarily imposed laws and determined punishments for violations which are called sins. Since He is a God of justice, evil stirs up His wrath which must be appeased by a sacrifice including the shedding of blood.** Those who finally reject salvation come under the awful curse of God Who will finally take vengeance by smiting sinners with fire from heaven – the second death. A sinner whose guilty conscience brings conviction for his sinfulness can confess and be granted forgiveness because the ransom price has been provided to legally cancel the debt. **The propitiation brings atonement for sins which**

are then blotted from the record books of heaven. The repentant sinner, by faith, is justified and **declared to be righteous.** Having received salvation, he grows in sanctification towards perfection and, in the final investigative judgment, will not come under condemnation.

"However, **in the biblical healing model of how God and His law should be understood, God designed laws as the basis of life, violations of which have intrinsic, natural consequences leading towards death. Those who rebel against His law of love will exhibit that rebellion in unrighteous acts – sins. This state of sinfulness causes condemnation in the conscience and has punishment built into it. When a person persists in rejection of and distrust in God, God honors that free-will choice and in wrath leaves the sinner to the consequences of his choices. If guilt brings conviction enough to cause a sinner to choose repentance, he will receive forgiveness which has already been granted by God to all. A realization of the grace and glory (character) of God to provide salvation leads the sinner to trust (have faith in) God; to be justified or set right with Him – what the Bible calls atonement – the condition of being 'at-one' with God. The repentant sinner then, as He beholds the righteousness of Christ, grows in sanctification towards perfection of character. Christ's life (typified by His blood) and sacrifice frees (ransoms) us from what held us captive – the lies of Satan about the character of God and our own sinful natures.**" (Ray Foucher, characterofgod.org, January 1, 2022)

In all of which this chapter has stated, we have struck a foundation which Antinomianism can never touch; now we know why the law can never change; it is because God's love never changes. He is the same yesterday, today, and forever; and He has loved us with an everlasting love. Jesus says, "it is easier for heaven and earth to pass, than one tittle of the law to fail" (Luke 16:17). This is no hyperbole; it is the simple statement of a fact that we can understand.

This revelation of the true context of God's law, being eternally ingrained into the very laws of nature, destroys the idea of two covenants separated by dispensations of time. Rather, there is but one covenant; one gospel—and it is everlasting.

> "And I will establish my covenant between me and thee and thy seed after thee in their generations **for an everlasting covenant,** to be a God unto thee, and to thy seed after thee." (Genesis 17:7)

> "And I saw another angel fly in the midst of heaven, **having the everlasting gospel to preach unto them that dwell on the earth,** and to every nation, and kindred, and tongue, and people..." (Revelation 14:6)

Within the realm of God's kingdom, law and grace are inextricably linked. No covenant of law existed without grace, just as no covenant of grace exists without law. Instead, these elements harmonize, becoming integral facets of the plan of redemption. The two covenants are not matters of dispensation, but are instead reflective of two frameworks of human experience. By strictly assigning the old covenant to the Old Testament, and the new covenant to the New Testament, men fall into confusion—and this is just how Satan would have it. Properly understood, one can be in the old or new covenant at any point in time depending upon the condition of the heart, and regardless of whether or not the individual lived before or after Christ's first advent.

To regard the old covenant as principally characterized by a strict legality and an absence of mercy is to misconstrue the Father's nature as revealed in Christ. In the same way, designating the new covenant as devoid of any moral framework desecrates the work which Christ came to do and effectively sanctions a disposition inclined towards unrestrained indulgence. Correctly understood, the divine law of God remains perpetual, mirroring the timeless nature of His grace and character.

> "For I am the LORD, **I change not...**" (Malachi 3:6)

> **"The New Testament does not present a new religion; the Old Testament does not present a religion to be superseded by the**

New. The New Testament is only the advancement and unfolding of the Old." (Ellen G. White, *Counsels for the Church,* pg. 90)

"**Night before last I was shown that evidences in regard to the covenants were clear and convincing.** Yourself [Uriah Smith], Brother Dan Jones, Brother Porter and others are spending your investigative powers for naught to produce a position on the covenants to vary from the position that Brother Waggoner has presented... **The covenant question is a clear question and would be received by every candid, unprejudiced mind,** but I was brought where the Lord gave me an insight into this matter." (Ellen G. White to Uriah Smith, Letter 59, March 8, 1890; in *1888 Materials,* pg. 604-605)

"**Now I tell you here before God, that the covenant question, as it has been presented [by Waggoner], is the truth. It is the light. In clear lines it has been laid before me.** And those who have been resisting light, I ask you whether they have been working for God, or for the devil. It is the clear light of heaven, and it means much to us." (Ellen G. White Manuscript 4, "Sermon," March 8, 1890; in *1888 Materials,* pg. 593-597)

Within the confines of the present publication, an in-depth examination of the covenants is unfeasible, as that discussion is beyond the scope of this treatise. However, the reader would do well to understand this matter. For this purpose, the author recommends the following works:

- *Studies in Galatians*, by Alonzo T. Jones
- *The Glad Tidings*, by E. J. Waggoner
- *The Everlasting Covenant*, by E. J. Waggoner
- *Stand by the Landmarks*, by Adrian Ebens

Before moving on, we must briefly address accusations of legalism. In most theological circles, to "stress obedience apart from faith is to produce legalism." Is that what we have done?

On the contrary!—We have contended that the law is not of *legal* value, but of *spiritual and moral* value—it is the very character of God transcribed; it is selfless love perfectly manifested. How could one hope to gain heaven by mere rule-keeping? Obedience born from a sense of obligation produces no real change in the character; no renewal of the heart. We are called to come into harmony with God, manifesting the righteous principles that the law points us toward, because these are the intrinsic principles upon which life operates. And how could it be possible for any sinful being to embody God's character of love without relying upon the merits of Christ? Let it be stated plainly: righteousness cannot possibly come by the law, but only by the faith of Christ.

> "**True sanctification is harmony with God, oneness with Him in character.** It is received through obedience to those principles that are the transcript of His character." (Ellen G. White, *Testimonies for the Church*, vol. 6, pg. 350)

> "**There are many who will be lost, because they depend on legal religion, or mere repentance for sin. But repentance for sin alone cannot work the salvation of any soul.** Man cannot be saved by his own works. **Without Christ it is impossible for him to render perfect obedience to the law of God; and heaven can never be gained by an imperfect obedience;** for this would place all heaven in jeopardy, and make possible a second rebellion. God saves man through the blood of Christ alone, and man's belief in, and allegiance to, Christ is salvation." (Ellen G. White, *Signs of the Times*, December 30, 1889)

> "**All true obedience comes from the heart. It was heart work with Christ. And if we consent, He will so identify Himself with our thoughts and aims, so blend our hearts and minds into conformity to His will, that when obeying Him we shall be but carrying out our own impulses.** The will, refined and sanctified, will find its highest delight in doing His service. When we know God as it is our privilege to know Him, our life will be a life of continual obedience. Through an appreciation of the character of Christ, through communion with God, sin will become hateful to us..." (Ellen G. White, *The Desire of Ages*, pg. 668)

In order to better understand the correlation between the law and faith, thereby dissuading all accusations of legalism, we will now quote directly from chapter 3 of *The Glad Tidings* by E. J. Waggoner, for the author has yet to encounter any work outside of the Bible that expounds upon this topic with such clarity and elegance. For the sake of the reader, I have placed emphasis upon the bodies of scripture from which Waggoner forms his claims. It begins by quoting from Galatians 3:9-10…

> "***So then, those who are men of faith are blessed with Abraham who had faith. For all who rely on works of the law are under a curse; for it is written, 'Cursed be everyone who does not abide by all things written in the book of the law, and do them.' [Galatians 3:9-10]…***
>
> "Note the sharp contrast in verses 9 and 10. 'Those who are men of faith are blessed,' but 'all who rely on works of the law are under a curse.' Faith brings the blessing. Works bring the curse, or, rather, leave one under the curse. The curse is on all, for 'he who does not believe is condemned already, because he has not believed in the name of the only Son of God.' John 3:18. Faith removes the curse.
>
> "Who are under the curse? 'All who rely on works of the law.' Note that it does not say that those who *do* the law are under the curse, for that would be a contradiction of Revelation 22:14, KJV: '*Blessed* are they that *do* His commandments, that they may have right to the tree of life, and may enter in through the gates into the city.' '*Blessed* are those whose way is blameless, who *walk* in the law of the Lord!' Psalm 119:1.
>
> "So, then, they who are of *faith* are keepers of the law; for they who are of faith are blessed, and those who do the commandments are blessed. By faith they do the commandments. Since the gospel is contrary to human nature, we become doers of the law not by doing but by believing. If we *worked* for righteousness, we would be exercising only our own sinful human nature, and so would get no nearer to righteousness, but farther from it. But by *believing* the 'exceeding great and precious promises,' we become 'partakers of the divine nature' (2 Peter 1:4,

KJV), and then all our works are wrought in God. 'The Gentiles, which followed not after righteousness, have attained to righteousness, even the righteousness which is of faith. But Israel, which followed after the law of righteousness, hath not attained to the law of righteousness. Wherefore? Because they sought it not by faith, but as it were by the works of the law. For they stumbled at that stumbling stone; as it is written, Behold, I lay in Sion a stumbling stone and rock of offense: and whosoever believeth on Him shall not be ashamed.' Romans 9:30-33, KJV.

"No one can read Galatians 3:10 carefully and thoughtfully without seeing that the curse is transgression of the law. Disobedience to God's law is itself the curse; for 'sin came into the world through one man and death through sin.' Romans 5:12. Sin has death wrapped up in it. Without sin death would be impossible, for 'the sting of death is sin.' I Corinthians 15:56. 'For all who rely on works of the law are under a curse.' Why? Because the law is a curse? Not by any means: 'The law is holy, and the commandment is holy and just and good.' Romans 7:12. Why, then, are all who rely on works of the law under a curse? Because it is written, 'Cursed be everyone who does not abide by all things written in the book of the law, and do them.'

"Mark it well: They are not cursed because they *do* the law, but because they do *not* do it. So, then, we see that relying on works of the law does not mean that one is doing the law. No! 'The carnal mind is enmity against God: for it is not subject to the law of God, neither indeed *can* be.' Romans 8:7, KJV. *All* are under the curse, and he who thinks to get out by his own works, remains there. Since the 'curse' consists in not continuing in all things that are written in the law, therefore the 'blessing' means perfect conformity to the law.

"'Behold, I set before you this day a blessing and a curse; a blessing, if ye *obey* the commandments of the Lord your God, which I command you this day: and a *curse*, if ye will *not obey* the commandments of the Lord your God.' Deuteronomy 11:26-28, KJV. This is the living word of God, addressed to each one of us personally. 'The law brings wrath' (Romans 4:15), but the wrath of God comes only on the children of *dis*obedience

(Ephesians 5:6). If we truly believe, we are not condemned, because faith brings us into harmony with the law, the life of God. 'Whoso looketh into the perfect law of liberty, and continueth therein, he being not a forgetful hearer, but a doer of the work, this man shall be blessed in his deed.' James 1:25, KJV.

"The Bible does not disparage good works. On the contrary, it exalts them. 'This is a faithful saying, and these things I will that thou affirm constantly, that they which have believed in God might be careful to maintain good works. These things are good and profitable.' Titus 3:8, KJV. The charge against the unbelieving is that they are 'unto every good work *reprobate*' Titus 1:16, KJV. Timothy was exhorted to 'charge them that are rich in this world,' 'that they do *good*, that they be rich in good *works*.' I Timothy 6:17, 18, KJV. And the apostle Paul prayed for us all that we might 'walk worthy of the Lord unto all pleasing, being fruitful in *every* good work.' Colossians 1:10, KJV. Still further, we are assured that God has created us 'in Christ Jesus for good works,' 'that we should walk in them.' Ephesians 2:10.

"He has Himself prepared these works for us, wrought them out, and laid them up for all who trust in Him. Psalm 31:19. 'This is the work of God, that you believe in Him whom He has sent.' John 6:29. Good works are commended, but we cannot do them. They can be performed only by the One who is good, and that is God. If there be ever any good in us, it is God who works in us. There is no disparagement of anything that He does. 'Now the God of peace, that brought again from the dead our Lord Jesus, that great Shepherd of the sheep, through the blood of the everlasting covenant, make you perfect in every good work to do His will, working in you that which is well pleasing in His sight, through Jesus Christ; to whom be glory forever and ever. Amen.' Hebrews 13:20, 21, KJV.

"Now it is evident that no man is justified before God by the law; for 'He who through faith is righteous shall live'; but the law does not rest on faith, for 'He who does them shall live by them.' [Galatians 3:11-12].

"When we read the frequent statement, 'He who through faith is righteous shall live,' it is necessary to have a clear idea of what the word 'righteous' means. The King James Version has it, 'The just shall live by faith.' To be justified by faith is to be made righteous by faith. 'All unrighteousness is sin' (I John 5:17, KJV), and 'sin is the transgression of the law' (I John 3:4, KJV). Therefore all unrighteousness is transgression of the law, and of course all righteousness is obedience to the law. So we see that the just, or righteous, man is the man who *obeys* the law, and to be justified is to be made a *keeper* of the law.

"Right doing is the end to be obtained, and the law of God is the standard. 'The law worketh wrath,' because 'all have sinned,' and 'the wrath of God cometh on the children of *dis*obedience.' How shall we become doers of the law, and thus escape wrath, or the curse? The answer is, 'He who through faith is righteous shall live.' By faith, not by works, we become doers of the law! 'With the heart man believeth *unto righteousness*.' Romans 10:10, KJV. That no man is justified by the law in the sight of God is evident. How? From this, that 'the just shall live by faith.' If righteousness came by works, then it would not be by faith; 'if it is by grace, it is no longer on the basis of works; otherwise grace would no longer be grace.' Romans 11:6. 'To him that worketh is the reward not reckoned of grace, but of debt. But to him that worketh not, but believeth on Him that justifieth the ungodly, his faith is counted for righteousness.' Romans 4:4, 5, KJV.

"There is no exception, no halfway working. It is not said that *some* of the just shall live by faith, or that they shall live by faith *and* works; but simply, 'the just shall live by faith.' And that proves righteousness comes not by their own works. All of the just are *made* just and *kept* just by faith alone. This is because the law is so holy. It is greater than can be done by man; only divine power can accomplish it; so by faith we receive the Lord Jesus, and He lives the perfect law in us.

"'The law does not rest on faith.' Of course it is the written law, no matter whether in a book or on tables of stone, that is here referred to. That law simply says, 'Do this,' or, 'Do not do that.' 'He who does them shall live by them.' That is the sole condition on which the written law offers life. Works, and works only, commend themselves to it. How those works are obtained is of no consequence to it, provided they are present. But none have done the requirements of the law, and so there can be no *doers* of the law; that is, none who in their own lives can present a record of perfect obedience.

"'He who *does* them shall live by them.' But one must be *alive* in order to do! A dead man can do nothing, and he who is 'dead in trespasses and sins' can do no righteousness. Christ is the only one in whom there is life, for He is the life, and He alone has done and can do the righteousness of the law. When, instead of being denied and repressed, He is acknowledged and received, He lives in us all the fullness of His life, so that it is no more we but Christ living in us. Then His obedience in us makes us righteous. Our faith is counted for righteousness simply because our faith appropriates the living Christ. In faith we yield our bodies as temples of God. Christ, the Living Stone, is enshrined in the hearts, which become God's thrones. And so in Christ the living law becomes our life, for 'out of the heart are the issues of life.'

"***Christ redeemed us from the curse of the law, having become a curse for us—for it is written, 'Cursed be everyone who hangs on a tree'—that in Christ Jesus the blessing of Abraham might come upon the Gentiles, that we might receive the promise of the Spirit through faith. [Galatians 3:13-14].***

"In this letter there is no controversy over the law as to whether or not it should be obeyed. No one had claimed that the law was abolished or changed or had lost its force. The letter contains no hint of any such thing. The question was not *if* the law should be kept but *how* it was to be kept. Justification—being made righteous—was admitted to be a necessity. The question was: 'Is it by faith, or by works?' The 'false brethren' were persuading the Galatians that they must be made righteous by their own efforts. Paul by the Spirit was showing that all such attempts were useless and could result only in fastening the curse more firmly on the sinner.

"Righteousness through faith in Jesus Christ is set forth to all men in all time as the only real righteousness. The false teachers made their boast *in the law,* but through breaking it caused the name of God to be blasphemed. Paul made his boast *in Christ,* and by the righteousness of the law to which he thus submitted, he caused the name of God to be glorified in him.

"That death is the curse is evident from the last part of verse 13: 'Cursed be everyone who hangs on a tree.' Christ was made a curse for us in that He hung on a tree, that is, was crucified. But *sin* [not God] is the cause of death: 'By one man sin entered into the world, and death by sin; and so death passed upon all men, for that all have sinned.' Romans 5:12, KJV. 'The sting of death is sin.' I Corinthians 15:56. So we have the substance of verse 10 thus, that those who do not 'abide by all the things written in the law' are *dead.* That is, disobedience is death.

"'When lust hath conceived, it bringeth forth sin: and sin, when it is finished, bringeth forth death.' James 1:15, KJV. Sin contains death, and men out of Christ are 'dead through trespasses and sins.' Ephesians 2:1. It matters not that they walk about seemingly full of life. The words of Christ are, 'Unless you eat the flesh of the Son of man and drink His blood, you have no life in you.' John 6:53. 'She that liveth in pleasure is dead while she liveth.' I Timothy 5:6, KJV. It is a living death—a body of death—that is endured. Romans 7:24. Sin is the transgression of the law. The wages of sin is death. The curse, therefore, is the death that is carried about concealed even in the most attractive sin. 'Cursed be everyone who does not abide by all things written in the book of the law, and do them.'

"'Christ redeemed us from the curse of the law.' Some who superficially read this rush off frantically exclaiming, 'We don't need to keep the law, because Christ has redeemed us from the curse of it,' as though the text said that Christ redeemed us from the curse of obedience. Such read the Scriptures to no profit. The curse, as we have seen, is *dis*obedience: 'Cursed be everyone who does *not* abide by all things written in the book of the law, and do them.' Therefore Christ has redeemed us from *dis*obedience to the law. God sent forth His Son 'in the likeness of sinful flesh and for sin, . . . in order that the just requirement of the law might be *fulfilled* in us.' Romans 8:3, 4.

> "Someone may lightly say, 'Then we are all right; whatever we do is right so far as the law is concerned, since we are redeemed.' It is true that all are redeemed, but not all have *accepted* redemption. Many say of Christ, 'We will not have this Man to reign over us,' and thrust the blessing of God from them. But redemption is for *all*. *All* have been purchased with the precious blood—the life—of Christ, and *all* may be, if they will, free from sin and death. By that blood we are redeemed from 'the futile ways inherited from your fathers.' I Peter 1:18.
>
> "Stop and think what this means. Let the full force of the announcement impress itself upon your consciousness. 'Christ redeemed us from the curse of the law'—from our failure to continue in all its righteous requirements. We need not sin anymore! He has cut the cords of sin that bound us so that we have but to accept His salvation in order to be free from every besetting sin. It is not necessary for us any longer to spend our lives in earnest longings for a better life and in vain regrets for desires unrealized. Christ raises no false hopes, but He comes to the captives of sin, and cries to them, 'Liberty! Your prison doors are open. Go forth.' What more can be said? Christ has gained the complete victory over this present evil world, over 'the lust of the flesh and the lust of the eyes and the pride of life' (I John 2:16), and our faith in Him makes His victory ours. We have but to accept it." (E. J. Waggoner, *The Glad Tidings*, pg. 66-74)

Waggoner makes it unmistakably clear! Life isn't derived from the law; yet, renewing us to life—restoring our capability to love—involves God inscribing the law upon our hearts. God is the sole Source of life; the law, on its own, lacks life. The law primarily exists to illuminate our sinful condition, prompting us to approach Him for restoration. The sole reason it was inscribed onto stone tablets at Sinai was due to its absence from the hearts of humanity. Its purpose is to realign us with the essence of life; to reveal to our wicked minds what perfect love is and how to walk in it. By coming into harmony with God through selfless love, we become reconnected to the Source of life, and it is Christ who facilitates this work.

> "**Christ in His humanity wrought out a perfect character, and this character He offers to impart to us...** By His perfect obedience He has made it possible for every human being to obey God's commandments. **When we submit ourselves to Christ, the heart is united with His heart, the will is merged in His will, the mind becomes one with His mind, the thoughts are brought into captivity to Him; we live His life.** This is what it means to be clothed with the garment of His righteousness." (Ellen G. White, *Christ's Object Lessons*, pg. 311)

It is not that we are simply given the *ability* to keep the law, but we are given the *mind* that finds delight in doing it; the mind of Christ. "Let this mind be in you, which was also in Christ Jesus" (Philippians 2:5). It is not that we comply with the law because we see no other way of escaping punishment, for this would not be of love but of fear. No. We comply with the law because it is not we that live, but Christ in us, fulfilling the promise that "he which hath begun a good work in you will perform it until the day of Jesus Christ" (Philippians 1:6).

> "...since all men are declared guilty by the law, there can be no righteousness in the law for any man, and that, as a consequence, **if men were left alone with the law there would be no hope for any. The law is only the written statement of the righteousness of God, and therefore can impart no righteousness; but God is a living God, and His righteousness is a living righteousness;** His Spirit has all-pervading power, and therefore **He can put His own righteousness into and upon all that believe; for faith is the reception of God into the heart.**" (E. J. Waggoner, *The Present Truth,* vol. 10, August 30, 1894, pg. 548)

> "'If a law had been given which could make alive, then righteousness would indeed be by the law.' [Galatians 3:21]. This shows us that righteousness is life. It is no mere formula, no dead theory or dogma, but is living action. Christ is the life, and He is, therefore, our righteousness. **The law written on two tables of stone could not give life any more than could the stones on which it was written. All its precepts are perfect, but the flinty characters cannot transform themselves into action. He who receives only**

> **the law in letter has a 'ministration of condemnation' and death.** But 'the Word was made flesh.' In Christ, the Living Stone, the law is life and peace. **Receiving Him through the 'ministration of the Spirit,' we have the life of righteousness which the law approves.**" (E. J. Waggoner, The Glad Tidings, pg. 94)

Let it be clearly understood that "the entering of the law" at Sinai was not the beginning of its existence. The law of God existed in the days of Abraham and was kept by him (Genesis 26:5). It existed before it was spoken upon Sinai (Exodus 16:1-4,27-28). And as this chapter has suggested, it existed from eternity. It was "added" in the sense that at Sinai it was given in such a manner so that fallen humanity could explicitly understand its precepts and that sin might abound. God would have put His law into their hearts even as He put it into Abraham's heart, if only the Israelites had believed.

> "Although **the law existed in all its force before the exode**, yet it 'came in,' 'entered,' was spoken or given, or 'added' [Galatians 3:19] at that time. And why? **That the offense might abound**, i.e., 'that sin by the commandment might become exceeding sinful;' that what was sin before might the more plainly be seen to be sin. Thus it entered, or was added, 'because of transgressions.' **If it had not been for transgressions there would have been no necessity for the law to enter at Sinai.** Why did it enter because of transgressions? **'That the offense might abound;' in order to make sin seem greater than ever before, so that men might be driven to the superabounding grace of God as manifested in Christ. And so it became a school-master, pedagogue, to bring men to Christ, in order that they might be justified by faith, and be made the righteousness of God in Him.** And so it is stated later that the law is not against the promises of God. It works in harmony with the promise, for without it the promise would be of no effect. **And this most emphatically attests the perpetuity of the law.**" (E. J. Waggoner, *The Gospel in Galatians*, 1888)

Claiming to have faith in Christ while, at the same time, purposefully behaving in opposition to His character implies the absence of the truth within us. Exercising faith that is not expressed through deeds of love, as exemplified by the law, is to make faith dead; it is to make void the law through faith. It is to say "I have faith in Christ, therefore I need not love others."

> "Do we then make void the law through faith? God forbid: yea, **we establish the law.**" (Romans 3:31)

> "We know that we have passed from death unto life, because we love the brethren. **He that loveth not his brother abideth in death.**" (I John 3:14)

> "**This is my commandment, That ye love one another,** as I have loved you." (John 15:12)

> "Owe no man any thing, but to love one another: **for he that loveth another hath fulfilled the law.** For this, Thou shalt not commit adultery, Thou shalt not kill, Thou shalt not steal, Thou shalt not bear false witness, Thou shalt not covet; and if there be any other commandment, it is briefly comprehended in this saying, namely, **Thou shalt love thy neighbour as thyself. Love worketh no ill to his neighbour: therefore love is the fulfilling of the law.**" (Romans 13:8-10)

> "**He that saith, I know him, and keepeth not his commandments, is a liar,** and the truth is not in him." (I John 2:4)

> "**For this is the love of God, that we keep his commandments:** and his commandments are not grievous." (I John 5:3)

> "If ye love me, **keep my commandments.**" (John 14:15)

Is it considered legalism to love the Lord your God? To refuse to bow down to idols? To honor your father and mother? To refrain from murder and adultery and thievery? Surely not! All these things are merely evidence that one is truly "a new creature" in Christ (2 Corinthians 5:17). Instead, the author would assert that *true* legalism involves viewing God's governance as an imperial system, along with all the hazardous implications that follow such a framework. This perspective envisions God as constrained by a mere judicial role. It depicts God's kingdom as exclusively a realm of laws and regulations. It reflects a viewpoint where the law is seen as an external constraint rather than an innate expression of God's principles for life. It is to make the law and the Law-Giver devoid of all love, portraying them as burdensome yokes of authority and dominance. It imagines God's entire character and governance as being synonymous with flawed human constructs of legality and justice.

The imperial view of God is plagued by the misleading assertion that Christ's work on behalf of the sinner is merely an illusion, a falsehood. This perspective suggests that our righteousness is a result of a legal decree rather than a true transformation; we are *legally* made righteous instead of *actually* made righteous. The record books in heaven are perceived as being altered in some way, rather than our own hearts and minds. The consequence of such a view, is that Christ lacks the definitive power to completely cleanse us of sin; He instead must resort to trickery and deception in order to convince the Father of our righteousness despite our actual state. It ultimately diminishes the role and power of Christ, and constrains the primary purpose of His labor to a mere judicial function. Instead of achieving unity with the Father, we ultimately require protection from Him. This perspective regards sin strictly as a legal issue—a transgression of imposed laws that is subject to punishment by an overseer or judge, rather than recognizing it for what it is: a hereditary and disharmonious condition that innately causes separation, destruction, and death. God's intention toward the sinner is no longer discerned as to heal and restore, but to condemn and execute. Moreover, God's law is perceived as a set of rules to test obedience, rather than guidelines meant to help humanity become aware of their sinful nature and seek restoration. This legal perspective often downplays the personal relationship, growth, and inner change that should accompany religious belief.

The purpose of God's law is to diagnose our sinful condition and direct us to Christ, who promises to impart unto us His righteousness of character. This empowers us to live a life of selfless love in accordance with the law. This transcendent work, on behalf of the sinner, entails a process of spiritual metamorphosis, wherein the resultant moral transformation is merely a consequential outcome thereof. The law is *not* the means by which we are saved, rather it demonstrates our salvation.

> "**A mere profession of discipleship is of no value. The faith in Christ which saves the soul is not what it is represented to be by many. 'Believe, believe,' they say, 'and you need not keep the law.' But a belief that does not lead to obedience is presumption.** The apostle John says, 'He that saith, I know Him, and keepeth not His commandments, is a liar, and the truth is not in him.' I John 2:4. Let none cherish the idea that special providences or miraculous manifestations are to be the proof of the genuineness of their work or of the ideas they advocate. **When persons will speak lightly of the word of God, and set their impressions, feelings, and exercises above the divine standard, we may know that they have no light in them...**" (Ellen G. White, *Thoughts from the Mount of Blessing*, pg. 146)

These succinct counterarguments to potential accusations of legalism adequately satisfy the author's intention. With these addressed, we may now proceed in our presentation of the matters relevant to the present work. Having elucidated the concepts outlined in this chapter, we now shift our attention toward the condition of sin and its intrinsic consequences. Here, our primary concentration rests on accentuating a lucid grasp of the inherent nature of sin according to our newfound understanding of God's character and government. Upon coming to the revelation that our God is not to be regarded with trepidation, and His character does not align with that of a rigorous autocrat dispensing arbitrary punishments upon those who err, we can then begin to uncover the source of death as an innate consequence of sin. This inquiry seeks to dissociate mortality from divine wrath and will be the core subject of our next chapter.

Chapter 7

Unveiling the Harvest of Sin: Consequences and Impact

*"…**since God's life is the standard of righteousness, it is evident that everything that is different from the life of God is unrighteousness; and 'all unrighteousness is sin.'** But if the life of any being is different from the life of God, it must be because His life is not allowed free course through that being. **But where God's life is not, there is death. Whoever is out of harmony with God—enmity against Him—has death working in him, and death for his inevitable portion. So it is not by an arbitrary decree that the wages of sin is death. That results from the very nature of things.** Sin is opposition to God,—rebellion against Him,—and is utterly foreign to His being. **It is separation from God, and separation from God is death, because there is no life outside of Him.** All that hate Him, love death…" (E. J. Waggoner, The Present Truth, vol. 9, September 21, 1893, pg. 386)*

*"Although many might hesitate to express it thus, the thought that lingers in their minds is about like this: 'God is arbitrary and obstinate, and will not permit the slightest variation from his laws without plunging us into eternal death.' **This is what Satan has ever said of God and of his government.** I desire to show the contrary so that all may see. **I desire to show that it is the variation itself that plunges us into eternal death, and not the arbitrary decree of God… The law of God is not simply his fiat; it rests on eternal principles of pleasure and pain,—principles as unchangeable in their very nature as the laws that govern the seasons or control the motions of the planets. The law is not so simply because God said so, but he said so because it was so, and because it must eternally and universally be so.**" (George Fifield, God is Love, pg. 37-38)*

As previously established in this volume, sin is a hereditary condition with inherent consequences. It's an ancestral ailment that has grossly marred the soul and character of humanity. The overarching message of the gospel, spanning from Genesis to Revelation, revolves around God's endeavor to remedy this condition and reinstate mankind to its pre-fallen state.

> "**For I will restore health unto thee,** and I will heal thee of thy wounds, saith the LORD..." (Jeremiah 30:17)

> "For God sent not his Son into the world to condemn the world; **but that the world through him might be saved.**" (John 3:17)

However, the restoration of our Edenic nature doesn't occur through a mere judicial decree or proclamation, as penal substitution theology implies. Instead, the transformation that unfolds is a genuine and profound change within the hearts and minds of humanity. By beholding Christ, we are brought into harmony with Him, and He imparts unto us His own righteousness of character. This is life to the soul, freely given, and we are nourished by His graceful intercession.

Yet, numerous individuals misconstrue the purpose of Christ's work. They misinterpret the genuine context of His intercession on behalf of humanity. Embracing the deceit propagated by the arch-deceiver, they perceive God as a Being to be shielded from. Under the imperial view, God becomes the author of suffering and death.

> "Satan came into our world, and led men into temptation. **With sin came sickness and suffering, for we reap that which we sow. Satan afterward caused man to charge upon God the suffering which is but the sure result of the transgression of physical [natural] law.** God is thus falsely accused, and his character misrepresented. **He is charged with doing that which Satan himself has done...**" (Ellen G. White, *The Christian Educator,* October 1, 1898)

For those with the imperial view of God, Christ's intercession is seen as protecting them from divine wrath, lest God should harm them. They imagine the Father as angry and vindictive, with the Son positioned in-between Him and the transgressor, preventing the fatal deathblow from the Father. This perspective instills fear and mistrust in God Himself.

However, within the context of our newly acquired comprehension of God's law and character, we understand that this cannot be so. The kingdom of heaven is not likened to a court room. The love of God and the love of Christ are the same. The Father loves the sinner just as much as the Son does—and His aim is to heal and restore. God is not offended because of our sin; rather, He is grieved at the state of our condition. He is empathetic toward our infirmities and seeks to deliver us.

> "**In all their affliction he was afflicted,** and the angel of his presence saved them: **in his love and in his pity he redeemed them;** and he bare them, and carried them all the days of old." (Isaiah 63:9)

> "**For we have not an high priest which cannot be touched with the feeling of our infirmities;** but was in all points tempted like as we are, yet without sin." (Hebrews 4:15)

> "But **God commendeth his love toward us,** in that, **while we were yet sinners, Christ died for us.**" (Romans 5:8)

We do not need protection from the Father—we need His help! But how can He aid us in our current state if we regard Him with apprehension and distrust? Christ's intercessory role, when correctly understood, is situated within the context of restoration rather than protection. The term "intercession" refers to the act of intervening on behalf of another. The interpretation of this matter could vary based upon the framework through which it is examined. From an imperial perspective, Christ necessarily intervenes and pleads before the Father, on behalf of the sinner, so that His wrath may be pacified, and destruction averted. Such a notion is not supported by the scriptures. Accurately understood within the context of the natural law system, the intercession of Christ becomes a requisite for the sinner to be restored to a state of righteousness. Our innate capability to address our sin-ridden condition, on our own, is futile. This necessitates Christ's intervention to undertake a corrective process within us. He assures us that God forgives and has the power to help us. Through this remedial intervention, we are empowered to overcome sin and attain alignment with the divine nature. This is true intercession.

> "…**I do not say to you that I will ask [intercede] the Father on your behalf; for the Father himself loves you,** because you have loved me and have believed that I came from God." (John 16:26-27, *ESV*)

Christ's intercession, though always on behalf of humanity, isn't aimed at the Father—this would be unnecessary, "for the Father himself loves you," (John 16:27, *ESV*). Instead, it's directed at the hearts and minds of men. Through Christ, God reconciles the world to Himself. In stark contrast, the penal legal (*imperial*) framework suggests that Christ's intercessory efforts are aimed at reconciling the Father to humanity.

> "…God was in Christ, **reconciling the world unto himself…**" (2 Corinthians 5:19)

Sadly, many choose to maintain the penal legal form of intercession wherein Christ acts as our defender against a most harsh and critical judge. This not only distorts the role of Christ as intercessor, but also suggests that the acquisition of righteousness remains an elusive prospect for the transgressor. This interpretation alleges that the repentant sinner remains in a continuous and eternal state of imperfection, yet is shielded from divine retribution through Christ's perpetual intervention. It implies that sin, by itself, does not inherently harm the individual who engages in it; rather, it is only when God discovers it that suffering and death result. It proposes an everlasting retention of human depravity and sinful inclination, merely camouflaged by Christ's scheme of concealing individuals beneath the cloak of His sacrificial blood. Our sinful condition becomes permanent, and true righteousness unattainable. This premise ultimately nullifies and extinguishes the power of Christ to fully cleanse humanity of sin. Righteousness is then degraded to a mere legal declaration, void of any tangible veracity. The problem of sin, rather than being eradicated by God, is merely ignored, and becomes prolonged and residual. Humanity is not restored or transformed, but instead our corrupt nature remains eternally veiled—merely obscured from the Father. Such a deception only serves to excuse the believer from true spiritual growth and constrains them to a state of spiritual infancy and paralysis; they remain under the curse of disobedience.

Dear reader, does this bear semblance of salvation for you? How can this be genuine salvation—a concept implying deliverance or rescue—when its very implication is that we are meant to remain in captivity?

> "Stand fast therefore in the liberty wherewith **Christ hath made us free, and be not entangled again with the yoke of bondage.**" (Galatians 5:1)

It is God "which giveth us the victory through our Lord Jesus Christ." (1 Corinthians 15:57). But what exactly is it that we gain victory over? Is it the wrath of God?—His punitive justice? No, it cannot be so, as it would suggest a scenario wherein God experiences some form of defeat. According to 1 Corinthians 15:54, it is in fact "death" that is "swallowed up in victory." Ah, so we gain victory over death. Yet, from where does death arise? "For the wages of sin is death" (Romans 6:23). And "sin, when it is finished, bringeth forth death" (James 1:15). Sin *is* death. Therefore, in Christ, we obtain victory over sin and all its deleterious outcomes, including death! Why is it, then, that so many refuse to believe in victory over sin? Why do so many settle for "righteousness so-called"?

Those who gain heaven will not retain their present wicked state only to have it veiled by the blood of Jesus and sheltered from the discerning gaze of the Father. Instead, a new character will be embraced—the very character of Christ. Nowhere in the scriptures is there an allusion to the idea that the realization of sanctification carries with it a symbolic or metaphorical meaning. Quite the opposite, inspiration plainly states that this work is an authentic spiritual transformation.

> "Whereby are given unto us exceeding great and precious promises: that **by these ye might be partakers of the divine nature, having escaped the corruption that is in the world through lust.**" (2 Peter 1:4)

> "For he hath made him to be sin for us, who knew no sin; **that we might be made the righteousness of God in him.**" (2 Corinthians 5:21)

> "But we all, with open face beholding as in a glass the glory of the Lord, **are changed into the same image from glory to glory, even as by the Spirit of the Lord.**" (2 Corinthians 3:18)

> "...we know that, when he [Jesus] shall appear, **we shall be like him;** for we shall see him as he is." (1 John 3:2)

If sin can be conceptualized as a degradation in condition, or moral state, rather than strictly a legal matter, it follows that righteousness should be regarded similarly, emphasizing it as a genuine condition of the person rather than merely a legal declaration. It was *our* nature—*our* character—that was impaired at the onset of sin. Our character, therefore, is to be renewed by the blood of Christ.

> "Day by day angels of God are watching the development of character, and weighing moral worth... All defects must be remedied. **The character must be assimilated to the character of Christ...** At an infinite cost a fountain has been prepared for our cleansing. **In the blood of the Son of God we may wash our garments of character, and make them white.**" (Ellen G. White, *Signs of the Times,* April 17, 1901)

> "**Remember your character is being daguerreotyped [photographed] by the great Master Artist in the record books of heaven** as minutely as the face is reproduced upon the polished plate of the artist. What do the books of heaven say in your case?

> **Are you conforming your character to the Pattern, Jesus Christ? Are you washing your robes of character and making them white in the blood of the Lamb?**" (Ellen G. White, *Letters and Manuscripts,* vol. 6, Letter 51, 1889)

But what is meant by the *blood* of Christ? If it is by the shedding of His blood that we are saved from sin (Hebrews 9:22), doesn't this denote a penal legal substitution?

> "And almost all things are by the law purged with blood; and **without shedding of blood is no remission.**" (Hebrews 9:22)

> "But now in Christ Jesus **ye who sometimes were far off are made nigh by the blood of Christ.**" (Ephesians 2:13)

Doesn't this mean that Christ's physical blood had to be spilt in order for us to come into a right standing with God? Isn't it true that the only way God could be appeased is by seeing blood flow?

In this instance, it is incumbent upon the author to underscore the prevalent human capacity for forgiveness without an insistence on acts of violence or the shedding of blood. We see regularly that payback of a "pound of flesh" is not necessary. Individuals routinely extend forgiveness, and appreciate receiving it, without demanding a vein be opened, or the sacrifice of an animal. Therefore, when contemplating the divine, the question arises: does God not possess the same capacity for unconditional forgiveness? Is man more willing to forgive than God? Is He unable to freely forgive?

> "**...even as the Lord has [freely] forgiven you,** so must you also [forgive]." (Colossians 3:13, *AMPC*)

> "Let the wicked change their ways and banish the very thought of doing wrong. **Let them turn to the Lord that he may have mercy on them. Yes, turn to our God, for he will forgive generously.**" (Isaiah 55:7, *NLT*)

Since when are there conditions for unconditional love, grace, mercy, and forgiveness? Is God's forgiveness of a lesser sort than ours? Certainly not!

It is here that we must ascertain the proper context of Christ's blood; we must determine whether it has a literal or spiritual application. In many instances of scripture, Christ's words were taken literally when, in fact, He was speaking of spiritual truths.

> "**All these things spake Jesus unto the multitude in parables; and without a parable spake he not unto them:** That it might be fulfilled which was spoken by the prophet, saying, I will open my mouth in parables; I will utter things which have been kept secret from the foundation of the world." (Matthew 13:34-35)

This led to a numerous multitude of His listeners grossly misunderstanding the principles of His ministry. An illustrative instance of this idea, relevant to our current discussion, may be found in the book of John:

> "I am the living bread which came down from heaven: if any man eat of this bread, he shall live for ever: **and the bread that I will give is my flesh, which I will give for the life of the world. The Jews therefore strove among themselves, saying, How can this man give us his flesh to eat?**" (John 6:51-52)

Here, Jesus explains how He is the bread of life, and that by consuming His flesh we may gain eternal life. The Jews, however, understood Him to be speaking of His *literal* flesh. Certainly, Jesus was not endorsing cannibalism! Rather, He was comparing Himself to the manna that Israel had eaten in the time of Moses:

> "Your fathers did eat manna in the wilderness, and are dead. **This is the bread which cometh down from heaven, that a man may eat thereof, and not die.**" (John 6:49-50)

Like manna, Jesus descended from heaven; and, like manna, Jesus gives life. Unlike manna, the life that Christ imparts lasts forever:

> "This is that bread which came down from heaven: not as your fathers did eat manna, and are dead: **he that eateth of this bread shall live for ever.**" (John 6:58)

The symbolism of the bread is further illustrated in His temptation in the wilderness. The devil tempts Jesus with bread, and Jesus answers:

> "But he answered and said, It is written, **Man shall not live by bread alone, but by every word that proceedeth out of the mouth of God.**" (Matthew 4:4)

In this instance, Jesus quotes Deuteronomy 8:3, and suggests that the nourishment for our spiritual well-being is found in God's word. In the first chapter of John, Jesus is called "the Word" of God "made flesh" (John 1:14). Further, in chapter 6, He claims:

> "I am that bread of life." (John 6:48)

All of this signifies that Christ Himself is sustenance for the weary soul. The words spoken by Christ and the spiritual truths He exemplified served the purpose of reuniting humanity with the Source of life. From His lips came illuminating and profound truths which served to unveil the character of the Father. Just as our words serve as a window into our heart—containing our nature, character, and purposes—Christ, as the Word of God, constituted the verbal embodiment of the Father, rendering His intrinsic nature, character, and divine purposes perceptible in human form. By internalizing the words of Christ, we may readily discern the heart of the Father.

> "...for **out of the abundance of the heart the mouth speaketh.**" (Matthew 12:34)

In every instance, and in every word, Christ was conveying the spiritual truths of the kingdom of heaven. It is by treasuring His words and applying them to our own life—patterning our life and character after that of Christ, allowing Him to work in us—that we may find nourishment for our souls and obtain everlasting life. This is what is meant by eating His flesh. It is digesting the word of God—the bread of life—and applying its truths to our lives. In doing so, we come into harmony with the heart of the Father.

Moreover, continuing in our analysis of the sixth chapter of John, Jesus states:

> "Then Jesus said unto them, Verily, verily, I say unto you, **Except ye eat the flesh of the Son of man, and drink his blood, ye have no life in you. Whoso eateth my flesh, and drinketh my blood, hath eternal life;** and I will raise him up at the last day. **For my flesh is meat indeed, and my blood is drink indeed. He that eateth my flesh, and drinketh my blood, dwelleth in me, and I in him.**" (John 6:53-56)

In this particular instance, Jesus extends the metaphor beyond a mere consumption of His flesh, incorporating the imperative to also partake of His blood. Regrettably, a considerable number among His audience misconstrued His speech. They took His words quite literally, resulting in their disillusionment and subsequent departure. This misunderstanding hindered their ability to apprehend the profound spiritual lesson that lay beneath His words.

> "Many therefore of his disciples, when they had heard this, said, **This is an hard saying; who can hear it?... From that time many of his disciples went back, and walked no more with him.**" (John 6:60,66)

Christ's graphic imagery concerning the consumption of His flesh and the drinking of His blood initially appears perplexing. However, as we have already seen, a deeper understanding is gained by a thorough contextual analysis. But why did Christ choose to speak symbolically in this instance? By examining the entirety of Jesus' teachings and actions in John chapter 6, the obscurity surrounding the reason for His veiled speech gradually diminishes.

Earlier in the chapter, Jesus fed the 5,000 (John 6:1-13). The next day, the same multitude continued to follow Him, seeking after another meal. Jesus pointed out their short-sightedness; they were only seeking physical bread, but as we have already established, there was something more important:

> "**Labour not for the meat which perisheth, but for that meat which endureth unto everlasting life,** which the Son of man shall give unto you..." (John 6:27)

At this point, Jesus endeavors to shift their focus from physical nourishment to their genuine need, which was of a spiritual nature. This contrast between physical food and spiritual food sets the stage for Jesus' statement that we must eat His flesh and drink His blood. To prevent being misconstrued, Jesus specifies that He is speaking symbolically of spiritual matters:

> "...the words that I speak unto you, **they are spirit,** and they are life." (John 6:63)

Nevertheless, a substantial portion of the audience remained firmly entrenched in a purely physical perspective, unable to bridge the cognitive gap to grasp the spiritual message which Jesus was conveying. It is the same with many today. A considerable number of Christians comprehend the symbolic nature of His speech in this particular instance but don't comprehend the symbolic nature of similar passages in other parts of scripture. They acknowledge the spiritual context of His words here but elsewhere understand Him in an exclusively physical and literal manner, thereby missing out on certain spiritual truths.

For our current discussion, we are not as concerned with the misapplication of the spiritual meaning of the bread as we are with the meaning of the blood. Having briefly explored the lesson conveyed through the bread, we now reorient our attention back to our initial focus: the significance of Christ's blood.

Numerous individuals believe that when the scriptures declare "without shedding of blood is no remission [of sin]" (Hebrews 9:22), it implies that, after-all, God *does* indeed require blood sacrifice for the forgiveness of sin. However, this boldly assumes the character of God to be predatory, merciless, and unforgiving—even bloodthirsty! This interpretation commits gross violence against all that the author has put forth in this volume. Not only this, but it likens the disposition of our God to that of a pagan god; no different than Baal of the Phoenicians that required human sacrifice—mostly of babies and young children—before his wrath could be appeased.

Does the reader see how Satan has drastically marred the character of God by this interpretation? But if the verse in question—namely Hebrews 9:22—isn't alluding to physical blood, then what is meant here? In order to discern its significance, we look to the book of Leviticus:

> "**For the life of the flesh is in the blood,** and I have given it for you on the altar to make atonement for your souls, for **it is the blood that makes atonement by the life.**" (Leviticus 17:11, *ESV*)

> "For the life of every creature is its blood: **its blood is its life.**" (Leviticus 17:14, *ESV*)

Letting the Bible interpret itself, we discover that the life is typified by the blood. And it is through the blood, or life, of Christ that atonement is made. By applying the interpretation of this symbol to the words of Christ, we place it in its proper context:

> "And as they were eating, Jesus took bread, and blessed it, and brake it, and gave it to the disciples, and said, Take, eat; this is my body. And he took the cup, and gave thanks, and gave it to them, saying, Drink ye all of it; **For this is my blood of the new testament, which is shed for many for the remission of sins.**" (Matthew 26:26-28)

Just as Christ is not speaking of His literal body in this instance, neither is He alluding to His physical blood. Rather, He employs metaphorical rhetoric. When we align His words with what's conveyed in the epistle to the Hebrews, it fosters a fresh understanding:

> "**...without shedding of blood is no remission [of sin].**" (Hebrews 9:22)

By reconciling all of these elements, we come to understand that in Hebrews 9:22, the reference to "blood" does not pertain to the literal shedding of blood but is instead symbolized by the life of Christ. The power is not in the blood itself, but rather in the One who shed His blood. It's not Christ's mere blood that is the atoning agent, but the life of Christ imparted and manifested in the sinner which completes this work.

The contextualization of this spiritual truth stands thus: that without the life of Christ—His righteousness of character—being imparted to the soul of the transgressor, the sinful nature could not be overcome. Expanding upon the foundations laid out earlier in this work; it's clear that without divine external help, humanity could not overcome its sinful disposition. This necessitates Christ interceding on man's behalf and imparting unto us His life-giving Spirit, for we are, of ourselves, "dead in trespasses and sins" (Ephesians 2:1). This is how we come into unity—or "at-one-ment"—with the Father. This is how God, through Christ, reconciles "the world unto himself" (2 Corinthians 5:19). Upon embracing the righteous life and character of Christ, our sinful nature begins to be remitted (*alleviated, remedied, sent away*) by the gentle and loving Spirit of our Savior.

> **"Just here somebody has remembered that it is said in Hebrews 9:22, 'Without the shedding of blood there is no remission;' and this makes him think that after all God did demand a sacrifice before He would pardon man. It is very difficult for the mind to rid itself of the idea received as a legacy from Paganism, through the Papacy, that God was so angry at man for having sinned, that He could not be mollified without seeing blood flow, but that it made no difference to Him whose blood it was, if only somebody was killed; and that since Christ's life was worth more than the lives of all men, He accepted Him as a substitute for them.** This is almost a brutal way of stating the case, but it is the only way that the case can be truly presented. The heathen conception of God is a brutal one, as dishonouring to God as it is discouraging to man; and **this heathen idea has been allowed to colour too many texts of Scripture.** It is sad to think how greatly men who really loved the Lord, have given occasion to His enemies to blaspheme.

"'Apart from shedding of blood there is no remission.' What is remission? It means simply 'sending away.' What is to be remitted, or sent away? Our sins, for we read that 'through faith in Christ's blood the righteousness of God is declared for the remission of sins that are past, through the forbearance of God.' Romans 3:20. **So we learn that apart from the shedding of blood there is no sending away of sins... But how is it that the shedding of blood, even the blood of Christ, can take away sins? Simply because the blood is the life.** 'For the life of the flesh is in the blood; and I have given it to you upon the altar to make an atonement for your souls, for it is the blood that maketh atonement for the soul.' Leviticus 17:11. **So when we read that apart from the shedding of blood there is no remission, we know it means that no sins can be taken away except by the life of Christ. In Him is no sin; therefore when He imparts His life to a soul, that soul is at once cleansed from sin...**" (E. J. Waggoner, *The Present Truth*, vol. 9, September 21, 1893, pg. 387-388)

The concept of Christ's blood is intricately connected to His life, embodying profound spiritual symbolism. Just as blood sustains physical life, Christ's life represents the spiritual sustenance He offers to believers. His sacrificial actions, teachings, and love epitomize the redemptive and saving power that flows from His veins. His blood signifies the shedding of His life for humanity's salvation, His longsuffering through man's rejection to deliver mankind, serving as a poignant reminder of the covenant between God and His people. The life Jesus lived typifies the essence of His blood. And by embracing His life and character, the transformative journey from sin to salvation is instigated in the hearts and minds of His followers.

However, there are those who will argue that the Father demanded Christ's blood be spilt as a prerequisite for forgiveness. With bold and fervent conviction, they proclaim, "Christ served as our substitute, settling our debt and absorbing the wrath of God on our behalf, making it possible for the Father to extend His forgiveness to us."

Let it be clearly stated: the author firmly believes that Christ's substitutionary death was necessary for humanity's salvation, but decisively rejects the notion that it was the Father who took the life of Christ on the cross. As has already been established in chapter 3 of this volume, Christ's mission was to reveal the true character of His Father and, therefore, the love of the Father and the love of Christ are the same. We steadfastly dismiss the notion that God required the brutal murder of His own Son as a prerequisite for Him to resume His role as a loving and forgiving Father. His love for His children never wavered; in fact, His love was so profound that He devised a plan for our salvation from the very moment sin entered the world.

> "**For God so loved the world, that he gave his only begotten Son,** that whosoever believeth in him should not perish, but have everlasting life." (John 3:16)

Instead, dear reader, consider this: was it the Father who demanded/necessitated Christ's sacrifice, or was it humanity? Who was it that needed to be reconciled and to whom? One's perspective on this matter directly affects how they will perceive the doctrine of substitutionary atonement.

The author finds fault with the perspective that penal substitution theology suggests—where "penal" signifies punishment, and "substitution" implies that Jesus took upon Himself divine punishment in the place of the sinner—as it misplaces the biblical context of the substitution while, at the same time, completely diminishes the true nature of atonement. Even worse is that this theological theory is only partially in error, making it an even more treacherous and subtle deception. There exists no substantive evidence in scripture for the notion that Christ assumed the role of bearing God's wrath as a substitute for the sinner. This interpretation would, in effect, imply that suffering and death originate in God—an inference not grounded in the biblical text. Scripture never indicates that it is the Father who requires reconciliation; instead, in every instance, it clearly conveys that it is humanity that needs to be reconciled to God. It underscores that God, through Christ, is actively facilitating this reconciliation.

The substitutionary aspect that is affirmed by the Bible and upheld by the author is the conviction that Christ assumed our sins, thereby allowing us to partake of His righteousness. He became man's substitute by taking our terminal condition upon Himself so that we would fully accept His attempts to impute us with His own righteous character.

> "The next day John seeth Jesus coming unto him, and saith, **Behold the Lamb of God, which taketh away the sin of the world.**" (John 1:29)

> "**For he hath made him to be sin for us,** who knew no sin; **that we might be made the righteousness of God in him.**" (2 Corinthians 5:21)

This is true substitutionary atonement. He was made "to be sin for us, who knew no sin" (2 Corinthians 5:21) in order that we might be cured of our fallen nature. On the cross, He endured the natural and inescapable outcome of sin, similar to those who, by rejecting God's remedy, will ultimately face the same fate.

Christ's death on the cross wasn't meant to settle a legal transaction between the sinner and an angry deity. The Father did not place Him there to be an object of His wrath. Instead, Christ's sacrifice is intended to rectify humanity's fallen condition, as originally promised by the Almighty.

> "**The mystery of the incarnation of Christ, the account of His sufferings, His crucifixion, His resurrection, and His ascension, open to all humanity the marvelous love of God.** This imparts a power to the truth. **The attributes of God were made known through the life and works of Christ. He was the representative of the divine character.**" (Ellen G. White, *Review and Herald,* June 18, 1895)

This perspective of the cross will receive comprehensive study in a subsequent section of this volume. We shall now redirect our attention back towards the primary theme of this chapter. It is noteworthy, however, that our reentry into the chapter's central discourse is instigated by the profound impact of the misguided theology of penal substitution—particularly its stance on the nature of sin—thus establishing the foundation for our forthcoming deliberation.

Owing to the effect of the theory of penal substitution, many falsely believe that Jesus died at the hands of the Father in the sinner's place. As a result, they reason that there must be no natural or innate consequence of sin, rather God personally administers punishment for transgression. Instead of viewing God's law as the inherent principles that govern life, they regard these rules as mere imperial inventions. They see the Almighty as capricious and authoritarian, imposing boundaries to manipulate human lives, hindering genuine happiness through His arbitrary decrees. In place of sin yielding the wages of death, it is seen as God who metes out the consequence of mortality. If the rules are merely made up, and there are no innate ramifications to sin, then God must be the One to enforce its punishment.

Dear reader, this is in direct contrast to the sacred precepts of scripture. By committing transgression, we inevitably reap that which we sow. The punishment of sin is built in and comes as naturally as night follows day.

> **"Those who live only to satisfy their own sinful nature will harvest decay and death from that sinful nature.** But those who live to please the Spirit will harvest everlasting life from the Spirit." (Galatians 6:8, *NLT*)

> **"For the wages of sin is death; but the gift of God is eternal life** through Jesus Christ our Lord." (Romans 6:23)

Anyone in disharmony with God, harboring enmity against Him, carries the burden of death within themselves, destined for its inescapable embrace. Thus, it is not by an arbitrary decree that the wages of sin is death; rather, it emerges from the fundamental order of existence. Sin represents defiance of God, a rebellion against His nature, and stands in stark contrast to His essence. It signifies a severance from God, and separation from God is synonymous with death, as life cannot exist outside of Him.

> "**For in him we live,** and move, and have our being..." (Acts 17:28)

God did not say "for in the day that thou eatest thereof I will surely kill you." Absolutely not! Rather, He warned us that, by embracing sin, we "shalt surely die." (Genesis 2:17).

> "**God does not stand toward the sinner as an executioner of the sentence against transgression;** but He leaves the rejectors of His mercy to themselves, to reap that which they have sown..." (Ellen G. White, *The Great Controversy*, pg. 36)

> "**We are not to regard God as waiting to punish the sinner for his sin. The sinner brings the punishment upon himself. His own actions start a train of circumstances that bring the sure result.** Every act of transgression reacts upon the sinner, works in him a change of character, and makes it more easy for him to transgress again. **By choosing to sin, men separate themselves from God, cut themselves off from the channel of blessing, and the sure result is ruin and death...**" (Ellen G. White, *Selected Messages*, vol. I, pg. 235)

Sadly, many erroneously pursue a belief wherein God stands as the progenitor of all sin's results. They interpret that, due to the transgression of Adam and Eve, the cursing of the earth under sin was driven by a spitefulness on the part of God. All of the woe that has entered the world as a result of sin is, therefore, attributed to the hand of the Almighty. To defend this belief, they cite Genesis chapter 3:

> "And unto Adam he said, Because thou hast hearkened unto the voice of thy wife, and hast eaten of the tree, of which I commanded thee, saying, Thou shalt not eat of it: **cursed is the**

> **ground for thy sake; in sorrow shalt thou eat of it all the days of thy life; Thorns also and thistles shall it bring forth to thee; and thou shalt eat the herb of the field...**" (Genesis 3:17-18)

How may we reconcile this passage with our newfound understanding of the character of God and the nature of sin? We must ask ourselves: in this particular instance, is God conveying to our first parents that, as a consequence of their disobedience, He intends to impose a punitive act by cursing the ground?—Or, is He primarily communicating that, given their transgression, these are the intrinsic and inescapable outcomes that shall occur as a result of the natural course of things?

To gain a broader perspective on this issue, we refer to the book of Isaiah. Within its pages, we can readily discern that the curse that befell the earth did not occur by forceful divine intervention, but rather emerged as a direct consequence of sin.

> "**The earth also is defiled under the inhabitants thereof; because they have transgressed the laws,** changed the ordinance, broken the everlasting covenant. **Therefore hath the curse devoured the earth,** and they that dwell therein are desolate..." (Isaiah 24:5-6)

The curse arose as a natural outcome of transgression, rather than being a consequence of God's punitive action. And the book of Romans tells us that, because of sin:

> "**...the whole creation groaneth and travaileth in pain** together until now." (Romans 8:22)

God is not the author of the decay or discomfort that man experiences as a result of sin. In the process of earth's creation, the Creator looked upon the works of His hands and saw "that it was good." To maintain that God, now, takes pleasure in the existence of thorns, thistles, and all the adversity associated with sin is to profoundly misrepresent both God's character and the nature of sin. Our God exclusively brings forth that which is good; nothing unfavorable arises from His craftsmanship.

"For everything created by God **is good...**" (I Timothy 4:4, *ESV*)

"**Every good gift and every perfect gift is from above, and cometh down from the Father of lights,** with whom is no variableness, neither shadow of turning." (James 1:17)

"**God, then, did not make this world a scene of sorrow. It was not His purpose that it should be such, but the contrary.** It became what it is by the deed of Satan, in opposition to the will of God." (William Matson, *The Adversary: His Purpose, Power and Person,* pg. 43, published in 1891)

Since sin is inherently evil, it logically entails that its results are likewise inherently evil. Conversely, since God is inherently good, it logically follows that He can only produce those things which are good. From a logical standpoint, it is inconceivable for God to bestow evil upon another, or even entertain the thought of creating evil, as this would contradict His very Being.

"**See that none render evil for evil unto any man;** but ever follow that which is good, both among yourselves, and to all men." (I Thessalonians 5:15)

"**He [God] is not the Author of evil, either of sin or of its terrible progeny, disease and death;** we have no right to say even that God sends sickness or death, or that such things are due directly to the Will of God." (Robert Eyton, *The Lord's Prayer: Sermons,* pg. 106, published in 1892)

Evidently, the adversity in which humanity often finds itself is a consequence of mankind's own actions.

"Let no man say when he is tempted, I am tempted of God: for **God cannot be tempted with evil,** neither tempteth he any man: But **every man is tempted, when he is drawn away of his own lust, and enticed.** Then when lust hath conceived, it bringeth forth sin: and **sin, when it is finished, bringeth forth death.**" (James 1:13-15)

Our fatal infatuation with sin, stemming from our fallen nature, places us in a condition of moral and spiritual disarray, leading inevitably to corruption and suffering.

> "Is it any wonder, then, when the spirit is in such a state of moral disorder, that the body, which has its life from the spirit, should be filled with impurity and disease also? and that, when a whole people or all mankind is in such a state, pestilences should break out and ravage whole countries and go through the world? **Let not men, then, (as they are too apt to do) ascribe these scourges of humanity to the Hand of their Heavenly Father above, who is Love and Goodness itself, -who is a Saviour, not a destroyer,-but to their own state of corruption and sin, which is the sole cause of their suffering.**" (Oliver Prescott Hiller, *God Manifest: A Treatise on the Goodness, Wisdom, and Power of God, as Manifested in His Works, Word, and Personal Appearing,* pg. 280)

By choosing to sin, we actively participate in our own destruction. By embracing sin, we inevitably choose death. It is God's aim to rescue us from death's firm grasp. As we grow in our understanding of the Father as He is revealed in Christ, we learn that He wholly refrains from any engagement in the realm of death—neither does He derive any pleasure in the demise of the wicked.

> "Say unto them, As I live, saith the Lord GOD, **I have no pleasure in the death of the wicked; but that the wicked turn from his way and live: turn ye, turn ye from your evil ways; for why will ye die,** O house of Israel?" (Ezekiel 33:11)

Rather, it is our adversary—the devil—who may aptly be designated as the harbinger of death. As Christ tells us, he was a murderer from the beginning:

> "Ye are of your father the devil, and the lusts of your father ye will do. **He was a murderer from the beginning, and abode not in the truth, because there is no truth in him.** When he speaketh a lie, he speaketh of his own: for he is a liar, and the father of it." (John 8:44)

The Apostle John goes on to affirm that an individual who manifests an affinity towards murder, or bears responsibility for the taking of another's life—any being who delights in death and destruction—stands devoid of eternal life.

> "**Whosoever hateth his brother is a murderer:** and ye know that **no murderer hath eternal life abiding in him.**" (I John 3:15)

Taking this verse as it reads, should we acknowledge that God is the source of death, we would be compelled to concede the flawed assertion that eternal life does not abide within Him. Furthermore, the Psalmist tells us that:

> "**Evil shall slay the wicked:** and they that hate the righteous shall be desolate." (Psalm 34:21)

Are we to say that God is evil? So it is with those who claim Him as the progenitor of death and destruction! The author, in good conscience, cannot endorse such a view. Such a conclusion as this should be wholly unacceptable to any Christian! God is not evil; therefore God does not kill.

> "A big question that soon comes up in discussions about God's character is: 'does God kill?' Even more important is the more specific question 'does God kill with the Second Death?' Again, in reference to Revelation 20:9, does God personally, actively and directly send fire to kill the lost? **If we mix literal fire directly from God with the mental anguish that will be part of the experience, we have what is defined as torture.** Torture - to inflict pain before execution - is something that civilized governments do not do. **Torture is of no benefit to the one being tortured (obviously), to anyone looking on (to them it should arouse sympathy, even indignation) or to the torturer, although some may feel that it is satisfying to a vindictive spirit. Any physical torture being imposed would make the penalty more severe than simply 'the wages of sin is death.' – The wages of sin is not torture!**
>
> **"God personally and actively terminating the sinner's life would demonstrate that death proceeds from Him, and that death is part of His way, His principles of government. That would**

mean that God brought death as the final solution to the sin problem. But we know that is not the case because death itself is an enemy of God. 'The last enemy that will be destroyed is death.' (I Corinthians 15:26). **Wouldn't it be rather strange if the last enemy that should be destroyed in the Great Controversy - death - was destroyed by an act of God Himself causing death?** God destroying death by using it as the final solution makes no sense whatsoever! That would establish death as a tool God uses to solve issues. Wouldn't death be more effectively destroyed (even in the sense of showing that it was never necessary in the first place) by God showing that death was never part of His plan? **The final, end result of sin is death.** The Bible says where death comes from: 'Then when lust hath conceived, it bringeth forth sin: and sin, when it is finished, bringeth forth death.' (James 1:15).

"**Sin brings forth death; that is its source. If we say that, in the end, the source of death is God, then what does that make God?** Consider what was said to Adam and Eve in the Garden of Eden: 'But of the tree of the knowledge of good and evil, thou shalt not eat of it: for in the day that thou eatest thereof thou shalt surely die.' (Genesis 2:17).

"**Was that a threat or a warning? It makes a difference.** If I tell you of danger from something or someone else, that is giving you a warning. However, if I tell you of possible danger coming from me - that is a threat. **God could never have won the love and loyalty of His created beings by threatening them with force. His 'weapons' are love and truth.** God was saying either: 'If you eat from that tree, there will be negative consequences and I don't want you to experience that' (a warning). Or 'If you eat from that tree, I will kill you.' (Sounds pretty harsh but that is exactly what it would amount to - a dire threat.) As we well know, much can be learned from the tone of voice in which words are said. Unfortunately, we don't get that in reading Genesis. But just think of it - God had just created Adam and Eve; He made everything perfect; designed everything for their happiness. Then He said to them basically 'do it My way, obey Me or I will kill you' (at least eventually). Does that seem to fit? Hardly!" (Ray Foucher, *The Lake of Fire and the Second Death,* pg. 36-39)

God is our Defender, Christ our Savior! The loving intention of the Godhead is to save us from sin and reinstate us to our pre-fallen condition. This *is* the good news!

> "...**If God be for us, who can be against us?** He that spared not his own Son, but delivered him up for us all, **how shall he not with him also freely give us all things?**" (Romans 8:31-32)

The Great Physician seeks to heal and restore. By demonstrating selfless love and kindness, our Father reconciles His estranged children back to Himself. Christ's advent should be understood as a means to deliver humanity from the fatal consequences of sin, rather than as a means to protect mankind from the wrath of an angry god. Inspiration is definitive on this point: that in all ways, God seeks to deliver His people from the bondage of sin and selfishness.

> "And she shall bring forth a son, and thou shalt call his name JESUS: for **he shall save his people from their sins.**" (Matthew 1:21)

> "This is a faithful saying, and worthy of all acceptation, that **Christ Jesus came into the world to save sinners;** of whom I am chief." (I Timothy 1:15)

To counteract this work, Satan has sought to divorce mercy from justice by asserting that, if God is to remain just, every sin must meet its punishment. Our adversary seeks to undermine the true definition of divine justice—and fallen man, by nature, believes his misconstruing of justice. God is then seen as an angry and wrathful god, void of mercy and forgiveness. This is just as Satan would have it. Therefore, he exerts all of his energy in manipulating the truth of this matter in the minds of men. An imperial net is cast abroad, and millions are caught in its deadly snare. The wrath of God, His anger, and His justice are all entirely misunderstood. In the next chapter, the author will seek to reconcile these attributes of God with the divine character as it is revealed in Christ.

"God's love has been expressed in His justice no less than in His mercy. Justice is the foundation of His throne, and the fruit of His love. **It had been Satan's purpose to divorce mercy from truth and justice.** He sought to prove that the righteousness of God's law is an enemy to peace. **But Christ shows that in God's plan they are indissolubly joined together; the one cannot exist without the other... By His life and His death, Christ proved that God's justice did not destroy His mercy, but that sin could be forgiven, and that the law is righteous, and can be perfectly obeyed.** Satan's charges were refuted. God had given man unmistakable evidence of His love." (Ellen G. White, *The Desire of Ages,* pg. 762)

Chapter 8

Love in the Shadow of Wrath: Exploring God's Divine Justice

*"**God has given to men a declaration of His character and of His method of dealing with sin.** 'The Lord God, merciful and gracious, long-suffering and abundant in goodness and truth, keeping mercy for thousands, forgiving iniquity and transgression and sin, and that will by no means clear the guilty.' Exodus 34:6, 7… **The power and authority of the divine government will be employed to put down rebellion; yet all the manifestations of retributive justice will be perfectly consistent with the character of God as a merciful, long-suffering, benevolent being.***

*"**God does not force the will or judgment of any.** He takes no pleasure in a slavish obedience. He desires that the creatures of His hands shall love Him because He is worthy of love. He would have them obey Him because they have an intelligent appreciation of His wisdom, justice, and benevolence. **And all who have a just conception of these qualities will love Him because they are drawn toward Him in admiration of His attributes.***

*"**The principles of kindness, mercy, and love, taught and exemplified by our Saviour, are a transcript of the will and character of God. Christ declared that He taught nothing except that which He had received from His Father. The principles of the divine government are in perfect harmony with the Saviour's precept, 'Love your enemies.'** God executes justice upon the wicked, for the good of the universe, and even for the good of those upon whom His judgments are visited. He would make them happy if He could do so in accordance with the laws of His government and the justice of His character. **He surrounds them with the tokens of His love, He grants them a knowledge of His law, and follows them with the offers of His mercy; but they despise His love, make void His law, and reject His mercy.** While*

constantly receiving His gifts, they dishonor the Giver... The Lord bears long with their perversity; but the decisive hour will come at last, when their destiny is to be decided. Will He then chain these rebels to His side? Will He force them to do His will?... What source of enjoyment could heaven offer to those who are wholly absorbed in earthly and selfish interests?... ***A life of rebellion against God has unfitted them for heaven. Its purity, holiness, and peace would be torture to them; the glory of God would be a consuming fire.*** *They would long to flee from that holy place. They would welcome destruction, that they might be hidden from the face of Him who died to redeem them.* ***The destiny of the wicked is fixed by their own choice. Their exclusion from heaven is voluntary with themselves, and just and merciful on the part of God.*** *" (Ellen G. White, The Great Controversy, pg. 541-542)*

The character of God serves as the cornerstone of all theological belief, completely shaping one's interpretation of the Bible. Yet, Christendom has struggled in their efforts to harmonize certain aspects of God's character with the embodiment of love demonstrated by Christ in His life and ministry. The Bible has been approached as a static manual, limiting the word of God to a strict literalism of interpretation rather than recognizing it as the revelation of divine love and the plan of salvation. Consequently, redemptive power is attributed solely to the book itself, rather than to the God it unveils. This results in a form of worship that meticulously adheres to the textual aspects of the Bible but lacks a genuine alignment with the God that is portrayed within its pages.

"Search the scriptures; **for in them ye think ye have eternal life: and they are they which testify of me.**" (John 5:39)

By neglecting the Bible's ability to interpret itself, we allow certain passages to distort our perception of God, failing to reconcile each piece of scripture with the overarching divine character that Christ came to exemplify.

> "The Bible is its own expositor. Scripture is to be compared with scripture. **The student should learn to view the word as a whole, and to see the relation of its parts.** He should gain a knowledge of its grand central theme, of God's original purpose for the world, of the rise of the great controversy, and of the work of redemption." (Ellen G. White, *Education,* pg. 190)

Historical and cultural context is disregarded; and individuals frequently interpret particular verses in a manner that grants them what *seems* like divine authorization to disregard the principal message intended by the inspired word. They passionately declare, driven by their earthly desires, "the Bible states it, therefore I am permitted to indulge!" or, "God *seems* to conduct Himself in this manner, therefore, it suggests that I am likewise permitted to do so!" This wayward form of religion can only result in a perversion of character. Such is in direct opposition to God's true plan for His children.

Evidence for this matter may be found in certain individuals' adherence to hellish beliefs such as polygamy, racism, sexism, the persecution of nonbelievers, slavery, and a host of other immoral actions. For all of human history, men have invented exceedingly clever ways of projecting onto God their own debased conduct.

The delinquent behavior of the believer is ardently defended by their own misinterpretation of the Godhead: "Should God reveal His anger, I might discern validation for my own indignation. If He releases His wrath upon His adversaries, it could embolden me to follow suit. In the event of swift divine judgment, it might stir within me a desire for retribution against those I hold in disdain. *And if God Himself takes life... it may inspire me to do likewise.*"

The ramifications, as the reader may plainly see, are profound. Without a proper grasp of the divine character as unveiled in Christ, humanity's quest to transcend its inherent sinful nature appears futile. In fact, a misconstrued perception of the true nature of God, as exemplified above, only serves to embolden sinful inclinations and self-centeredness.

This chapter is dedicated to the reconciliation of God's attributes with the character exemplified by Christ. His justice, His wisdom, His power, His mercy, and even His wrath and anger, are only different faces of the many-sided but all-embracing and eternal love. It follows that the motive of God's action must ever be love's own. The overarching objective of the author is to demonstrate that, at its core, God's character finds its expression in selfless love despite some of these seemingly negative characteristics. To accomplish this, we will embark upon a structured journey, beginning with an exploration of God's anger and wrath, and culminating with a precise delineation between divine justice and "justice-so-called." Through this systematic approach, we will come to perceive that these aspects of God's nature seamlessly correspond with the loving character manifested in the life and teachings of Christ.

Dissecting Misconceptions: God's Anger and Wrath in Perspective

*"**The entire Christian world has taught that God will put up with sinners only so long, and then His patience runs out;** He gets mad and angry with them, and then lets 'em have it. What a pity. **The truth is that God never loves the sinner less. Never.**" (Gary Hullquist, The Loving Wrath of God, pg. 2)*

*"The wrath of God. That is, the divine displeasure against sin, resulting ultimately in the abandonment of man to the judgement of death… God does not force His love upon those who are unwilling to receive His mercy… Thus, **God's wrath against sin is exercised in the withdrawal of His presence and life-giving power from those who choose to remain in sin and thus share in its inevitable consequences.**" (Seventh-Day Adventist Bible Commentary, vol. 6, pg. 477)*

In light of the insights presented in this volume concerning the loving and nonviolent character of God, how should we understand His anger and wrath? Is it possible for these attributes to coexist with love and righteousness? Could it be that we have misinterpreted these characteristics of the Almighty and inadvertently misrepresented His revealed nature? While many today reject this notion, they do so by thrusting an imperial framework upon God and contending that, in order to remain just, His anger and wrath must be swiftly demonstrated against the disobedient. Such a stance diminishes that which the author has gone so far to outline: that God's intentions toward the sinner are to heal and restore rather than to condemn and punish. We serve a God of love and mercy, not a retaliatory and outraged seeker of retribution. "But," says one, "what about all the instances in the Bible which speak of God's wrath being poured out against the sinner? Are these not evidence of His divine malpractice?" In order to adequately address these verses, we must position God's anger and wrath within the context of His revealed qualities of love and nonviolence, thereby achieving a harmonious perspective of His overall nature.

One instance which is frequently cited by those who perceive God as an aggressive and punitive figure, yet also serves as a compelling initial reference for the author to establish their argument, is located in the book of Psalms:

> "**He [God] cast upon them the fierceness of his anger,** wrath, and indignation, and trouble, **by sending evil angels among them.**" (Psalm 78:49)

This verse seemingly appears clear and straightforward to the undiscerning religionist. Nevertheless, if we accept this verse as it stands, we must acknowledge that God is the commander of evil angels; directing their actions—bidding them go forth, and they obey. This places God in league with Satan, who we recognize as the leader of fallen and malevolent angels. Such an interpretation should be wholly unacceptable to the genuine Christian. Furthermore, how can we reconcile this verse with the apparent contradiction in 1 Thessalonians?

> "**See that no one repays anyone evil for evil,** but always seek to do good to one another and to everyone." (I Thessalonians 5:15, *ESV*)

If God doesn't respond to evil with evil, even with regard to sinners, then how can He justify sending evil angels among those who have defied Him? They are presumably sent with the intent to cause harm—and how does this align with the concept of a loving God?

In order to harmonize this, we must define the terms. It is worthy to note that the word used for "anger" in Psalm 78:49 is the very same Hebrew word used for "longsuffering" in Exodus 34:6, when God is proclaiming His character to Moses.

> "And the LORD passed by before him, and proclaimed, The LORD, The LORD God, **merciful and gracious, longsuffering, and abundant in goodness and truth...**" (Exodus 34:6)

Is it to be rightly understood that God is merciful and gracious, "*long in anger*," and abundant in goodness and truth? This cannot be so!—for such a rendering does evident violence to the inspired text. The very same term is also translated as "nostrils" earlier in the book of Exodus:

> "And **with the blast of thy nostrils** the waters were gathered together, the floods stood upright as an heap, and the depths were congealed in the heart of the sea." (Exodus 15:8)

The Hebrew word, אַף ('ap̄), used in each of these instances, literally means, "a rapid breathing through the nostrils in passion" (Strong's H0639). In the appropriate context, when would an individual engage in rapid breathing through their nose? In anger, perhaps—but we must understand that a loving God does not experience anger the same way we do, *if at all.* Another instance of rapid breathing through the nose might occur when someone is very sad or deeply grieved. It is this understanding that allows us to place the attribute of God's anger in its proper context: intense grief. God's anger can be understood as His profound sorrow, knowing that He will have to withdraw Himself and allow the unconverted sinner to pursue their own selfish desires.

Simultaneously, this represents a particular aspect of His justice, for it would be *unjust* for Him to compel the individual to obey His will—something that selfless love, as stated in 1 Corinthians, does not do.

> "[Love] does not insist on its own way..." (I Corinthians 13:4, *ESV*)

This correlation between anger and grief is further illustrated in the following event contained in Israel's history. Notice the very same Hebrew word, אַף ('ap̄), is used here to denote the anger of God:

> "I [God] gave thee a king **in mine anger...**" (Hosea 13:11)

The text seems to suggest that God, in His anger, appointed a king to rule over Israel. But is such the truth of the matter? As we have previously laid out in this volume, adverse outcomes that are merely *permitted* to occur by God are often attributed to His direct intervention and causation. By adopting a wider context of the verse in question, we learn that it was actually Israel who, upon rejecting the solemn reproofs of the Almighty, chose to ordain a king for themselves.

> "Now therefore behold **the king whom ye have chosen, and whom ye have desired!** and, behold, the LORD hath set a king over you." (I Samuel 12:13)

This was what the people had desired! God, in His Providence, foresaw that it would ultimately lead to their downfall. For so long He had served as their King and sole Protector. However, being influenced by their envy of neighboring nations and their lust for conformity to worldliness, the people now set their eyes upon the establishment of an earthly ruler.

> "Nevertheless the people refused to obey the voice of Samuel; **and they said, Nay; but we will have a king over us; That we also may be like all the nations;** and that our king may judge us, and go out before us, and fight our battles." (I Samuel 8:19-20)

Although God was fully aware of the destructive path they were choosing, He had to allow Israel to exercise their free will. It pained Him deeply to remove His protective hand from His children and allow them to appoint a ruler in His stead, fully cognizant of the ensuing dangers. Nevertheless, it can be seen that God often grants in displeasure that which humanity sinfully desires. When He suffered Israel to establish an earthly ruler, it was not driven by anger or tantrum, for God woefully lamented this decision and had instead aspired to be their standalone King.

> "**O Israel, thou hast destroyed thyself; but in me is thine help. I will be thy king:** where is any other that may save thee in all thy cities? and thy judges of whom thou saidst, Give me a king and princes?" (Hosea 13:9-10)

Upon applying due discernment, we may see that in the course of His intense grief, God merely *allowed* Israel to pursue their self-serving ambitions, ultimately culminating in their own ruin. He did not powerfully intervene to establish a monarch for the children of Israel, nor did He punish them for doing so. Instead, because of their firm rejection of His council, all He did was withdraw His presence and allow His people to set up a king for themselves.

> "But the thing displeased Samuel, when they said, **Give us a king to judge us.** And Samuel prayed unto the LORD. **And the LORD said unto Samuel, Hearken unto the voice of the people in all that they say unto thee: for they have not rejected thee, but they have rejected me, that I should not reign over them.**" (I Samuel 8:6-7)

> "And when ye saw that Nahash the king of the children of Ammon came against you, **ye said unto me, Nay; but a king shall reign over us: when the LORD your God was your king...** And all the people said unto Samuel, Pray for thy servants unto the LORD thy God, that we die not: for we have added unto all our sins this evil, to ask us a king." (I Samuel 12:12,19)

Returning back to the context of Psalm 78:49, where it appears that God directed evil angels be sent among the population, we may rightly judge that He experienced a deep sense of bereavement due to the wayward actions of His children. Through their persistent transgression and rejection of His grace, they placed themselves beyond His hedge of protection. Consequently, God had no option but to withdraw His presence, allowing them to face the consequences of their own choices. Following God's withdrawal of His safeguarding proximity, malevolent angels were unleashed among the people. His restraining power, which for so long had contended against these infernal forces, was at last relinquished and their sinister inclination towards pain and suffering was allowed to envelop the populace. This course became unavoidable because God's children had willfully pushed away their Father's protective hand, making it impossible for Him to both safeguard them and, at the same time, honor their free will. This grieved Him tremendously! Our God may fittingly be labeled as One who is *long-suffering*.

> "**The Spirit of God, persistently resisted, is at last withdrawn from the sinner,** and then there is left no power to control the evil passions of the soul, **and no protection from the malice and enmity of Satan...**" (Ellen G. White, *The Great Controversy*, pg. 36)

Have we gone too far in our estimation of this matter? It would do the reader well to remember that, in many instances of scripture where Hebrew idiom is employed, God is said to directly cause that which He merely *allows* to happen. In the case of Psalm 78:49, when it says that He acted in sending "evil angels among them," it may be more properly understood that He *allowed* evil angels to roam free among the camp.

Due to the aforementioned, many will accuse the author of reading too much into the text—of not taking the Bible as it reads. To this, we contend that the primary aim of God's word is to guide individuals toward a proper understanding of His character and His redemptive plan for humanity. Allowing verses like those we've examined to remain colored by the biases of popular theology would be to do the very opposite; it would be to muddle the entirety of God's character as it is revealed in Christ. It would be to turn His love into malice; His patience into irritability; His grief into anger and fury. A gross failure to reconcile the character of the Father with that of the Son can only result in absurd theological doctrines that serve the devil more than they do Jehovah. The Father's disposition must be conformed to the character revealed by Christ, otherwise we call Christ a liar and a fraud.

Let's continue our investigation into the matter of God's anger and wrath. Might we discover similar instances of scripture that corroborate the author's interpretation?

Notice what happens when Jesus enters the synagogue on the Sabbath to worship:

> "And he [Jesus] entered again into the synagogue; and there was a man there which had a withered hand. **And they [the Pharisees] watched him, whether he would heal him on the sabbath day; that they might accuse him.** And he saith unto the man which had the withered hand, Stand forth. **And he saith unto them, Is it lawful to do good on the sabbath days, or to do evil? to save life, or to kill?** But they held their peace. And when he had looked round about on them **with anger, being grieved for the hardness of their hearts,** he saith unto the man, Stretch forth thine hand. And he stretched it out: and his hand was restored whole as the other." (Mark 3:1-5)

In this particular passage of scripture, several observations warrant our consideration. In verse 4, a significant contrast emerges as Christ associates doing good with the preservation of life and doing evil with the cessation of life. This statement contributes to a growing body of scriptural evidence supporting the nonviolent disposition of God. The underlying premise here is that the deliberate taking of life is inherently aligned with evil, a stance incongruous with the intrinsic goodness attributed to God. God does not kill. Consequently, this interpretation serves as a counterpoint to the prevailing theological school of thought that construes the Father's wrath and anger as agents of annihilation, for in this instance, Jesus offers a different perspective into how the anger of God is manifested. In verse 5, Jesus looked upon the Pharisees "with anger, being grieved for the hardness of their hearts" (Mark 3:5). This text reinforces the author's point that divine anger is correlated with grief. Jesus, in His anger, did not seek to condemn or destroy the Pharisees. Rather, He was grieved because they had hardened their hearts against the restorative and healing truths He was attempting to present to their carnal minds. The condition of the Pharisees saddened the countenance of our Savior. It did not incite within Him a spiteful desire for violent and punitive justice.

God is grieved by all those that stubbornly reject the truth of His love and mercy because He knows that, in doing so, they will ultimately reap the natural result of being disconnected from the Source of life: namely, death. Sorely He mourns for His children, that they might choose to trust Him and be delivered from their sinful and wretched condition. We may see this idea typified in the life of King David, upon the death of his son Absalom:

> "**And the king was much moved, and went up to the chamber over the gate, and wept:** and as he went, thus he said, **O my son Absalom, my son, my son Absalom!** would God I had died for thee, O Absalom, my son, my son!" (2 Samuel 18:33)

> "And it was told Joab, **Behold, the king weepeth and mourneth for Absalom.**" (2 Samuel 19:1)

In the same way that King David mourns for his son, so too does God mourn for those who are embracing sin and death. In Hosea, we find God speaking in like manner unto the children of Israel who were steeped in paganism and idolatry, far removed from His divine will:

> "**How can I give you up, O Ephraim? How can I hand you over, O Israel?** How can I make you like Admah? How can I treat you like Zeboiim? **My heart recoils within me;** my compassion grows warm and tender." (Hosea 11:8, *ESV*)

Here, God expresses His reluctance to abandon His people, as doing so would mean to remove His Spirit entirely, leaving them vulnerable to the perils of their sinful nature. This hesitation reflects His intention to withdraw His protective presence only in the case where their persistent transgression leaves Him no other choice. He genuinely desires to shower His children with signs of His love and truth, but their hearts remain closed to their Father's appeals. They persist in their willful disobedience until, finally, God must let them alone. He must permit them the freedom to act according to their own will, even if it means they exist outside of His protective care.

"Ephraim is joined to idols: **let him alone.**" (Hosea 4:17)

In certain instances throughout scripture, this withdrawal of the divine presence is illustrated by God either hiding His face or turning away. To grasp the nature of this action, envision it not as an expression of anger or disgust, where one averts their gaze, but rather as an act of profound sorrow and dismay. It's akin to someone covering their face with their hands in utter grief, or turning away to shield themselves from witnessing a heart-wrenching outcome.

"But **the king covered his face**, and the king cried with a loud voice, O my son Absalom, O Absalom, my son, my son!" (2 Samuel 19:4)

"But **your iniquities have separated between you and your God, and your sins have hid his face from you,** that he will not hear." (Isaiah 59:2)

"For a small moment have I forsaken thee; but with great mercies will I gather thee. **In a little wrath I hid my face from thee for a moment**; but with everlasting kindness will I have mercy on thee, saith the LORD thy Redeemer." (Isaiah 54:7-8)

"And they caused their sons and their daughters to pass through the fire, and used divination and enchantments, and sold themselves to do evil in the sight of the LORD, **to provoke him to anger. Therefore the LORD was very angry with Israel, and removed them out of his sight...**" (2 Kings 17:17-18)

"And the LORD said unto Moses, Behold, thou shalt sleep with thy fathers; and this people will rise up, and go a whoring after the gods of the strangers of the land, whither they go to be among them, and will forsake me, and break my covenant which I have made with them. **Then my anger shall be kindled against them in that day**, and I will forsake them, **and I will hide my face from them**, and they shall be devoured, and many evils and troubles shall befall them; so that they will say in that day, **Are not these evils come upon us, because our God is not among us? And I will surely hide my face in that day** for all the evils which they shall have wrought, in that they are turned unto other gods." (Deuteronomy 31:16-18)

As our comprehension deepens, we discern that God does not approach the sinner with deadly intent. Death and destruction are not inflicted by any external divine agency, but rather, they steadfastly pursue their inexorable course as natural results of sin.

Considering the inherent dangers associated with sin, what basis is there for God's involvement in the adverse fate of the wrongdoer? Rather than defining God's anger as the channel by which punitive measures unfold—a meaning made entirely redundant by the innate consequences of sin—a more accurate interpretation may be found in the context which the author has outlined in this chapter. Divine anger, properly understood, is God's reluctant and painful obligation to give His children over to the dominion and unbridled power of Satan. This causes Him insurmountable grief and sorrow.

"Wherefore **God also gave them up** to uncleanness through **the lusts of their own hearts**, to dishonour their own bodies between themselves: Who changed the truth of God into a lie, and worshipped and served the creature more than the Creator... For this cause **God gave them up** unto vile affections..." (Romans 1:24-26)

"And even as they did not like to retain God in their knowledge, **God gave them over** to a reprobate mind, to do those things which are not convenient..." (Romans 1:28)

"And he **[God] shall give Israel up** because of the sins of Jeroboam, who did sin, and who made Israel to sin." (I Kings 14:16)

"And the heathen shall know that the house of Israel went into captivity for their iniquity: because they trespassed against me, **therefore hid I my face from them, and gave them into the hand**

> **of their enemies:** so fell they all by the sword. According to their uncleanness and according to their transgressions have I done unto them, **and hid my face from them.**" (Ezekiel 39:23-24)

The rationale behind God's engagement in such actions, despite the resultant anguish it causes Him, primarily stems from His repudiation of coercive measures. God will never impose Himself upon another. Instead, His only recourse is to appeal to the hearts and minds of man through the gentle work of the Holy Spirit. This course of action necessitates affording us, as conscious beings, the liberty to exercise our own free will. We must have the innate ability to accept or reject His entreaties. Such autonomy is a divine gift from our Creator, and it is one that He is resolute in safeguarding, refraining from any inclination to revoke it. In our folly, we frequently deviate from the path that God intends for us. By stubbornly resisting His efforts to restore us, He is eventually compelled to withdraw and allow us to pursue our own course.

> "...The LORD is with you, while ye be with him; and if ye seek him, he will be found of you; **but if ye forsake him, he will [must] forsake you.**" (2 Chronicles 15:2)

> **"What is the fate of those who reject the Lord? It is clear enough that it is separation from Him, for that is what they have chosen.** They were naturally separated from the Lord by their sins. God, however, would not let them go without an effort to induce them to accept His ways. But **their refusal of His kind offers showed their determination to be for ever separated from Him, and He is at last compelled to give them up to their own choice.**" (E. J. Waggoner, *The Present Truth,* vol. 9, February 23, 1893, pg. 54)

This, however, serves a unique purpose. By affording us the liberty to chart our own course, His ultimate aim is to illuminate our profound dependence on His divine aid. By tasting of the bitter consequences of sin and selfishness, He aspires for us to recognize our need for His mercy and regenerative power, which He stands ready to generously impart.

> "I will go and return to my place, till they acknowledge their offence, and seek my face: **in their affliction they will seek me early.**" (Hosea 5:15)

> "Don't you see how wonderfully kind, tolerant, and patient God is with you? Does this mean nothing to you? **Can't you see that his kindness is intended to turn you from your sin?**" (Romans 2:4, *NLT*)

After numerous unsuccessful attempts to reach our hardened hearts, and only when there is no inclination left in us to heed His gentle reproofs, our Father must permit us to reap the consequences of our own actions. Saddened by the obstinacy of our constant rejection, He withdraws His presence. This is what it means to grieve the Holy Spirit.

> "And **grieve not the holy Spirit of God,** whereby ye are sealed unto the day of redemption." (Ephesians 4:30)

By casting off God's protective agency, we place ourselves at Satan's disposal. The sin-stricken nature which corrupts our soul, when cherished and indulged, becomes our inevitable downfall.

> "**Those who live only to satisfy their own sinful nature will harvest decay and death from that sinful nature.** But those who live to please the Spirit will harvest everlasting life from the Spirit." (Galatians 6:8, NLT)

> "**When the Lord sees unbelief in the heart against light and evidence, all he has to do is to let the human agent alone;** for the seed put into the soil will bring forth seed after its kind. Many have been sowing the seed of unbelief, and if this seed is cultivated, it will produce a harvest that will not be so pleasant to reap as the seed is to sow… **God destroys no man; but after a time the wicked are given up to the destruction they have wrought for themselves.**" (Ellen G. White, Youth's Instructor, November 30, 1893)

This highlights the unavoidable end result of un-remedied sin: death and decay. By satisfying our carnal nature, we inevitably place ourselves at its mercy. Unable to break the chains which bind us to its yoke, and unwilling to turn to the One who can offer relief, we turn to despair. The sinner, through their willful transgression, is laying the snare for their own destruction. By choosing to instill separation between themselves and the only Being who can offer them refuge, the results of sin are fondly embraced as if they were welcomed companions.

> "O Israel, **thou hast destroyed thyself;** but in me is thine help." (Hosea 13:9)

> "O Israel, return unto the LORD thy God; **for thou hast fallen by thine iniquity.**" (Hosea 14:1)

> "The Jews had forged their own fetters; they had filled for themselves the cup of vengeance. In the utter destruction that befell them as a nation, and in all the woes that followed them in their dispersion, **they were but reaping the harvest which their own hands had sown.** Says the prophet: 'O Israel, thou hast destroyed thyself;' 'for thou hast fallen by thine iniquity.' Hosea 13:9; 14:1. **Their sufferings are often represented as a punishment visited upon them by the direct decree of God. It is thus that the great deceiver seeks to conceal his own work.** By stubborn rejection of divine love and mercy, **the Jews had caused the protection of God to be withdrawn from them, and Satan was permitted to rule them according to his will.** The horrible cruelties enacted in the destruction of Jerusalem are a demonstration of Satan's vindictive power over those who yield to his control..." (Ellen G. White, *The Great Controversy*, pg. 35)

The absence of the safeguarding presence of the Almighty means certain destruction. For any poor soul that places themselves outside of His loving arms, death is their inevitable portion. The results of sin constrict their victim, shrouding them in darkness; the sinner is consumed by their own rebellion. God's hand is not in the destruction of the wicked, as many foolishly believe. Rather, God is our Protector!—Our Stronghold against the powers and principalities of evil!

> "**The LORD is good, a strong hold in the day of trouble;** and he knoweth them that trust in him." (Nahum 1:7)

> "**God is our refuge and strength,** a very present help in trouble." (Psalm 46:1)

> "The LORD of hosts is with us; **the God of Jacob is our fortress.** Selah" (Psalm 46:7, *ESV*)

If it were not for His protective agency, even at the current moment, we would all be destroyed by the sheer force of sin's unyielding effects. We see this principle demonstrated in the book of Numbers, when Miriam is stricken with leprosy.

> "And Miriam and Aaron spake against Moses because of the Ethiopian woman whom he had married: for he had married an Ethiopian woman... **And the anger of the LORD was kindled against them; and he departed.** And the cloud departed from off the tabernacle; **and, behold, Miriam became leprous,** white as snow: and Aaron looked upon Miriam, and, behold, she was leprous." (Numbers 12:1,9-10)

Notice how it was only *after* God's presence had departed from Miriam that she became leprous. We may readily discern in this instance that God, in His anger, did not cause harm to Miriam by marking her with disease. Rather, it was through the withdrawal of His presence—the only barrier between Miriam and her sudden calamity—that she was stricken with leprosy. God, in His grace, shields His children from all that might do them harm. It is only by a constant rejection of His mercy that we force Him to depart from us. In His grief, God's Spirit retreats and it is this abrupt movement away from the sinner that permits destruction to exact its toll.

> "When Miriam and Aaron spoke against Moses, 'the anger of the Lord was kindled against them; and He departed. And the cloud departed from off the tabernacle; and, behold, Miriam became leprous.' **God's ways are truly different from ours. When our anger is kindled against someone we move toward them, to attack, to strike out! But God moves away. He departs...** And at the cross

God personally showed how He will ultimately deal with sin... On the cross Jesus took the sinner's place and God treated Him exactly as He will treat every sinner who ever lived. There our Saviour died the final death of complete separation from God: the equivalent of the second death. Jesus assumed the very position of the sinner who wants nothing of God and demands that He leave him alone. **Sadly God leaves, and as He does, His sustaining, life-giving, protective power is withdrawn. Now nothing can save from the awful power of sin as it crushes the life forces into extinction.** No wonder Jesus cried out, 'My God, My God, why have You forsaken me?' Why have you given me up? Why have you let me go? But it wasn't at the hand of an offended God that Christ died. The Father didn't slay His Son. Jesus did not say, 'My God, why are you executing me?' We may have gotten that impression... But the Bible often speaks of God as doing that which He permits. Because God is sovereign over the events of the entire universe, He also assumes full responsibility for what takes place within it. 'We esteemed Him [Jesus] smitten, stricken of God and afflicted.' [Isaiah 53:4]. We thought that God was smiting Him. But, in fact, 'He was wounded for [or, by] our transgressions, He was bruised for [or, by] our iniquities.' [Isaiah 53:5]." (Gary Hullquist, *The Loving Wrath of God*, pg. 9-11)

Ever since the fall of man and the onset of sin, God has been intervening to hold back its conclusive results. Death has been relentless in its pursuit, determined to overcome humanity. It is only by God's grace, His protective power against the ultimate consequences of sin, that we have been able to continue living despite our current condition. Even now, angelic agencies are directed to hold back the winds of strife from being unleashed upon the earth, as Revelation aptly tells us.

"**And after these things I saw four angels standing on the four corners of the earth, holding the four winds of the earth, that the wind should not blow on the earth, nor on the sea, nor on any tree.** And I saw another angel ascending from the east, having the seal of the living God: and he cried with a loud voice to the four angels, to whom it was given to hurt the earth and the sea, Saying,

> **Hurt not the earth, neither the sea, nor the trees, till we have sealed the servants of our God in their foreheads.**" (Revelation 7:1-3)

How do we understand this text? Do we perceive these winds as a form of God's punitive judgement soon to be loosed? Is He merely commanding His angels to wait until the proper time to bring harm to His children? Instead, by positioning this passage within the context we've been exploring throughout this chapter, all becomes clear and harmonious. In this particular instance, one may discern the tangible demonstration of God's sheltering influence. He bids His angels to stand guard against death's approach, to restrict its destructible course. At the same time, this text alludes to a period when the wicked will have passed the boundary of their probation. When this occurs, God's Spirit will be fully withdrawn and no longer will His angels be directed to constrain the elements of strife. The sinner will be destroyed, not by a divine decree, but rather by the natural outcome of their own stubborn rebellion.

> **"Why is it that all this wickedness does not break forth in decided violence against righteousness and truth? It is because the four angels are holding the four winds,** that they shall not blow upon the earth. But human passions are reaching a high pass, and **the Spirit of the Lord is being withdrawn from the earth. Were it not that God has commanded angelic agencies to control the satanic agencies that are seeking to break loose and to destroy, there would be no hope.** But the winds are to be held until the servants of God are sealed in their foreheads..." (Ellen G. White, *In Heavenly Places*, pg. 96)

> **"The restraint which has been upon the wicked is removed, and Satan has entire control of the finally impenitent. God's long-suffering has ended. The world has rejected his mercy, despised his love, and trampled upon his law. The wicked have passed the boundary of their probation; the Spirit of God, persistently resisted, has been at last withdrawn. Unsheltered by divine grace, they have no protection from the wicked one.** Satan will then plunge the inhabitants of the earth into one great, final trouble. As the angels of God cease to hold in check the fierce winds of

> human passion, all the elements of strife will be let loose. The whole world will be involved in ruin more terrible than that which came upon Jerusalem of old." (Ellen G. White, *The Great Controversy 1888*, pg. 614)

> "Satan works through the elements also to garner his harvest of unprepared souls. He has studied the secrets of the laboratories of nature, and **he uses all his power to control the elements as far as God allows.** When he was suffered to afflict Job, how quickly flocks and herds, servants, houses, children, were swept away, one trouble succeeding another as in a moment. **It is God that shields His creatures and hedges them in from the power of the destroyer. But the Christian world have shown contempt for the law of Jehovah; and the Lord will do just what He has declared that He would—He will withdraw His blessings from the earth and remove His protecting care from those who are rebelling against His law and teaching and forcing others to do the same. Satan has control of all whom God does not especially guard.** He will favor and prosper some in order to further his own designs, and he will bring trouble upon others **and lead men to believe that it is God who is afflicting them...**" (Ellen G. White, *The Great Controversy*, pg. 589)

As irrefutably evidenced, the manifestation of divine anger distinguishes itself markedly from human expressions of wrath. When approached with theological precision, God's anger assumes a character more closely aligned with profound lament and sorrow. This disposition arises from God's ethical obligation to permit sinners the autonomy to willingly distance themselves from His benevolent love and nurturing care, should they elect to do so. In accordance with this principle, they must be allowed the freedom to pursue their own desires, as divine coercion is incompatible with the endeavor to elicit the affection of the sinner.

God's anger finds expression not through overt acts of punishment but rather through the gradual withdrawal of His protective presence and omnipotence. This withdrawal inevitably paves the way for impending destruction, as God is the only safeguard against such peril. Regrettably, mankind often misconstrues these adverse consequences, perceiving them as punitive judgments stemming directly from the hand of God in response to their transgression. It is in this misperception that Satan finds cause for rejoicing, recognizing the effectiveness of his subterfuge in obscuring the true nature of the Father. God's sentiment towards us is not one of anger but rather immense grief, brought about by the severity of our fallen condition. He does not seek to condemn and destroy, but to heal and restore.

However, many Christians contend that in order for God to remain just, He must promptly enact punitive judgments. Regrettably, some erroneously conflate the concept of human justice with that of the divine. The prevailing perception of justice that many attribute to the Father is the kind that would have been met by the summary death of our sinful race. More aptly labeled as "justice-so-called," this imperialist distortion does not even begin to approach the form of elevated and enlightened justice that belongs to heaven.

The concept of God's justice encompasses a fundamentally distinct definition as compared to the form of justice observed in fallen humanity. In the latter portion of this chapter, the author will introduce a novel perspective on divine justice, likely unfamiliar to many readers. By harmonizing God's justice with the insights we've gained about the true context of His anger and, in essence, His entire character as it is unveiled in Christ, we attain a deeper comprehension of the divine nature. In doing so, we aim to disentangle divine justice from punitive action and reinstate it to its rightful role as an attribute of the righteousness of God; as a quality to be eagerly anticipated rather than fearfully apprehended.

Jurisprudence Beyond Mortals: Unbinding God's Justice from Punitive Paradigms

*"**I was shown that the judgments of God would not come directly out from the Lord upon them [sinners], but in this way: They place themselves beyond His protection.** He warns, corrects, reproves, and points out the only path of safety; **then if those who have been the objects of His special care will follow their own course independent of the Spirit of God,** after repeated warnings, if they choose their own way, **then He does not commission His angels to prevent Satan's decided attacks upon them...**" (Ellen G. White, Manuscript Releases, vol. 14, pg. 3)*

Continuing our discussion regarding the attributes of God, we now shift our focus to His justice. In doing so, we aim to challenge conventional notions of justice and explore the transcendental realm of divine justice. This half of our chapter delves into the profound question of how human societies have historically interpreted and applied the concept of God's justice, inviting the reader to contemplate the boundless possibilities of reimagining this age-old paradigm. Many contend that God's justice is synonymous with the deluge of severe judgements that follow transgression, administered by the mighty hand of a powerful potentate. However, a more nuanced understanding of His justice reveals a different perspective.

Upon a consideration of this subject, we must ask ourselves: may God's justice be likened to our own? Does the justice of a vengeful and worldly nation accurately reflect the justice of God? Is it right to conceive that God runs His universe in the same way sinful beings run earthly governments? And by asserting that God is "just," do we in any way diminish the attributes of His love and mercy? These are the questions which must be reconciled if we are to come to a proper revelation of

God's character and government. Failing to correct mistaken assumptions about how God's justice operates incites the risk of misrepresenting Him. By constraining the concept of divine justice to a purely punitive framework, we ultimately fail to situate it correctly within its true context.

Numerous individuals assert that the essence of the gospel is rooted in the idea that Jesus' death was for the purpose of satisfying the requirements of God's punitive justice. This interpretation of the atonement is known as *penal substitution.* The author's proposition fundamentally challenges the prevailing interpretation, asserting that it deviates substantially from the teachings of the Bible. This divergence, the author contends, arises from individuals imposing their secular comprehension of justice onto the biblical narrative. The New Testament, in contrast, is actually an exhaustive critique of punitive justice. It presents it as a problem to be solved, not as a means to the solution. The problem of wrath—that is, punitive justice—is effectively overcome through the cross. The cross is, in essence, an act of restoration, bringing humanity back into a harmonious relationship with God. To put it differently, God operates through a restorative form of justice, rather than a retributive and vindictive form that is enforced via a penal legal framework.

As we have already established in previous chapters of this work, the fundamental disposition of God revolves prominently around the principles of love and nonviolence. Notably, even within moments of divine indignation, God's intention does not incline towards retribution. In light of this, if we concede that God's anger is more accurately construed as a manifestation of divine grief, a profound shift in our understanding of His justice system becomes imperative. In such a framework, God's justice, rather than being aligned with punitive measures born from anger, ought to be more aptly aligned with the concept of restoration. God's justice involves setting things right—not punishing wrongs! This context of divine justice is underscored by God's intrinsic characteristics of love and nonviolence. It effectively harmonizes mercy with justice. For God to maintain His justice, it suffices for Him to extend mercy to the sinner.

> "If we confess our sins, **he is faithful and just to forgive us our sins, and to cleanse us from all unrighteousness.**" (I John I:9)

The demand for punitive action against transgressors is rendered unnecessary, as the natural consequences of their sins will manifest on their own. Thus, God's justice, instead of being grounded in punishment, is rightly exemplified by His efforts to heal and restore the sinner to harmony with Himself.

What a glaring disparity when compared to human concepts of justice! The kind of justice sinful beings prefer, and the kind which they project onto God, would have been met by the summary death of fallen humanity; all people had sinned, and, if justice were to take its regular course, all must perish. But God's love for us "while we were yet sinners," (Romans 5:8) could not suffer that. Instead, He strived to rectify all that had been distorted by the condition of sin, working to redeem that which had become corrupted, and endeavoring to rescue those who had wandered astray. This is true justice at work.

And it is here that we will urge that such an interpretation does not in any way diminish God's justness. The author has no intention of undermining this attribute of the Almighty. Rather, it is merely by a more elevated definition of the term that He is, indeed, just. The concept of divine justice and the justice exhibited by wickedly sinful beings must in fact be two markedly distinct modes of expression. Unfortunately, there has been a universal readiness to conclude that heaven's justice system operates in the same manner as mankind's. Such an idea is erroneous and only serves to cast ambiguity upon what God's justice truly is.

> "**For my thoughts are not your thoughts, neither are your ways my ways, saith the LORD.** For as the heavens are higher than the earth, so are my ways higher than your ways, and my thoughts than your thoughts." (Isaiah 55:8-9)

> "...thou thoughtest that I was altogether **such an one as thyself...**" (Psalm 50:21)

Many have endeavored to establish a philosophical schism between the divine attributes of love and justice. As per the commonly held interpretation of divine justice, it is often inferred that the scope of God's love and mercy is circumscribed. Beyond a certain delineation, it is suggested that He is compelled to suspend His benevolence and compassion towards the sinner, instead manifesting anger and meting out punitive measures for their transgressions. As a consequence of this view, His disposition of love is diminished, His nonviolent nature becomes compromised, and mercy appears to be in direct conflict with justice. The consequences of sin are then attributed to the hand of God, His expression of justice becomes overshadowed by an imperial framework, and God becomes a malevolent dictator rather than the benevolent Creator. This is just as Satan would have it.

> "In discussions of God's character, it is often said that 'God is love but He is also just.' That saying is found nowhere in the Bible. It does say that God is love and it does say that God is just (Deut 32:4, Isa 45:21). **However, combining them with the 'but' puts the two in opposition. It suggests the idea that God is love but if you cross Him, watch out - He will change His attitude towards you and show His just side.** As I said, the Bible does say God is just, **but every use of just or justice reflects a loving action.** It will say to show justice to the poor, to widows or the old. **Never does it reflect the idea of retribution as many suggest...** God's justice in the Traditional Legal Model and the thinking of most Christians is all about payment for sin. Someone has to pay the penalty. You do the crime, you do the time. **Such a view diminishes God's mercy and forgiveness; it makes Him subject to justice itself which must be satisfied. According to the Biblical Healing Model, God's justice is doing the right thing according to the law of love which is to restore to a right state, to heal and to save. Justice, if it is truly done in love, is first seeking the good of others, it is not about keeping track of wrongs in order to even**

the score. Justice is restorative but, if it is not able to restore, it simply releases the offender to the inevitable results of sin which is death." (Ray Foucher, *Justice*, characterofgod.org, February 7, 2018)

Until the cross, Satan was successful in pitting justice and mercy at odds with one another. His idea of justice was that every sin must be punished—an idea which is abhorrent to God. This counterfeit justice system is so wide in its reach and intricate in its cunning, and is so deeply instilled in our minds today, continually being reinforced in our systems of law, within our families and schools, and in all of the media that we consume. This deception paints the sacrifice at Calvary in an altogether different light than intended—one where the Father brutally murders His own Son in order to satisfy divine justice.

"In the opening of the great controversy, **Satan had declared that the law of God could not be obeyed, that justice was inconsistent with mercy,** and that, should the law be broken, it would be impossible for the sinner to be pardoned. **Every sin must meet its punishment, urged Satan; and if God should remit the punishment of sin, He would not be a God of truth and justice.** When men broke the law of God, and defied His will, Satan exulted. It was proved, he declared, that the law could not be obeyed; man could not be forgiven. Because he, after his rebellion, had been banished from heaven, Satan claimed that the human race must be forever shut out from God's favor. **God could not be just, he urged, and yet show mercy to the sinner…**" (Ellen G. White, *The Desire of Ages*, pg. 761)

"**The condemning power of Satan would lead him to institute a theory of justice inconsistent with mercy.** He claims to be officiating as the voice and power of God, claims that his decisions are justice, are pure and without fault. Thus he takes his position on the judgment seat and declares that his counsels are infallible. **Here his merciless justice comes in, a counterfeit of justice, abhorrent to God…**" (Ellen G. White, *Christ Triumphant*, pg. 11)

Christ's mission to the world served as a stark revelation of humanity's predicament, one ensnared beneath the looming menace of a form of justice invented and propagated by Satan, characterized by wrath and the prospect of eternal ruin. In a state of helplessness and ignorance, mankind found itself under the shadow of this punitive justice system; under a god that found no joy in their deliverance. It was within this context that Jesus emerged as our Deliverer, providing the utmost assurance of salvation and liberation from this perilous condition.

> "**And this is life eternal, that they might know thee** the only true God, and Jesus Christ, whom thou hast sent." (John 17:3)

For the purpose of revealing to humanity what the Father's true intentions were, and thereby illuminating how His justice system truly operated, Christ was sent. He demonstrated that God's character diverged significantly from the claims urged by Satan—including the ultimate manifestation of His concept of justice.

> "Christ came to give to the world an example of what perfect humanity might be when united with divinity. He presented to the world a new phase of greatness in his exhibition of mercy, compassion, and love. **He gave to men a new interpretation of God. As head of humanity, he taught men lessons in the science of divine government, whereby he revealed the righteousness of the reconciliation of mercy and justice. The reconciliation of mercy and justice did not involve any compromise with sin, or ignore any claim of justice;** but by giving to each divine attribute its ordained place, mercy could be exercised in the punishment of sinful, impenitent man without destroying its clemency or forfeiting its compassionate character, and **justice could be exercised in forgiving the repenting transgressor without violating its integrity...**" (Ellen G. White, *Review and Herald*, December 22, 1891)

It is Satan who pronounces condemnation upon us, not God. Satan's ultimate aim is to witness our eternal estrangement from the Father. His theory of punitive justice finds its very foundation in this desire. He accuses us of the very sins he has tempted us to commit, asserting that these actions render us unforgivable in the eyes of a just and holy God. Yet, this is a falsehood that, regrettably, many continue to accept even today.

> "And the great dragon was cast out, that old serpent, called the Devil, and Satan, which deceiveth the whole world: he was cast out into the earth, and his angels were cast out with him. And I heard a loud voice saying in heaven, Now is come salvation, and strength, and the kingdom of our God, and the power of his Christ: **for the accuser of our brethren is cast down, which accused them before our God day and night.**" (Revelation 12:9-10)

God's expression of justice, demonstrated by the mercy and selfless love of Christ, is aimed at the restoration of humanity to their ordained position as children of the Most High. His purpose is to restore His universe to its rightful, or *just*, state by realigning humanity with the divine principles for life, consequently purging the stain of sin from His creation forever.

> "There is therefore now **no condemnation to them which are in Christ Jesus,** who walk not after the flesh, but after the Spirit." (Romans 8:1)

> "God grants men a probation in this world, that their principles may become firmly established in the right, thus precluding the possibility of sin in the future life, and so assuring the happiness and security of all. **Through the atonement of the Son of God alone could power be given to man to establish him in righteousness, and make him a fit subject for heaven. The blood [life] of Christ is the eternal antidote for sin.**" (Ellen G. White, *Signs of the Times,* December 30, 1889)

Through the commissioning of His Son to be sent to this earth, the Father aimed to fulfill His mission of establishing justice—of restoring matters to a rightful state; of healing sin and conferring righteousness. Furthermore, He sought to share the true nature of His justice with humanity by pouring out His Spirit, enabling people to comprehend and embrace it.

While our central emphasis remains rooted in the exploration of the theme of divine justice, it becomes imperative at this time to briefly recognize and engage with the intricately intertwined concept of judgment. This recognition is necessitated due to the repeated interplay of judgment with our understanding of divine justice.

Across the biblical text, justice and judgment are closely connected; portrayed as interdependent principles that underpin the divine order of God's kingdom. But rather than being channels through which divine wrath is expressed, as many suppose, they actually signify the benevolent attributes of mercy and truth.

> "**Justice and judgment** are the habitation of thy throne: **mercy and truth** shall go before thy face." (Psalm 89:14)

This verse employs a classic Hebraic parallelism—a literary technique wherein two phrases are juxtaposed to amplify and expound upon one another's meaning. In this particular context, the term "justice" finds its interpretation in "mercy," while "judgment" is elucidated by "truth." Despite the nuanced distinctions inherent between these two concepts, they nevertheless share an intrinsic interrelation. In select scriptural contexts, the two terms may even be employed interchangeably. The biblical narrative frequently emphasizes the importance of both justice and judgement—both mercy and truth—in God's dealings with humanity.

So what does inspiration tell us in regards to divine justice? Are there any instances in scripture where justice is applied in the context of mercy and restoration rather than condemnation and punishment? The short answer, dear reader, is a resounding yes!

In Zechariah, executing true judgement—or justice—is illustrated by showing *mercy* and compassion to your neighbor:

> "Thus speaketh the LORD of hosts, saying, **Execute true judgment, and shew mercy and compassions every man to his**

brother: And oppress not the widow, nor the fatherless, the stranger, nor the poor; and let none of you imagine evil against his brother in your heart." (Zechariah 7:9-10)

In the book of Ezekiel, justice is defined by dispelling imposed violence and inflicted hardships from among the people:

"Thus saith the Lord GOD; Let it suffice you, O princes of Israel: **remove violence and spoil, and execute judgment and justice,** take away your exactions from my people, saith the Lord GOD." (Ezekiel 45:9)

Jeremiah declares that the righteous and enlightened justice of God is demonstrated by the deliverance of the oppressed from the hand of the oppressor:

"O house of David, thus saith the LORD; **Execute judgment** in the morning, and **deliver him that is spoiled out of the hand of the oppressor...**" (Jeremiah 21:12)

"Thus saith the LORD; **Execute ye judgment and righteousness, and deliver the spoiled out of the hand of the oppressor:** and do no wrong, do no violence to the stranger, the fatherless, nor the widow, neither shed innocent blood in this place." (Jeremiah 22:3)

The same concept of justice is conveyed by the Psalmist, highlighting the benevolence of God in His dealings with humanity:

"**Defend the poor and fatherless: do justice to the afflicted and needy.** Deliver the poor and needy: rid them out of the hand of the wicked." (Psalm 82:3-4)

"Happy is he that hath the God of Jacob for his help, whose hope is in the LORD his God: Which made heaven, and earth, the sea, and all that therein is: **which keepeth truth for ever: Which executeth judgment for the oppressed:** which giveth food to the hungry. The LORD looseth the prisoners: The LORD openeth the eyes of the blind: the LORD raiseth them that are bowed down: the LORD loveth the righteous: The LORD preserveth the strangers; he relieveth the fatherless and widow: but the way of the wicked he turneth [allows to be turned] upside down." (Psalm 146:5-9)

In Isaiah, God's justice may be seen as relieving the oppressed and cleansing individuals of their evil affections:

"Wash you, make you clean; put away the evil of your doings from before mine eyes; **cease to do evil; Learn to do well; seek judgment,** relieve the oppressed, judge the fatherless, plead for the widow." (Isaiah 1:16-17)

As can be readily discerned, biblical justice is characterized by the emancipation of the oppressed rather than the exaction of punitive measures against the oppressor.

"**God's justice involves setting things right, not punishment. God's justice involves compassionate intervention in the world against all injustice, with a special attention to those who are being abused.** God's justice is something in which we're taking part as we make things right in the world." (Louis Johnson, as quoted in *Did God Kill Jesus Instead of Killing Us?*, pg. 9, by Kevin J. Mullins)

Describing the justice system implemented through Moses in the Old Testament, Ben Carson, M.D., states the following:

"**They focused on reparation to the victim rather than punishment** or fines levied on the perpetrator..." (Ben Carson, M.D., *America the Beautiful: Zondervan,* 2012, pg. 29)

Within this theological framework, God's law is regarded as the foundational blueprint for life, with deviations being inherently injurious to those who transgress it. God's justice is revealed through allowing persistent sinners to bear the natural outcomes of their destructive decisions, rather than imposing external punishments by His own intervening power.

"The righteousness of the perfect shall direct his way: but **the wicked shall fall by his own wickedness.**" (Proverbs 11:5)

"**Thine own wickedness shall correct thee, and thy backslidings shall reprove thee:** know therefore and see that it is an evil thing and bitter, that thou hast forsaken the LORD thy God, and that my fear [reverence] is not in thee, saith the Lord GOD of hosts." (Jeremiah 2:19)

"**God is a just judge;** he is angry [grieved] throughout the day... **See the one who is pregnant with wickedness, who conceives destructive plans, and gives birth to harmful lies – he digs a pit and then falls into the hole he has made. He becomes the victim of his own destructive plans and the violence he intended for others falls on his own head.**" (Psalm 7:11,14-16, *NET*)

"The LORD is known by the judgment which he executeth: **the wicked is snared in the work of his own hands.** Higgaion. Selah." (Psalm 9:16)

In the end, the ascendancy of Good over Evil is not achieved through the virtue of Good performing Evil, but rather by Good steadfastly upholding its moral integrity in the face of Evil. In other words, Good will not ultimately triumph over Evil by resorting to Evil's methods, but instead by upholding that which is Good *in spite of* Evil. Evil, by its inherent nature, is the architect of its own downfall, while the essence of Goodness lies in its unwavering inclination towards righteousness and edification. Goodness, true to its nature, even extends a compassionate effort to redeem Evil from its self-inflicted demise by illuminating the path toward truth and restoration to right principles. Through this achievement, that which is Evil may become that which is Good, but inherent Good will never succumb to the wicked state in which inherent Evil finds its comfort.

"**He is a God of love; a God who cannot do evil; who would not do evil even that good might result...** God has not sent evil to bring about strengthening. **The evil has fallen through some cause or from some source that is contrary to His will for man.**" (Henry B. Wilson, *Does Christ Still Heal?*, pg. 16, 37)

This is the kind of justice which our Creator exemplifies. He does not resort to malevolence and stern punishment in order to overcome evildoers, as this would only embolden them in their rebellion. Rather, by demonstrating the truth of His love and mercy, and illuminating to the sin-stricken mind those perils which must certainly come to pass if transgression is indulged, He fervently attempts to save evildoers from the consequences of sin and restore them to the righteous nature they were made to inherit prior to the fall of mankind.

"But," says one, "I supposed that God's justice required legal payment for sin; that He must punish someone—anyone—if justice was to be satisfied and the debt of sin forgiven." However, this argument does gross *injustice* to the character of God and the nature of sin. It fails to reconcile the character that Christ demonstrated with the character that the Father must therefore uphold. It implies that God is unforgiving, that sin has no innate consequence of its own but rather that God must mete out its punishment, and that God's government resides within an imperial, penal legal framework. This represents a distinct contrast to the truths which Christ came to reveal of His Father. Sin was forgiven by God from the very moment it took place. If this were not the case, then God need never have instigated His plan of salvation in the first place. He merely would have let humanity perish. But what has God done?

> "**For God so loved the world, that he gave his only begotten Son,** that whosoever believeth in him should not perish, but have everlasting life." (John 3:16)

Divine justice, rather than finding its satisfaction in punitive actions, required that the condition of sin be resolved and God's universe restored to its originally intended state of perpetual love and selflessness. God's justice is not found in wrath, but in redemption.

To illustrate this idea more clearly, the author will employ a number of relevant analogies, some of which have been borrowed from the brilliant mind of Dr. Timothy Jennings.

If you were to encounter someone who had just hanged themselves, thereby defying the law of respiration, what would "justice" require of you? Should you immediately administer punishment for their transgression of natural law by beating them? Should you initiate a formal trial, present evidence, and render a judicial verdict? Or, more fittingly, should your aim be to rescue and revive them from their breathless state, thus restoring them to harmony with the inherent laws of life? Which is the right, or *just*, course of action in this particular instance?

Furthermore, when contemplating the tragic occurrences of school shootings in America, what form of "justice" do you think the parents of the slain children would prefer: punishing the shooter via legal penalties, or resurrecting and restoring their children?

One more illustration begs our consideration. If you told your child, "But of the weed killer in the garage, thou shalt not drink of it: for in the day that thou drinkest thereof thou shalt surely die." Upon receiving this instruction, your child must then discern whether your statement is presented as a threat or a solemn warning. They must decide if, by drinking thereof, they will reap *inherent consequences* from ingesting the weed killer, or if they will reap *imposed consequences* for disobeying your orders. The question arises: does ingesting the weed killer inevitably result in their demise?—Or, will they "not surely die" (Genesis 3:4)? Will they meet their end through the natural consequences of consuming weed killer, or will you be compelled to impose punitive measures for their disobedience? Then, if your child drinks the weed killer and lies on the floor in apparent distress, should your response be one of anger, withholding forgiveness until they atone for their transgression?—Or are you grieved for the perilous condition which they now find themselves in? What does "justice" call upon you to do in this situation? Is it to further their suffering by punishing them while they are already in morbid distress?—Or is it to endeavor to heal them of their ailment, recognizing that without your direct intervention, they are certain to succumb? And if we, as inherently sinful and selfish beings, can extend compassion to our children, exerting ourselves not merely to preserve their existence but also to foster their prosperity, then it stands to reason that our heavenly Father, in His sublime benevolence, aspires to affect our healing and restoration to an even greater degree.

> "If ye then, being evil, know how to give good gifts unto your children, **how much more shall your Father which is in heaven give good things to them that ask him?**" (Matthew 7:11)

While these clear and succinct analogies effectively fulfill the author's objective of illustrating the manner in which God's justice ultimately unfolds, skepticism and doubt will continue to persist among many minds. A considerable number continue to hold fast to a punitive system of justice. Such an adherence serves two primary purposes: firstly, it bestows a perceived mandate upon those who delude themselves into a false sense of virtue, allowing them to consider themselves instruments of divine wrath, similar to the self-conception held by Saul of Tarsus. Similar to Saul, they disregard the moral principles of true religion and, in doing so, become persecutors themselves, thereby putting Christ to an open shame. Thinking to be wheat, they present themselves as tares. Secondly, it absolves this same class from the obligation of extending love and forgiveness to those whom they regard as wicked or undeserving of God's pardon. It represents a brand of justice which is contrary to the characteristics of love and nonviolence.

How can altruism be fostered amongst such a system? Surely it could only be thwarted and disfigured. Hate and wrath, instead, find their regular modes of expression and become familiar, cherished, and exalted. Through this artifice, Satan can extend his subterfuge, ensnaring not only those in the secular realm but also those within the very walls of the church. When individuals harbor a misconceived notion of God's character and, by extension, His approach to justice, they inadvertently become conduits for the adversary. The Lord is dishonored by the contention and strife caused by the un-sanctified disposition of professing Christians. Such individuals may unwittingly disseminate the pernicious doctrines of the devil, even from the sacred pulpit of the congregation.

In defense of punitive justice, many cite from the twenty-first chapter of the book of Exodus:

> "And if any mischief follow, then **thou shalt give life for life, Eye for eye, tooth for tooth, hand for hand, foot for foot, Burning for burning, wound for wound, stripe for stripe."** (Exodus 21:23-25)

In the first instance, this verse seems to support a form of punitive justice. But such an attempt proves ineffective when compared to the words of Christ.

> **"Ye have heard that it hath been said, An eye for an eye, and a tooth for a tooth: But I say unto you, That ye resist not evil:** but whosoever shall smite thee on thy right cheek, turn to him the other also." (Matthew 5:38-39)

The question then emerges: how may we reconcile these passages of scripture? In the book of Exodus, God appears to be imparting guidance to His people on a form of justice that aligns with inflicted punishments for wrongdoers, whereas the teachings of Christ seemingly run contrary to this instruction. One undeniable fact is that the character of the Father and the character of the Son cannot be in opposition; they must exhibit harmony. This necessarily implies that their expressions of justice should be consistent. Therefore, it becomes pertinent to inquire why, in this particular instance, God's sense of justice seems to assume a punitive role distinct from the perception of justice expounded by Christ? In order to harmonize this, we must employ historical context.

In the circumstance of the Exodus, the Israelites had just been led out of Egypt—a nation governed by an imperial ruler and steeped in pagan idolatry. The culture of the early Hebrews, especially their spiritual and political beliefs, was influenced by sources common to their environment. As a result of the Israelites' captivity, they had adopted many of the administrative protocols and religious customs of the Egyptians, including punitive justice.

> "**The influence of Egypt on the surrounding cultures, including ancient Israel, was significant** and comparable to the influence of dominant cultures like the US in the modern world." (Gary A. Rendsburg, M.D., professor of biblical studies, Hebrew language, and ancient Judaism at Rutgers University)

> "Egyptian authority was not only manifested in political and military control, but was a strong cultural influence that contributed to shaping society… **Along with an administration of Egyptian officials in Israel, a group of the local elite evolved in the country who adopted many of the Egyptian customs** and their artistry." (Amir Golani, M.D., Israel antiquities authority, interviewed by *The Jerusalem Post* in an article entitled, *"Egyptian culture influenced ancient Israel after Exodus, unearthed antiquities reveal,"* by Daniel K. Eisenbud, April 1, 2015)

Consequently, the Israelites began to view God in a manner reminiscent of how the Egyptians regarded their deities—as a being meriting worship primarily through its demonstration of power and authority; a pagan god. Such a god was believed to bestow or withhold blessings based on the actions and performances of its adherents. It was a deity poised to swiftly pass judgment upon those who defied its commands or failed to execute the prescribed rituals. Such a god would zealously demand the offering of blood as a means of propitiation. Thus, in order to mollify the deity, adherents endeavored to placate its wrath and secure its favor through sacrificial offerings and ceremonial rites of worship. As we shall later observe, this heathen perception of God has persisted as a blemish upon Christian doctrine, enduring even into contemporary times.

Unbeknownst to them, the Israelites had unwittingly embraced a pagan and imperialist interpretation of Jehovah. Their hearts and minds, over centuries of apostasy and idolatry, had become dark and hardened—they did not know their God's true disposition.

For this very reason, God conveyed the concept of justice we find described in Exodus 21:23-25. It wasn't a divine endorsement of punitive justice, but rather an effort to guide the ethical growth of the children of Israel away from spiritual infancy—a "move in the right direction," so to speak. He endeavored to gradually decouple the Israelites from their imperialistic interpretation of justice by instructing them to mete out punitive measures *exclusively* when they themselves were the victims of wrongdoing. The procedures provided in the referenced verse do not grant authorization for the punishment of merely any transgressor of the law, but rather restrict it to those directly causing harm to the offended party.

At this period in history, with the Israelites at such an early stage of their spiritual development, it was not feasible for God to promptly bestow upon their veiled understanding the profound truths inherent to His celestial system of governance. Such an immediate revelation would have likely resulted in rejection and contempt rather than acceptance and reverence. Due to their deep attachment to paganism and imperialistic ideals, the Israelites yearned for a deity who symbolized power and dominion—a being who would employ strength to eradicate its adversaries and punish dissenters. This was the system of justice ingrained in them from Egypt and what they were accustomed to since birth. Abandoning it at such an early stage in their spiritual development would have likely yielded disadvantageous results. It wasn't that God favored this form of justice, but rather it was the preference of the Israelites themselves. God simply *allowed* them the freedom to embrace their inclination for this particular brand of justice which was already rooted in their hearts—a principle we have firmly established in earlier segments of this volume. However, He introduced a minor adjustment to this system which represented a modest advancement over the principles they had left behind in Egypt. His goal was to guide them gradually, step by step, towards embracing the principles of love and nonviolence on their own initiative. It was because of the hardness of their hearts that God suffered them this form of justice, hoping that through this incremental improvement, He could initiate the process of softening their hearts and restoring them to right principles.

We may readily observe the same concept demonstrated in the Old Testament regulation on divorce, followed by the subsequent directive provided by Christ in the New Testament:

> "When a man hath taken a wife, and married her, and it come to pass that she find no favour in his eyes, because he hath found some uncleanness in her: **then let him write her a bill of divorcement, and give it in her hand, and send her out of his house.**" (Deuteronomy 24:1)

Referring to this Old Testament edict on divorce, Christ says the following:

> "And the Pharisees came to him, and asked him, Is it lawful for a man to put away his wife? tempting him. And he answered and said unto them, What did Moses command you? And they said, Moses suffered to write a bill of divorcement, and to put her away. And Jesus answered and said unto them, **For the hardness of your heart he wrote you this precept.**" (Mark 10:2-5)

> "They say unto him, Why did Moses then command to give a writing of divorcement, and to put her away? He saith unto them, **Moses because of the hardness of your hearts suffered you to put away your wives: but from the beginning it was not so.**" (Matthew 19:7-8)

Notice the latter half of verse 8 here in Matthew; "but from the beginning it was not so." (Matthew 19:8). Jesus, here, indicates that the Old Testament regulation on divorce, much like the punitive justice described in Exodus 21:23-25, was far removed from the core intent of God's original design for mankind. These antiquated conducts for governing behavior were not intended to be the ultimate apex of the moral principles which God sought for His people to embrace. Rather, these regulations were merely a concession on the part of God, prompted by the spiritual hardness of the people's hearts.

Numerous precepts pertaining to conduct in the Old Testament were designed to act as instruments for the softening of the Israelite's hearts and to facilitate their progression towards a more profound understanding of the principles that God wished for them to embrace—notably those of selfless love and nonviolence. But the Israelites, perceiving God in a predominantly imperialistic manner, prioritized meticulous compliance with the letter of the law over a deeper comprehension of the moral and spiritual principles which the law sought to convey. Their entrenched spiritual stagnation persisted to such an extent that even subsequent generations continued to adhere to antiquated notions of punitive justice, finally culminating in the merciless torture and crucifixion of the very One who had arrived to emancipate them from their predicament.

To ignore the rich historical and cultural context that has been exhibited here and instead maintain an advocacy for punitive justice, despite the overwhelming biblical evidence to the contrary, will undoubtedly lead to an erroneous theology which only serves to dishonor God's revealed character of love. In doing so, one substitutes the altruistic, nonviolent Creator God for an arbitrary, unmerciful, and imperial tyrant.

Such is the perilous outcome of adhering to punitive justice and penal substitution theology. In the current climate of Christianity, many suffer from this gross delusion. The system of punitive justice, historically, finds its exaltation in the very entity which endeavors to rival the kingdom of Jehovah, notably, the beast of Revelation 14—the little horn power of Daniel 7—the system of antichrist; none other than the Roman Papacy itself.

For a substantiation of this claim, one need only to examine the annals of history, particularly the gruesome and blood-stained episodes that unfolded under the auspices of the papal Inquisition, where the power of the State was used to enforce the conscience and silence any religious deviation from the ruling authority—whether by trial, torture, or execution. To suggest that the heavenly dominion functions in a manner that is similar to this horrific and beastly system is to pervert the truth and invite a most detrimental heresy into the midst of God's assembly. Punitive justice is *not* the application of true justice, but rather "justice-so-called." To align with its principles, in any way, is to champion the very method of conduct which Christ came to refute.

Divine justice, rather than being expressed through wrath and punishment, is actually God's compassionate effort to counter injustice and liberate His children from the yoke of bondage. It is His initiative to make right all that has been wronged by the condition of sin. In the pursuit of divine justice, God employs the virtues of mercy, truth, and love as instruments to evoke in us an unwavering trust in Him. This trust serves as the catalyst for our turning to Him for the purpose of healing and restoration, ultimately culminating in a harmonious reconciliation with the Divine. Through the redemptive work of Christ, the Father seeks to relegate sin to remission and deliver humanity from its morbid clutches. This divine endeavor, committed to establishing justice, strives to initiate a renewed order of spiritual health and well-being; new hearts and minds. Christ's righteousness then becomes reproduced in the sinner unto salvation.

> "The Spirit of the Lord GOD is upon me; because the LORD hath anointed me to preach good tidings unto the meek; **he hath sent me to bind up the brokenhearted, to proclaim liberty to the captives [of sin], and the opening of the prison to them that are bound [by sin]...**" (Isaiah 61:1)

The imperial fallacy of punitive justice, on the other hand, fundamentally misunderstands the exact nature of humanity's bondage to sin. Within the confines of this imposed, human-devised construct, it is suggested that mankind finds itself ensnared by the shackles of sin through a legalistic form of divine condemnation. Our transgressions ostensibly culminate in an impending capital sentence, which a righteous magistrate is compelled to execute. Within the scope of the imperial framework, this is construed as an embodiment of justice. Consequently, we find ourselves inexorably destined for death at the hands of an all-powerful potentate, unless a benefactor intercedes to discharge our indebtedness, thereby effecting our exoneration. In simple terms, someone must pay the legal penalty for sin if God is to forgive us. This theological perspective inevitably leads to the conviction that Christ's purpose was to shoulder this indebtedness and assume God's retribution on our behalf, thereby granting us absolution; Christ died to protect us from the Father's wrath. Ultimately, it suggests that God murdered His own Son as an alternative to us, with the intent of appeasing the demands of justice. Our righteousness subsequently assumes the nature of a legal transaction, while our innate carnal nature persists unchanged. God's forgiveness becomes the requisite for our salvation, rather than a transformation of character facilitated by the ministration of Christ. The Father's anger becomes the obstacle barring mankind from heaven, instead of sin itself. God becomes the source of death and suffering, instead of sin.

This position signifies a notable misinterpretation of self-evident truths. It strips Christianity of its transformative power and negates the redemptive work of Christ. A "form of godliness" is venerated, while "the power thereof" is denied (2 Timothy 3:5). It implies that, in the aftermath of sin's emergence, it was not humanity's nature that was affected, but rather God's. On account of transgression, God is provoked to take offense and subsequently imposes a verdict condemning man to death. Man becomes shackled by the judicial ruling of God rather than the harmful condition of sin. Instead of Satan, it is God who passes judgment—He assumes the role of the accuser. He temporarily suspends His capacity for forgiveness until this legal transgression is expiated. This interpretation, inspired by the punitive justice theory and imperial law model, diverges considerably from the truth as articulated in scripture. Inspiration tells us that God's disposition never changes. His character remains true for everlasting.

> "For I am the LORD, **I change not...**" (Malachi 3:6)

> "Every good gift and every perfect gift is from above, and cometh down from the Father of lights, **with whom is no variableness, neither shadow of turning.**" (James 1:17)

Sin had no impact upon the loving nature of God, save for causing Him immense grief over His creation's altered state. It should be readily apparent that it was the nature of mankind, rather than the nature of God, that became corrupted as sin made its treacherous debut. Consequently, it was necessary that humanity should be reconciled back to God. To achieve this purpose, the Father gave His only begotten Son.

> "And all things are of God, **who hath reconciled us to himself by Jesus Christ,** and hath given to us the ministry of reconciliation..." (2 Corinthians 5:18)

> **"For God so loved the world, that he gave his only begotten Son,** that whosoever believeth in him should not perish, but have everlasting life." (John 3:16)

The Father's love remained unwavering; He sought to save us from the very moment sin entered the world, never requiring appeasement or persuasion to extend His forgiveness and mercy. To suggest that God, for a time, rendered dormant His forgiving nature contradicts the explicit teachings conveyed by the prophet Isaiah. The notion that the Father required reconciliation through punitive measures before He could forgive sin signifies a profound misunderstanding of His character. His forgiveness was never withheld; His reconciliation never required. His love and forgiveness stand eternally available for us to embrace. He freely forgives all.

> "The wicked need to abandon their lifestyle and sinful people their plans. They should return to the Lord, and **he will show mercy to them,** and to their God, for **he will freely forgive them.**" (Isaiah 55:7, *NET*)

The theory of punitive justice starkly rejects this reality, instead furnishing it with a veneer of falsehood. It ascribes to God an unforgiving and unrelenting character that is incongruent with His true nature as it is revealed in Christ. This viewpoint insinuates that were God to merely restrain His anger, the sinner could persist in their wicked state perpetually because sin, on its own, isn't fundamentally harmful. Instead, God arbitrarily renders it injurious by His own judicial compulsion to punish transgression. It is God that punishes sin; therefore, it is God that we must be saved from.

This falsehood is then exacerbated by the doctrinal mistake of equating God's forgiveness with salvation. Many contend that the achievement of salvation, and the process of atonement, involves the payment of our legal penalty, resulting in God's extension of forgiveness and the subsequent absolution of our sins. Nevertheless, this perspective is subject to critique, for it essentially construes salvation as a judicial pronouncement, similar to a pardon granted by a judge.

Our sinful state, in this framework, remains an imprisoning force upon our soul, with no substantive emancipation from its profound and wretched influence. God is portrayed as unyielding, with the concession of forgiveness contingent upon disturbing displays of blood-sacrifice. As a result of this misconception, humanity ardently believes that they must endeavor to reconcile God to themselves, by any means necessary, if His loving and forgiving disposition is to be reawakened, His retributive punishment evaded, and salvation obtained. This delusion is so deeply instilled in the human psyche that many today maintain the belief that the act of killing God's own Son was the solitary means by which divine forgiveness could be procured—as if such a wicked gesture was meant to elicit compassion from the Father. This interpretation of salvation is inconsistent with the theological principles of the gospel.

Certainly, Christ's crucifixion was essential for humanity's salvation, but it did not serve to appease the wrath of an angry god, nor was it intended to secure the Father's forgiveness. Instead, it was required so that humanity could believe that God was willing to forgive sin; we demanded it. Once we obtained the belief that God could forgive, then, and only then, could we open ourselves up to His restorative plan to affect our salvation.

The claim that equates God's forgiveness with salvation is fundamentally flawed. Salvation, in theological terms, ought not to be construed as deliverance from the wrath of God, but rather as deliverance from the inherent condition of sin. We are to attain *genuine* righteousness, not *legal* or *formal* righteousness. Moreover, God's forgiveness cannot be regarded as synonymous with salvation, as it has already been offered to all—and to embrace the doctrinal position of universalism would be unwise. It is true that forgiveness has been universally granted for sin, but it is also true that not all individuals have been redeemed from the entanglements of their sinful condition. This does not arise from any deficiency in God's ability to purify humanity from sin; rather, it emanates from the deliberate and willful choice of individuals to endure in an unwavering state of sinfulness, despite God's efforts and influence. There is no limit to God's mercy and love; but as righteousness in the individual soul is the result of God's working in and through that soul, when it is of its own free will submitted to Him, the power of God to save men from sin into righteousness is limited by their willingness to submit themselves to Him. When that willingness or power is lost through rebellion continued till the habits of the mind have become fixed, and the nobler desires are either wholly obliterated or entirely under the control of the baser passions, then the case is hopeless.

In the biblical text, neither forgiveness nor salvation are construed as matters of legality. Thus, to regard salvation as merely a judicial declaration of sin's remission by the agency of God's forgiveness finds its proper place solely among discussions of an irrational nature. In such a context, the condition of sin is not authentically rectified; instead, it is merely disregarded or overlooked. It implies that our sins are purged from the ledgers of heaven rather than from the actual heart of the sinner.

Given that God's forgiveness extends to all and that His forgiveness, in and of itself, does not inherently change the sinful state of humanity, it is unreasonable to contend that God's forgiveness directly equates to salvation. For a substantiation of this claim, one need only to look to those individuals whom Jesus forgave while He was being crucified.

> "Then said Jesus, **Father, forgive them; for they know not what they do.** And they parted his raiment, and cast lots." (Luke 23:34)

Here, Jesus is not petitioning the Father for forgiveness toward those responsible for His crucifixion, as if the Father lacked the capacity to do so without Christ's direct appeal. Instead, He was unveiling the compassionate heart and nature of the Father. Christ was illustrating what the Father had *already* wrought within His heart for all those who had stood in opposition to Him. Christ's words exemplified the preexisting benevolence of the Father's disposition toward every sinner.

> "Then said Jesus unto them, When ye have lifted up the Son of man, then shall ye know that I am he, and that **I do nothing of myself; but as my Father hath taught me, I speak these things.**" (John 8:28)

> "For I have not spoken of myself; but the Father which sent me, **he gave me a commandment, what I should say, and what I should speak.**" (John 12:49)

As Christ uttered these words on the cross, He was revealing the attitude of the Father toward all who have ever transgressed. Thus, all of humanity may know with certainty that God's heart is one of mercy and forgiveness. Should Christ or His Father have ever nurtured feelings of anger or enmity towards those who had sinned, thereby abstaining from forgiveness, they would have undoubtedly sown the precursors of hypocrisy, as illuminated by the teachings of Christ Himself:

> "You have heard that it was said to those of old, You shall not murder; and whoever murders will be liable to judgment. **But I say to you that everyone who is angry with his brother will be liable to judgment...**" (Matthew 5:21-22, *ESV*)

Those who orchestrated the crucifixion of the Savior remained oblivious to the profound implications of their actions. They erroneously perceived it as the termination of Christ's existence, yet paradoxically, they were unwittingly solidifying their own spiritual callousness against the very Redeemer who held the power to heal them of their sinful condition. In hardening their hearts against Him, they inadvertently sowed the seeds of self-destruction. God had forgiven them, *but that forgiveness was not received* by them due to their own steadfast rejection of His regenerating Spirit.

This mistaken idea that forgiveness equates to salvation may be traced back to ancient Hebrew tradition. In accordance with our prior discourse, the early Hebrews, in the wake of the Exodus, construed God within the confines of a strict imperialistic paradigm. Due to their preexisting indoctrination in punitive justice, the Israelites ascribed to God the role of enacting punishment for sin, rather than recognizing that sin carried with it inherent and natural consequences. They likened God's kingdom and His justice to a judicial system of penal legality and capital repercussions. Few are truly aware just how much of this perspective continues to permeate contemporary Christian doctrine. Numerous individuals maintain the belief that God's government operates in a manner similar to human governments. It is no wonder, therefore, that a persistent association between forgiveness and salvation endures, much like the viewpoint held by the Israelites of old. After all, to be pardoned (*forgiven*) of a crime is to be set free (*saved*) from the consequences of a guilty verdict. However, this does not constitute the operational methodology of the kingdom of God. In truth, sin is a matter of the heart, not a matter of legality. It is a spiritual condition that needs to be remedied, not a judicial record that needs to be expunged. Jesus aimed to demonstrate this very truth to the Jewish nation when He healed the paralytic.

> "And, behold, they brought to him a man sick of the palsy, lying on a bed: and Jesus seeing their faith said unto the sick of the palsy; Son, be of good cheer; **thy sins be forgiven thee.**" (Matthew 9:2)

In this context, Christ was not granting forgiveness to the paralytic in the present moment; instead, He was affirming that the paralytic's sins had already been forgiven by God *preemptively*.

> "And, behold, certain of the scribes said within themselves, This man blasphemeth. And Jesus knowing their thoughts said, Wherefore think ye evil in your hearts? **For whether is easier, to say, Thy sins be forgiven thee; or to say, Arise, and walk? But that ye may know that the Son of man hath power on earth to forgive sins,** (then saith he to the sick of the palsy,) Arise, take up thy bed, and go unto thine house. And he arose, and departed to his house." (Matthew 9:3-7)

For the purpose of refuting the Israelites' traditional views regarding the nature of sin, forgiveness, salvation, and divine justice, Christ here amalgamates all four into a single demonstration.

In Jewish culture, there was a prevailing belief that if an individual experienced disease or physical ailments, it was regarded as a consequence of God's punitive justice, implying that they must've committed certain sins to incur such afflictions. In this instance, the scribes and Pharisees undoubtedly looked upon this paralytic man as egregiously wretched and sinful—someone to be shunned for fear of contaminating their own self-perceived piety. Jesus aspired to dismantle this misperception by engaging the Pharisees at their level of understanding. His exposition was meticulously crafted to impart a particular spiritual lesson, tailored to the spiritual infancy of the Pharisees. In full view of their gaze, He publicly displayed the act of forgiving the individual whom they deemed to be a grievous sinner. By their understanding, He had seemingly proclaimed salvation to a flagrant violator of the law—something they deemed incompatible with reason.

However, His instructional narrative did not end there. Christ continued His endeavors by affecting the healing of the paralytic's physical ailment, thereby restoring his ability to walk. This action served a profound and purposeful role in the lesson which Christ was conveying. It functioned as an enlightening revelation to those who observed it, demonstrating that the forgiveness of sin—which the Jewish nation conflated with salvation—was, in reality, the first step in a comprehensive restoration of one's entire condition, rather than being solely a legal or formal exoneration. He extended forgiveness and restored the physical condition of the paralytic to impress upon their understanding that salvation encompasses a spiritual healing of the whole being. If Christ had merely forgave the paralytic for his sins, a simple declaration would have proved insufficient to cure his condition. Instead, Christ undertook to provide a complete remedy for his infirmity, thereby illustrating the genuine nature of sin, forgiveness, salvation, and divine justice.

The adversary has made considerable efforts to distort the genuine nature of God's law, consequently shrouding the true nature of sin in ambiguity. This deliberate misrepresentation also leads to a perverted perception of God's justice, portraying it in an entirely erroneous manner, and subsequently falsifying His benevolent character. Heaven assumes the semblance of an authoritarian tribunal, where the earnest seeker could only encounter difficulties in deriving genuine delight.

This imperial deception leads Christians of all denominations to exert efforts to attain everything except genuine salvation. Hearts and minds remain untransformed, and God is misrepresented—His radiance and grandeur remain concealed by the stifling falsehoods propagated by Satan. Christianity has relinquished its transformative potential and instead pursues legal formalities that pale in comparison to the transcendent realities of heaven. A semblance of godliness has been embraced instead of genuine godliness, and many remain unaware. Divine justice has been supplanted by "justice-so-called" and the results, as one may plainly see, are damning.

In brief, from Satan's standpoint, the concept of God's justice assumes a forensic nature, necessitating a judicial verdict and subsequent punishment for its fulfillment. Within this analytical framework, it is not the inherent state of sin that holds humanity in bondage, but rather the legal penalty enforced by God, coupled with His apparent unwillingness to extend forgiveness.

On the other hand, in accordance with God's true framework, divine justice assumes a diagnostic function, emerging as an exhibition of healing and restoration. It seeks to counter injustices by delivering those who are oppressed instead of punishing the oppressor. The forces that restrain us in bondage to sin are the very misconceptions we harbor regarding the nature of God, coupled with our inherent carnal nature and propensity toward sin and selfishness.

> "**Ye are of your father the devil, and the lusts of your father ye will do.** He was a murderer from the beginning, and abode not in the truth, because **there is no truth in him.** When he speaketh a lie, he speaketh of his own: for **he is a liar, and the father of it.**" (John 8:44)

Christ's mission to liberate us from bondage was comprised of two distinct components. Firstly, He sought to reveal the truth about God, creating a basis upon which we could place our unwavering trust in Him. Secondly, by triumphing over the sinful condition ingrained in the human nature which He assumed, He furnished a remedy for our carnal struggle and endeavors to impart unto us the same righteousness which He personified. In this process, He initiates a profound transformation in our character through His redemptive efforts within the innermost recesses of our hearts. In submitting to His purposes, we inevitably trade lies for truth, blindness for discernment, fear and selfishness for love and trust, depravity of soul for Christ-like character, evil for righteousness, spiritual ailment for spiritual well-being, and the icy grip of death for the warm embrace of life.

> "**Love is the agency which God uses to expel sin from the human soul.** By it he changes pride into humility, enmity and unbelief into love and faith. **He does not employ compulsory measures; Jesus is revealed to the soul, and if man will look in faith to the Lamb of God, he will live...**" (Ellen G. White, *Signs of the Times,* June 9, 1890)

And yet, as a counter to this work, many continue to draw upon doctrines from the heretical annals of the Papacy—yes, even the likes of contemporary Adventists! We not only persist in adhering to their perspective of God's law as an imposed and imperial system, as the author tediously demonstrated in chapter 6, but we also hold dear the theory of punitive justice they forcefully project onto the Almighty. In tandem with this antichrist system, we assert that there is no distinction in function between the governance of heaven and the administrations of humankind. And while Adventists have effectively distanced themselves from doctrinal alignment with the Roman Church on matters such as the Sabbath, hellfire, and the immortality of the soul—the fundamental perception of God remains unaltered.

Dear reader, the Reformation cannot be complete until we Protestants wholly separate ourselves from the punitive justice and imperial law system that has come into the church and set itself up most prominently in the Roman Papal system, being as it is a continuation of the Roman Empire in religious garb. We all have inherited and been affected by these ideas that have been passed down for millennia; it is the "daily" (Daniel 8:13), the pagan ideas of deity that have continued and developed since the fall of Lucifer. And we are called by God to work with Him in cleansing His temple of these heinous ideas and bringing the controversy over God to an end.

Adventists have rightfully advocated the position that a benevolent God would never subject His children, including those who have rejected Him, to eternal torment. Nevertheless, many Adventists simultaneously adhere to the concept of punitive justice, acknowledging that God Himself still chooses to subject His children to the ordeal of burning, albeit for a shorter duration compared to the beliefs of some other Christian denominations. The comprehensive biblical perspective on the truth about hellfire, in its proper understanding, should ultimately direct attention to the genuine nature of the Father, portraying Him as a Being characterized by altruistic love and nonviolence. Not only does He abstain from subjecting His wayward children to an eternity of fiery torment, but He refrains from subjecting them to the act of burning altogether! Rather, they suffer eternal separation from the Father—the second death—as a direct and natural result of sin.

As is distinctly apparent in the account of Elijah, the manifestation of God's power cannot be found among the tumultuous flames.

"...And, behold, the LORD passed by, and a great and strong wind rent the mountains, and brake in pieces the rocks before the LORD; but the LORD was not in the wind: and after the wind an earthquake; but the LORD was not in the earthquake: **And after the earthquake a fire; but the LORD was not in the fire: and after the fire a still small voice.**" (I Kings 19:11-12)

Yet, a considerable number of Christians, including those adhering to the Adventist faith, tend to conceptualize God in a manner reminiscent of the pagan King Nebuchadnezzar as delineated in the historical narrative concerning his imperial edict, which mandated worship under the penalty of facing fiery retribution.

"Then an herald cried aloud, To you it is commanded, O people, nations, and languages, That at what time ye hear the sound of the cornet, flute, harp, sackbut, psaltery, dulcimer, and all kinds of musick, ye **fall down and worship the golden image that Nebuchadnezzar the king hath set up: And whoso falleth not down and worshippeth shall the same hour be cast into the midst of a burning fiery furnace.**" (Daniel 3:4-6)

Why should we even begin to entertain the idea that God would emulate the actions of this ancient Babylonian king?—Especially when we are instructed to disassociate ourselves entirely from spiritual Babylon and its perilous teachings?

"And there followed another angel, saying, **Babylon is fallen, is fallen,** that great city, because she made all nations drink of the wine of the wrath of her fornication." (Revelation 14:8)

"And he cried mightily with a strong voice, saying, Babylon the great is fallen, is fallen, and is become the habitation of devils, and the hold of every foul spirit, and a cage of every unclean and hateful bird. For all nations have drunk of the wine of the wrath of her fornication, and the kings of the earth have committed fornication with her, and the merchants of the earth are waxed rich through the abundance of her delicacies. And I heard another voice from heaven, saying, **Come out of her, my people, that ye**

be not partakers of her sins, and that ye receive not of her plagues." (Revelation 18:2-4)

If God were to use His own formidable power to threaten His children with fiery death—or worse, eternal torment—as a consequence of withholding worship from Him, it would only serve to further incite fear and rebellion. Such an ultimatum is fundamentally incapable of fostering love, trust, or reconciliation. Instead, it effectively deprives the human will of its freedom; genuine autonomy becomes a fleeting and illusory concept.

Sure, in the case of Nebuchadnezzar, Daniel and his friends would not have burned forever; nevertheless, their infernal demise would still have occurred at the very hands of Nebuchadnezzar himself. How could the implications of such a mandate constitute liberty of conscience? Could one truly make an authentic decision under such a circumstance? If God forewarns the sinner about the inevitable consequences of their transgressions and later enacts these punitive measures Himself, it may be aptly characterized as a form of coercion, albeit with delayed effects.

Imagine if someone presented you with an ultimatum: "Love me or in 5 days I'll douse you in gasoline and burn you alive." In such a scenario, there would be little room for genuine free will. Instead, fear would compel an attempt at love, yet it would lack sincerity, originating from a place of trepidation rather than genuine affection. Instead of cultivating a legitimate relationship, such an ultimatum would likely elicit a superficial and uninspired response of admiration. In the long run, this approach would only lead to intensified rebellion.

"**Its [Christ's kingdom] principles of development are the opposite of those that rule the kingdoms of this world. Earthly governments prevail by physical force; they maintain their dominion by war; but the founder of the new kingdom is the Prince of Peace.** The Holy Spirit represents worldly kingdoms under the symbol of fierce beasts of prey; but Christ is 'the Lamb of God, which taketh away the sin of the world.' John 1:29. **In His plan of government there is no employment of brute force to compel the conscience...**" (Ellen G. White, *Christ's Object Lessons,* pg. 77)

"Force is the last resort of every false religion." (Ellen G. White, *Signs of the Times,* May 6, 1897)

The very existence of the adversities which accompany the second death such as torment, destruction, pain, and anguish may be attributed to the *absence* of God's protective agency. Without His intervention, sin follows its inexorable course, suffocating the life force of its victim into oblivion, ultimately culminating in the second death—utter and eternal annihilation. It is not the hand of God that brings about the demise of the wicked by means of the inferno of hellfire; rather, it is the very nature of sin itself that begets their complete and eternal destruction.

How is it that Adventists have fallen short in apprehending the overarching implications to which these doctrines allude? Satan's subterfuge extends so far that, even amidst the realm of truth, error may still find a place of reverence.

Satan's artful deception in the garden, "Ye shall not surely die" (Genesis 3:4), extended beyond a mere lie about the immortality of the soul; it also served to conceal *the means* by which our ultimate destruction would materialize. Through the subtle suggestion that we would not surely die by our act of transgression, two distinct purposes were effectively realized: firstly, the acceptance of the intrinsic immortality of the soul, fostering the belief in eternal existence, be it in heaven or hell. Secondly, the assumption that there would be no destructive consequences entailed by the indulgence of sin. Sin did not inherently carry the burden of death; instead, it bore only the arbitrarily imposed verdict of death by a despotic deity. Consequently, the punitive justice system was conceived, giving rise to fear and apprehension toward the very Being intent on our salvation.

The doctrine of inherent immortality comes to its legitimate fruitage in the terrible God-defaming belief in eternal conscious misery for all the multitudes of the lost. It is not too much to say that all false religion is a logical development from that lie, although we cannot here take time and space to show this definitely. Given our constraints in the current volume, we will move on from this matter, having effectively addressed the author's objectives for the present discourse. However, if one would like to more fully understand the topics of hellfire and the immortality of the soul, we would recommend these informative selections:

• *The Fire That Consumes*, by Edward Fudge

• *Hell-Fire: A Twisted Truth Untangled*, by Joe Crews

• *Which? Mortal, Or Immortal? An Inquiry into the Present Constitution and Future Condition of Man*, by Uriah Smith

For now, the author's discourse on punitive justice has served its intended purpose and effectively presented its arguments. We pray that the egregious implications of one's adherence to such a devilish doctrine have been duly realized. Now we must endeavor to address particular scriptural instances that may act as refutations to this chapter's claims.

If the consequences of sin are not imposed upon transgressors via God's own formidable power and intervention, then why does the Bible seem to assert otherwise? It is at this juncture that we inevitably encounter the difficult challenge of reconciling this volume's aforementioned assertions with the myriad instances in the Old Testament where it ostensibly portrays God Himself as the executor of punitive measures and resolute judgments aimed at correcting those who have contravened His divine will. Having articulated this, let us now engage in an examination of God's *apparent* acts of punitive judgment in the Old Testament, with the purpose of reconciling them with His character as manifest through the person of Jesus Christ.

> "Yes, God does destroy as the Bible plainly says He does, but **He destroys in the sense of not restraining or preventing the natural consequences of man's choice and actions from occurring.**" (Ray Foucher, characterofgod.org, November 28, 2020)

> "**All who are conversant in the language of the Old Testament know, that it speaks of every event which God permits, as proceeding directly from him;** and describes his as hardening the hearts of those who abuse the divine dispensations." (Richard Graves, *Lectures on the Four Last Books of the Pentateuch,* pg. 194)

> "**The NT teaches us to base all of our thinking about God on Jesus.** In contrast to the way God spoke in the past, the author of Hebrews teaches, Jesus is the one and only 'exact representation of God's being' (Heb. 1:3). He is the one Word of God (Jn 1:1) and the one image of God (Col. 1:15). When Philip asked Jesus to show them God the Father, Jesus said, 'If you see me, you see the Father. Why then do you ask, 'Show us the Father'?' (Jn 14:7-9). John 1:17-18 even suggests that no one really knew God until Jesus...

> "**The bottom line is that, however we explain violent portraits of God in the OT, and even if we can't explain them, we must never allow anything we find in the OT to compromise or in any way disqualify the revelation of God we have in Christ.** Jesus isn't *part* of what God is like, the *fullness* of God's deity was in Christ (Col. 2:9). And **Jesus reveals a God who chooses to die on behalf of enemies rather than to use force against them... Whenever we find portraits of God in the OT that fall below the character of God revealed in Christ — all portraits that have God commanding or engaging in violence — we should see a reflection of the cross in them. That is, we should view these portraits as an example of God humbly stooping to enter the limited and fallen worldview of the authors.** They reflect God meeting people where

they are, working through the limited and fallen worldviews that they hold, in order to bring humanity to the place where he could reveal what he is really like — which is what he does in Christ…

"**Since Jesus reveals what God is always like, we should read the Bible with the understanding that God may appear to do what he merely allows.** In my book [*The Crucifixion of the Warrior God*], I have two chapters of material demonstrating that, as a matter of fact, **biblical authors frequently depict God doing things when the narrative itself makes it clear God merely allowed it.** For example, in Ex. 12 Yahweh says he will slay the firstborn children of Egypt, but the narrative makes it clear that he simply did not prevent 'the destroyer' (12:23) from killing the children. **And if we base all of our thinking about God on Jesus, we should envision God weeping whenever he feels he must allow evil to run its course, since Jesus weeps as he announces a judgment coming on Jerusalem (Lk. 19).**

"**In this light, I view all judgments involving violence to be a matter of God withdrawing his protection — always with a grieving heart — and thereby allowing the ever-present 'thief' who comes 'only to kill, steal and destroy' (Jn 10:10) to carry out the evil that is in his heart.** I thus believe that, in response to David's sin, God allowed Satan or some other destructive cosmic power to take the life of his newborn [2 Samuel 12]. **Because the biblical author did not have the full revelation of God that we have in Christ, he ascribed this violence directly to God. But as we read this narrative in the light of Christ, I believe we should understand that this was something God merely felt he had to allow, and he did so with a grieving heart.**

"We find Paul re-reading the Old Testament in the light of Christ along these lines. In I Cor. 10:5 he refers to the 'grumblers' who were slain by the 'the destroying angel' in the OT — referring to the judgment of Korah and his followers when the earth opened up and some rebels fell into it and when fire came down from the sky and incinerated others. If you read the OT account of this judgment, however, there's no mention of a destroyer. It simply looks like Yahweh did it. And I don't doubt that the author of the OT narrative believed Yahweh did this. **But**

in the light of Christ, Paul had more insight into how God judges than people in the OT had. With a grieving heart he allows evil to run its course, but he does not kill." (Greg Boyd, *Would God Kill a Baby to Teach Parents a Lesson?*, reknew.org, October 9, 2012)

Section 3

The God of the Old Testament Reinterpreted

Chapter 9

Divine Agency: Unveiling the Hand of God in the Old Testament

"But their minds were blinded: ***for until this day remaineth the same vail untaken away in the reading of the old testament; which vail is done away in Christ.*** *" (2 Corinthians 3:14)*

"The context of Scripture will help us to understand how to put some Old Testament passages in perspective with God's love. The ultimate way, however, is to look to Christ. Christ is the ultimate revelation of God Himself. *Christ is the Word of God (John 1:1-14).* ***So everything said or thought about God must be examined in the light of Jesus Christ. If I have an interpretation which is contrary to the nature of God as revealed in Christ, then I must reinterpret, because God is faithful, and He does not contradict Himself.*** *" (Joe Blair, When Bad things Happen, God Still Loves, pg. 96, published in 1986)*

It has been the object of this little book to show that all God's acts in His dealings with humanity come from the motive of love. Against this proposition it is often urged that His vengeful wrath destroyed the old world by a flood, and that a little later that same wrath obliterated entirely the fair cities of the plain. It is also said that He exterminated the tribes of the Canaanites—men, women, and children—and gave their lands and homes to others. These things, as recorded in the Bible, it is thought reveal the character of the Christian's God as anything but love. The author may agree that there are some instances of scripture that we cannot fully explain, because we do not know all the circumstances connected with them. We firmly believe, however, that the application to these special cases of the principles already made plain in these chapters will relieve them of very much of their difficulty.

While engaging with the Old Testament, a recurring phenomenon emerges where readers often acquire a misconstrued interpretation of the divine character of God. In the absence of a comprehensive knowledge of historical context and Hebrew literary technique, reconciling the depiction of God in the Old Testament with His portrayal in the New Testament becomes a formidable challenge. This difficulty proves even more daunting without a thorough understanding of Christ's purpose and mission. Consequently, many are led to contemplate whether there was a discernible shift in God's disposition across the epochs of history, with some even suggesting that the method of salvation somehow changed altogether. However, as we've previously ascertained, the pages of inspiration declare that God's ways never change:

> "For I am the LORD, **I change not...**" (Malachi 3:6)

> "Every good gift and every perfect gift is from above, and cometh down from the Father of lights, **with whom is no variableness, neither shadow of turning.**" (James 1:17)

In continuity with the representation of God in the New Testament, we find that His character remains as steadfast and as unchanging throughout the entirety of the Old Testament narrative as well. In this regard, the sentiment articulated by John resonates profoundly:

> "...God is love." (I John 4:8)

Yet, a significant number of individuals—including professed Christians—often cast doubt upon the apostle's inspired claim. Even in instances where they do not outright reject this fundamental truth, they tend to affix to it contrastive conjunctions and distorted doctrinal assertions which are laden with antithetical and paradoxical connotations, thereby introducing a profound level of ambiguity into the matter. These assertions can range from "God is loving, *but* He is also just," to even statements such as "God is merciful and forgiving, *but* sin stirs up His anger and He must lash out against transgression."

Through human agency, the pure love of heaven is blemished and far removed from its proper context by its association with a punitive system of justice. This union leads the believer into a state of intellectual inebriation, wherein incorrect understandings of God take root through the adhesion of conflicting principles. As a result, the narrative encompassing the Father's intentions toward humanity undergoes a profound transformation, transitioning from a paradigm of benevolent mercy and restorative grace to one marked by stern condemnation and penal infliction. This dilemma comes as a result of misunderstanding the true nature of God as revealed in Christ.

These diametric suggestions only serve to oppose and contradict His divine character of love and nonviolence. They are artfully insinuated into the receptive ears of believers by the arch-deceiver and subsequently enshrined in the fundamental tenets of the church. An effort to reconcile the character of the Father in the Old Testament with how He appears in the New Testament then becomes an exceedingly intricate endeavor, serving only to accentuate and amplify a seemingly impassable disharmony.

However, upon closer examination, we come to realize that the apparent discordance does not originate within God Himself, but instead resides within our imperfect and constrained comprehension of scripture. Numerous individuals tend to set aside their understanding of Christ when embarking upon a study of the Old Testament because they mistakenly suppose that this portion of the biblical narrative is not centered upon the Son, but rather the Father. In their omission of Christ, they inadvertently forfeit the singular conduit through which they may establish the Old Testament within its proper contextual framework. Undoubtedly, such an approach can only lead to an adverse perception of God—one that may potentially pose risks to the unperceptive adherent of faith. An insufficient familiarity with Christ prevents them from acquiring an authentic comprehension of the Father. And by refusing to interpret the God of the Old Testament through the lens of Christ—who is the "express image" of the Father's "person" (Hebrews 1:3)—the believer is only left with preposterous and unbecoming conclusions of the divine character.

It is Christ that revealed the Father to fallen humanity. The necessity for the revelation of the Father, by Christ, arose from prevalent and profound misunderstandings of His character. Consequently, a reading of the Old Testament devoid of the insight furnished by Jesus not only fails to rectify these misconceptions but also consigns us to a position similar to those individuals in the Old Testament who ascribed to God attributes incongruent with His true nature. Through the pursuit of understanding Christ, we attain the means to comprehend the Father.

> "Jesus saith unto him, Have I been so long time with you, and yet hast thou not known me, Philip? **he that hath seen me hath seen the Father;** and how sayest thou then, Shew us the Father?" (John 14:9)

> "Jesus saith unto him, I am the way, the truth, and the life: **no man cometh unto [a knowledge of] the Father, but by me.**" (John 14:6)

> "To this end was I born, and for this cause came I into the world, **that I should bear witness unto the truth.**" (John 18:37)

> "And **ye shall know the truth,** and the truth **shall make you free.**" (John 8:32)

> "And this is life eternal, **that they might know thee the only true God,** and Jesus Christ, whom thou hast sent." (John 17:3)

Therefore, it is exclusively through the light of Christ that we may reconcile the occurrences in the Old Testament where God's actions seemingly diverge from the divine attributes of love and nonviolence. By a knowledge of Christ, the entire Old Testament, heretofore concealed by misapprehension, becomes clear and illumined.

> "But their minds were blinded: **for until this day remaineth the same vail untaken away in the reading of the old testament; which vail is done away in Christ.**" (2 Corinthians 3:14)

If we adhere steadfastly to the conviction that Jesus embodies the full revelation of the Father, then in circumstances of scripture where we encounter a seemingly incongruous portrayal of the Father's character, we must contemplate the presence of an underlying, more nuanced understanding that remains to be unearthed—an overlooked explanation to consider. As our present discussion unfolds, it will become evident that certain passages of the Old Testament where God seems harsh or severe, when situated within a wider perspective, are shown to align with the conclusions expounded in this volume regarding the loving and nonviolent nature of God. And while there are many instances of scripture that suit our claims which we might urge, on account of our limited space we shall reduce them to only a select portion. These instances we will remark upon briefly in their order. However, in many of the passages which have been omitted from this publication where a broader context is of no immediate aid, or our personal understanding of the scripture fails, we must not despair. If a biblical statement appears to conflict with the revelation of God given to humanity in the person of Jesus Christ, we must reinterpret, because "God is love" (1 John 4:8) and He does not contradict Himself.

> "What seems literal and plain on the surface may not be. God wants us to dig more—**especially when the direct statement may seem at odds with the revelation of God given to humans in the person of His Son Jesus Christ.**" (Ben Kramlich, *Plain Statements on the Character of God*, pg. 9)

The Hardening of Pharaoh's Heart

"And the LORD said unto Moses, When thou goest to return into Egypt, see that thou do all those wonders before Pharaoh, which I have put in thine hand: ***but I will harden his heart, that he shall not let the people go.****" (Exodus 4:21)*

*"****And I will harden Pharaoh's heart,*** *and multiply my signs and my wonders in the land of Egypt." (Exodus 7:3)*

Upon an initial glance, these verses in Exodus seem to suggest that God, through a formidable intervention, is directly implicated in the hardening of Pharaoh's heart. These verses seem to suggest that Pharaoh had no capacity to influence his own fate or exercise his own free will. This perspective contends that Pharaoh couldn't have opened his heart to God's appeals even if he had desired to do so, as God had seemingly rendered him incapable of responding to His grace by some arbitrary divine decree. Consequently, God's methodologies undergo a distortion, and through this substantial misinterpretation, they become ever increasingly entwined with the attributes of imperialism.

However, the reader would do well to bear in mind the previous sections of this volume where the author underscores a specific literary convention associated with Hebraism, wherein God is frequently depicted as engaging in actions He does not forcefully obstruct. In other words, within numerous passages of scripture, events that God merely permits are often credited to His direct intervention, as if He actively initiated them. We may readily see this principle employed in the context of 1 Samuel:

"But **the Spirit of the LORD departed** from Saul, and an evil spirit **from the LORD** troubled him." (I Samuel 16:14)

Drawing from the author's formerly established groundwork, we may know with certainty that God, in every circumstance, is absolved of all responsibility for the coming and going of malevolent beings. Our God does not repay evil with further evil, nor does He task the hosts of hell with the objects of their torment. This compels us to seek an alternative explanation for the occurrences delineated in this verse.

In the context before us, we are supplied with the knowledge that the Spirit of the Lord *departed* from Saul—implying that God's protection was wholly removed. Consequently, this must've *allowed* the evil spirit to take its inexorable course. Without God's safeguarding presence, Saul became a conspicuous and vulnerable target. Commenting on this verse specifically, the *Seventh-Day Adventist Bible Commentary* seems to endorse the author's claim:

> "The Scriptures sometimes represent God **as doing that which He does not specifically prevent.**" (*Seventh-Day Adventist Bible Commentary*, vol. 2, pg. 531; on I Samuel 16:14)

Applying this same principle to instances where God seemingly hardens the hearts of His people, we find in Isaiah:

> "O LORD, **why hast thou made us to err from thy ways, and hardened our heart from thy fear?** Return for thy servants' sake, the tribes of thine inheritance." (Isaiah 63:17)

Does this appear to be an accurate representation of God? In this particular instance, it suggests that He induces His own people to stumble into error and disregard His divine will by intentionally hardening their hearts. Surely, this notion cannot hold true, for it defies all rationality. A more proper understanding of the passage may be obtained by applying the principle which we have been outlining thus far. In doing so, we can infer that God, in accordance with His endowment of free will, sanctioned His children to pursue their individual inclinations, even if it meant a deviation from the divinely ordained course. By their wayward decisions and unyielding tenacity, they obstinately closed their hearts to His gentle admonitions, resisting the call to return to His prescribed way, until His Spirit was wholly withdrawn from their midst.

In agreement with the author's interpretation of this verse in Isaiah, Bible commentator and clergyman William Lowth states the following:

> "The Words might better have been rendered, Why hast thou suffered [permitted] us to err from thy ways? for **the Form called Hiphil in Hebrew often denotes only Permission,** and is rendered elsewhere to that Sense by our translators." (William Lowth, *A Commentary Upon the Prophet Isaiah,* pg. 501, published in 1714)

Revisiting our initial inquiry into the matter of Pharaoh's heart, it is reasonable to assume that the very same principle is being invoked in this instance. Furthermore, when we consider the broader context of the Exodus narrative, we uncover corroborative evidence that effectively dispels any lingering obscurity or doubt surrounding this subject:

> "And **Pharaoh hardened his heart** at this time also, neither would he let the people go." (Exodus 8:32)

> "And when Pharaoh saw that the rain and the hail and the thunders were ceased, **he sinned yet more, and hardened his heart,** he and his servants." (Exodus 9:34)

It becomes apparent that Pharaoh, through his relentless commitment to sin, consciously fortified his heart in opposition to divine influence. Upon a thorough examination of the book of Exodus, it may be seen that God exerted profound and extraordinary effort in His attempts to reach Pharaoh, employing an unwavering commitment to appeal to his innermost sentiments and redirect him from the morally depraved and destructive course he tread. To then propose that God purposefully contributed to the hardening of Pharaoh's heart, thereby opposing His own divine effort, constitutes a significant departure from the intrinsic context of the biblical text. In such a scenario, God would be working contrary to His own intentions. In a comprehensive interpretation, it may be ascertained that when it is stated that God hardened Pharaoh's heart, what transpired was, in fact, that God, in response to the continuous rejection of divine guidance and entreaty by the Egyptian monarch, simply permitted him to persist in his transgression, culminating in the progressive hardening of Pharaoh's heart. God offered Pharaoh mercy, which when rejected, hardened Pharaoh's heart.

> "**All those who have read the Scriptures with care and attention, know well that God is frequently represented in them as doing what he only permits to be done. So because a man has grieved his Spirit and resisted his grace he withdraws that Spirit and grace from him, and thus he becomes bold and presumptuous in sin.** Pharaoh made his own heart stubborn against God, Exodus 9:34; and God gave him up to judicial blindness, so that he rushed on stubbornly to his own destruction." (Adam Clarke, *Commentary on the Whole Bible,* Exodus 4:21)

> "When God is said to harden men's hearts,-to deliver them up to a reprobate mind,-to send them strong delusions, that they should believe that God is acting unrighteously — **meaning He is acting against His character** — it is infinitely far from being meant of an efficacious impulse in God Almighty. **That all those verbs,-to harden, to blind, to deliver up, to send delusions, to deceive, and the like,-are by an ordinary Hebraism only permissive in signification, though active in sound, is placed without all controversy.**" (Thomas Pierce, I, pg. 23-24 edition of 1658 as quoted in Jackson, *The Providence of God,* pg. 401)

It is worth emphasizing that, throughout His life and ministry, Jesus never attempted to induce hardness of heart in His audience. To the contrary, His steadfast efforts were characterized by earnest and tender supplications, even in the face of the people's profound moral waywardness. So it is now; Christ stands at the threshold of our hearts, not with any nefarious intent to induce rigidity, but rather so that our hearts may become softened by His loving entreaty and we may submit to His transformative influence in our own lives.

> "**Behold, I stand at the door [of the heart], and knock:** if any man hear my voice, and open the door, I will come in to him, and will sup with him, and he with me." (Revelation 3:20)

By Christ's example, we can establish with certainty that the Father consistently endeavors to tenderize the hearts of His adherents. This pursuit is aimed at facilitating His divine presence among them and effecting the rejuvenation of their spiritual vitality. To postulate that God actively seeks to harden individuals' hearts, including notable instances like that of Pharaoh, stands in stark contradiction to His true character as manifest in Christ.

David Provoked to Number Israel

"And again ***the anger of the LORD was kindled against Israel, and he moved David against them to say, Go, number Israel*** *and Judah." (2 Samuel 24:1)*

Another instance of scripture which warrants our consideration is when David was moved, or persuaded, to number Israel. In the ancient world, rulers would take a census either to levy taxes or to draft an army, and the counting of men "that drew the sword" (2 Samuel 24:9) indicates that David, in this particular context, had the latter purpose as his aim. Joab warned David that to perform the census would be to transgress his trust in the Lord, most likely because it reflected a reliance upon human strength in the form of a large standing army. Joab aptly reminded David that they need not rely on the strength of mere mortals, but rather on God alone, and to do otherwise would be to cause all of Israel to sin:

> "And Joab answered, **The LORD make his people an hundred times so many more as they be:** but, my lord the king, are they not all my lord's servants? **why then doth my lord require this thing? why will he be a cause of trespass to Israel?** Nevertheless the king's word prevailed against Joab. Wherefore Joab departed, and went throughout all Israel, and came to Jerusalem." (I Chronicles 21:3-4)

Nonetheless, David had adopted a lack of faith in God's capacity to safeguard His people, leading him to be concerned about the nation's military strength, ultimately prompting him to conduct a census. Upon its conclusion, David came to comprehend the true implication of his actions:

> "**And David's heart smote him after that he had numbered the people. And David said unto the LORD, I have sinned greatly in that I have done:** and now, I beseech thee, O LORD, take away

> the iniquity of thy servant; for **I have done very foolishly.**" (2 Samuel 24:10)

At this juncture, many find themselves compelled to pause and reflect, considering that it was, after all, God Himself who had moved David to conduct a census of Israel, as suggested in 2 Samuel 24:1. But wouldn't this mean that God tempted David to commit sin? The narrative makes it appear as if God, driven by His anger with Israel, coerced David to do that which would be intolerable in His sight, with the ultimate aim of exacting punishment upon the entirety of Israel for the very act which He Himself seemingly enticed David to perform. This would imply that God deliberately engineered David's situation to affect the punitive outcome which He desired to manifest. Such an interpretation wholly disregards the biblical understanding of God's anger that the author outlined in chapter 8. Furthermore, it not only ascribes to Him the attributes of vengeance and malice, but even ventures to insinuate His direct involvement in temptation and sin. The idea that God is in any way implicated in the act of temptation may be sufficiently refuted by the words of James:

> "Let no man say when he is tempted, I am tempted of God: for **God cannot be tempted with evil, neither tempteth he any man...**" (James 1:13)

But this isn't our only clue in this instance. The verse in question—notably, 2 Samuel 24:1—specifically makes mention of how God's "anger" was "kindled against Israel" (2 Samuel 24:1). In light of the profound distinction between divine anger and its human counterpart, it is discernible that, within this particular context, God experienced a sense of deep lamentation in response to the errant trajectory of Israel. Consequently, He ceased in extending His heartfelt supplications aimed at rectifying their course, given that their unyielding stubbornness served as a clear evidence of their disdain for His counsel. In the action of His anger (grief) God elected to withdraw from the Israelites, thus affording them the autonomy to act in accordance with their own inclinations and sinful affections—David included. It necessarily follows that God was unable to preempt David's exercise of free will in guiding the direction of Israel, nor could He perpetually safeguard him from the allurements presented by the adversary. Commenting on this verse, the *Seventh-Day Adventist Bible Commentary* supplies the following remark:

> "In the verse under consideration we have another instance in which **God is said to do that which He does not prevent.**" (*Seventh-Day Adventist Bible Commentary*, vol. 2, pg. 710; on 2 Samuel 24:1)

The Spirit of God, persistently resisted by the Israelites, no longer intervened to restrain the infernal forces from their decided prey. As a result, the people became more susceptible to temptation. In the absence of the prudence imparted by the Spirit's guidance, the sinful passions of the Israelites became increasingly amplified, leading to a more fervent pursuit of worldly dominion through unrestrained ravenous ambition. Unsheltered by divine grace, David and the people succumbed to the subtle and deceptive provocations of the adversary.

This interpretation finds ample support in the comprehensive exposition of the same narrative, as expounded further within the pages of 1 Chronicles:

> "And **Satan stood up against Israel, and provoked David to number Israel.** And David said to Joab and to the rulers of the people, Go, number Israel from Beersheba even to Dan; and bring the number of them to me, that I may know it." (1 Chronicles 21:1-2)

Though the passage in 2 Samuel attributes the prompting of David to number Israel to God, the parallel account in 1 Chronicles reveals that it was, in fact, Satan who enticed David to conduct the census. The case which we have been outlining thus far serves to reconcile this apparent discrepancy. In light of this broader context, we can infer that it was not a direct provocation by God that led David to sin in the act of numbering Israel; rather, He merely did not act to prevent David from pursuing his own personal inclinations. Due to God's allowance of this event, it was attributed to His direct agency, in accordance with the convention of a common Hebraic linguistic expression. As God's protective presence was withdrawn, David became increasingly vulnerable to temptation, enabling Satan to have the monarch's ear and urge him forward along this sinful path. This vulnerability led David down a treacherous road, as he fell into the snare set by his own wicked desires and the persuasive whispers of the adversary.

Within the context of our central thesis for this chapter, it becomes prudent for the reader to attribute the character of Christ to the actions of the Father across the various scenarios presented in the Old Testament if His true disposition is to be properly discerned among these difficult passages. In this particular instance, owing to our comprehension of Christ's teachings and actions, it becomes evident that the prevailing interpretation of 2 Samuel 24:1 requires reassessment. Christ, in the course of His earthly ministry, did not seek to entice individuals into temptation under any circumstance; rather, His mission was directed towards the liberation of humanity from such seductions. Therefore, it is reasonable to deduce that, as evidenced by the conduct of Christ, the same principle applies to the Father as well: He would never prompt any individual, including King David, to purposefully transgress His divine will. Our God leads us *away* from temptation, not into it. To suggest otherwise would be to imply a cooperation between the Christian God and the devil; a collaboration between all that is good and all that is bad.

The Death of King Saul

*"**So Saul died for his transgression which he committed against the LORD,** even against the word of the LORD, which he kept not, and also for asking counsel of one that had a familiar spirit, to enquire of it; And enquired not of the LORD: **therefore he [the LORD] slew him, and turned the kingdom unto David the son of Jesse.**" (I Chronicles 10:13-14)*

Following a brief analysis of the death of King Saul, proponents advocating for a punitive interpretation of divine justice discover cause for celebration. They perceive this particular instance of scripture as an affirmation of their theological stance. After all, here it is explicitly mentioned that Saul was slain of God as a consequence of his transgression, and the kingdom was subsequently given over to David.

Nonetheless, this analysis is susceptible to criticism, as it neglects to acknowledge the enduring literary principles which we have consistently employed in similar circumstances of the Bible. It also disregards the broader contextual nuances of the account as a whole. As a result, God becomes venerated as a Being who kills the disobedient—as if this were cause for celebration and rejoicing. In such an interpretation, the loving character of Christ remains elusive within the framework of the Father's representation, and establishing harmony between the two becomes a most difficult initiative. The author is deeply troubled by the premature exultation of religionists who, in their misguided interpretation, depict God as a murderous despot. Overzealous and unaware, they perceive their argument as robust and unassailable—yet it is feeble, devoid of substance, and readily susceptible to refutation.

As this volume has previously outlined, God does not kill for any reason or under any circumstance. Our heavenly Father is the perfect embodiment of selfless love and nonviolence. In order to invalidate the prevailing interpretation of this particular verse, one need only to possess a discerning knowledge of Christ's nonviolent nature and undertake a concise analysis of the broader contextual framework of this account. For in the very same chapter, we read:

> "Then said Saul to his armourbearer, Draw thy sword, and thrust me through therewith; lest these uncircumcised come and abuse me. But his armourbearer would not; for he was sore afraid. **So Saul took a sword, and fell upon it.**" (I Chronicles 10:4)

And earlier, within the pages of 1 Samuel, we find an identical record of this event:

> "Then said Saul unto his armourbearer, Draw thy sword, and thrust me through therewith; lest these uncircumcised come and thrust me through, and abuse me. But his armourbearer would not; for he was sore afraid. **Therefore Saul took a sword, and fell upon it.**" (I Samuel 31:4)

Evidently, the Bible supplies its own counterpoints to those who might find opportunity to slander and defame the beneficent character of the Almighty. In this particular case, it is readily apparent that when God permitted Saul to take his own life in a moment of despair, this was ascribed to His own divine intervention by an ordinary Hebraism. Through his transgression, Saul inevitably incurred the innate consequences of his own wayward conduct. In order to circumvent the deadly harm from those who found reason to "thrust" him "through, and abuse" him (1 Samuel 31:4)—implying their desire to torture the wicked ruler, thus prolonging his death—he endeavored to swiftly complete the task himself with the sword. The narrative does not provide any indication that Saul encountered the formidable retribution of God. In this instance, as in every other, God's nonviolent disposition is upheld—and it is *this* fact that is cause for celebration and rejoicing.

The Tribulations of Job and Fire from Heaven

"Then Satan answered the LORD, and said, Doth Job fear God for nought? ***Hast not thou made an hedge about him, and about his house, and about all that he hath on every side?*** *thou hast blessed the work of his hands, and his substance is increased in the land.* ***But put forth thine hand now, and touch all that he hath, and he will curse thee to thy face.****" (Job 1:9-11)*

Within the narrative of Job, several elements merit contemplation. Observe closely that in this context, Satan accuses God of erecting a protective barrier, or "an hedge [of protection]" (Job 1:10), around His faithful servant, Job. Satan contends that if God were to simply remove this sheltering influence and unleash the destruction that for so long has been restrained, Job would afterward openly renounce Him.

This particular instance serves as an exemplification of the principle which we have previously considered, namely that God extends special protection to those individuals who harbor genuine love and unwavering trust in Him. His presence is a safeguard against the destructive forces of the devil. To deliberately call for the relinquishment of His safeguarding proximity is to beckon disorder and devastation.

Another principle which we have previously examined, and continue to explore in the current chapter, is expressed in verse 11. Notice how Satan directs God to "put forth" His "hand" and "touch all that he [Job] hath" (Job 1:11), as if to insinuate that God was the agent behind the onset of Job's forthcoming calamity. Upon reading the next verse, it becomes evident that this constitutes yet another instance wherein God is ascribed actions that, in reality, merely fall under His permissive will.

> "**And the LORD said unto Satan, Behold, all that he hath is in thy power;** only upon himself put not forth thine hand. So Satan went forth from the presence of the LORD." (Job 1:12)

Considering this broader contextual framework, it emerges unmistakably that the power of desolation lies with the adversary, as all of Job's possessions were surrendered into Satan's control. The reader is encouraged to pay particular attention to this observation as we proceed in our brief examination of the narrative of Job.

> "While he was yet speaking, there came also another, and said, **The fire of God is fallen from heaven, and hath burned up the sheep, and the servants, and consumed them;** and I only am escaped alone to tell thee." (Job 1:16)

In this circumstance, Job's attendants are conveying the extent of the destruction that has begun. Observe the peculiar perspective of Job's servant as he ascribes this sudden calamity to the immediate agency of God. The servant fervently declares that God Himself has dispatched fire from the heavens, resulting in the incineration and demise of all of Job's sheep and laborers. It is lamentable to witness the persistent adherence by many present-day Christians to this severe and lethal interpretation of God as articulated by Job's servant. We should possess a more transcendent and benign understanding, as the pages of inspiration have recently informed us in verse 12 of this very chapter, clarifying that *all* of this devastation is attributable to the influence of Satan. To Job's servant, it simply *appeared* as though this was God's celestial reckoning—a perspective influenced by the prevailing cultural beliefs of that age. In the Old Testament era, many regarded God as a deity characterized by wrath and retribution. Therefore, it is unsurprising that Job's servant attributed these catastrophes directly to the divine agency of Jehovah.

"But," says one, "I supposed that God was the harbinger of fire. After all, aren't there many instances of scripture that demonstrate His role as a purveyor of devastation and judgment?—Notably, by fire and brimstone?" And while there are many texts of scripture which make it *appear* as if God rains down fire from heaven—such as this particular instance in Job, the narrative of Elijah, and most famously, the destruction of Sodom and Gomorrah—it is prudent to bear in mind the central thesis of this section: God does not, under any circumstance or at any time, directly instigate death or destruction. Rather, these adversities are often incorrectly ascribed to His active intervention, when in reality, they are merely permissive in signification. This is a peculiarity of the Hebrew language, which does not always distinguish between permission and commandment. Often the scripture attributes to God what He only permits to be done; or what in the course of His Providence He does not powerfully obstruct. To instead promulgate the assertion that He actively precipitates death, wreckage, and ruin is to inadvertently bolster the devil's machinations aimed at subverting God's benevolent and nonviolent nature as it is exemplified in the person of Christ.

Christ never once invoked fire from heaven, nor did He harbor any intention to ever harm a single soul—even those guilty of the gravest sins. Instead, His mission was one that endeavored to heal and restore the hearts and minds of all whom He could influence. In fact, Christ openly issued a stern rebuke to His disciples, James and John, who harbored the same fiery and retributive misconceptions about the nature of the Father as did the servant of Job. So misguided were they in their cognition of Him, that they even sought to summon fire from heaven to consume the Samaritans, unaware of whose power they were really soliciting.

> "And it came to pass, when the time was come that he [Jesus] should be received up, he stedfastly set his face to go to Jerusalem, And sent messengers before his face: and they went, and entered into a village of the Samaritans, to make ready for him. And they [the Samaritans] did not receive him, because his face was as

> though he would go to Jerusalem. **And when his disciples James and John saw this, they said, Lord, wilt thou that we command fire to come down from heaven, and consume them, even as Elias did? But he turned, and rebuked them, and said, Ye know not what manner of spirit ye are of. For the Son of man is not come to destroy men's lives, but to save them.** And they went to another village." (Luke 9:51-56)

Does this passage indicate a disparity between the attributes of the Father and the Son? On the one hand, it appears that the Father employs the element of fire as a means to afflict and bring destruction upon numerous peoples in the Old Testament. Conversely, Christ condemns the use of such searing and devastating force. Heretofore, numerous individuals have viewed God as the dispenser of fire from heaven. Nonetheless, here, Christ repudiates such a notion. Instead, He highlights that to nurture this misconception of the Father is to foster the same malevolent disposition as the devil. To actively wish death and destruction upon those who offend you, and to hold the belief that God endorses such an endeavor and even goes so far as to actively contribute to its fulfillment, is to align oneself with the spirit of antichrist, for "Ye know not what manner of [wicked] spirit ye are of. For the Son of man is not come to destroy men's lives, but to save them." (Luke 9:55-56).

In *all* situations, Christ consistently manifested love and compassion towards those in His proximity, even extending these virtues to individuals who openly declared themselves to be His enemies. Therefore, we may have confidence that the Father does the very same. By failing to align one's own character with Christ's embodiment of love and nonviolence, and instead striving to bring about devastation upon those whom one deems irredeemable and undeserving of God's mercy, constitutes actions contrary to Christ's teachings—it is to act *anti* to *Christ*; it is to transgress God's very character; it is to actively work against the fulfillment of His objective for humanity. It is impossible to stand in allegiance with Christ while simultaneously pursuing the harm of others. And one cannot hope to gain an authentic comprehension of the Father if the veracity of His loving and nonviolent nature remains undiscerned.

God, as elucidated by Christ's example, cannot be the source of retributive fire from heaven. He eschews any involvement in actions which would result in excruciating degrees of torment. To raise this proposition would suggest that God resorts to severe modes of anguish against those who reject Him; base and vulgar methods of torture that not even worldly governments are willing to employ. As evidenced in the account of Job which we have considered, it is Satan who wields the power of fire to incite catastrophe and demise. And he will persist in employing this deception, skillfully creating the illusion that it is God who is the source of these lethal burnings, extending this narrative down even until the culmination of history. At that point, he will summon fire from heaven—as he has done throughout the course of scriptural history—in order to compel the adoration of all those who remain susceptible to his guile through their ignorance of the true disposition of the Father.

> "**And he [the beast/Satan] doeth great wonders, so that he maketh fire come down from heaven on the earth in the sight of men, And deceiveth them that dwell on the earth** by the means of those miracles which he had power to do in the sight of the beast…" (Revelation 13:13-14)

The miracle separated from the motive of love reveals its maker. Satan always has his miracles, but they have no love in them, and so no spiritual power for good. He is to work in the last days with "all power and signs and lying wonders, and with all deceivableness of unrighteousness in them that perish" (2 Thessalonians 2:9-10). When he works thus, Jesus Himself calls him a false christ, with power to deceive all but the very elect. Why has Satan no power to deceive the elect?—Because they are kept by the power of God through faith unto salvation; because they have learned that God is love, and that a miracle, to be any evidence of the divine mission and divine power of the worker, must be such a miracle as manifests only love's power. Such were the miracles of Jesus. Every one was wrought for love's sake; not to exhibit mere physical power, not to gain popularity or fame, but rather to reveal to the world the power of the divine love, which is the only power that can heal the soul as well as the body, and unite it to Him. It is only by love that love can be awakened, and Christ's miracles sought to demonstrate the love which God holds for His children, thereby awakening love within them. On the other hand, in Satan's deceptive wonders, love will not be present—and instead of being provoked to gratitude and adoration, many will be provoked to fear. In their misunderstanding, they will believe these demonstrations of power and force to come from the Lord and will consequently bow down to worship. Just as in the days of Elijah, fire from heaven will be employed by the adversary to coerce the conscience and awaken the unwavering devotion of men.

> "And he sent again a captain of the third fifty with his fifty. **And the third captain of fifty went up, and came and fell on his knees before Elijah, and besought him,** and said unto him, O man of God, I pray thee, let my life, and the life of these fifty thy servants, be precious in thy sight. **Behold, there came fire down from heaven, and burnt up the two captains of the former fifties with their fifties: therefore let my life now be precious in thy sight.**" (2 Kings 1:13-14)

Through the establishment of this connection to the narrative of Elijah, do we in any way detract from the integrity of the Lord's prophet? Does the author insinuate an affiliation between Elijah and the devil? Most assuredly not, for such a proposition would be fundamentally flawed. It is imperative, though, to briefly harmonize Elijah's testimony with the content covered in this section thus far. This endeavor will challenge the reservations that many individuals often harbor when confronted with the prospect of relinquishing the belief in God burning men alive.

In the context of 2 Kings 1:13-14, we witness Elijah's invocation of fire as a punitive response directed towards those individuals who persisted in their idolatrous practices, despite the prophet's impassioned admonitions. Upon the violent conflagration of two entire regiments of men, a third appears. The "captain of the third fifty" (2 Kings 1:13) approaches Elijah in a state of extreme trepidation. He had just beheld, alongside Elijah himself, the manifestation of what *appeared* to be an act of divine judgement upon the iniquitous and idolatrous forces aligned with King Ahaziah who were attempting to capture the Lord's prophet. Owing to the captain's constrained comprehension of the unfolding events, and motivated by profound fear, he earnestly implores both God and Elijah for clemency, seeking to avert their wrath. Only for the purpose of preserving his life and the lives of his comrades did he seek mercy. His request was not rooted in a sincere conviction of the wrongdoing committed by him and the rest of King Ahaziah's adherents; rather, it stemmed solely from his apprehension of imminent destruction, prompting him to an outward display of repentance. In a deliberate effort to evade the impending ordeal, he assumed a posture of supplication.

However, in the midst of the wealth of evidence elucidating God's benevolent and nonviolent nature within the context of this volume, are we to postulate an exception in this instance? Does God, in this case, choose to employ deadly force as a means to compel the captain and his fifty to a change of heart? The answer appears unequivocally negative, considering the well-established essence of His character. The utilization of coercive power contradicts the very methodologies attributed to God. Neither does He seek to instill fear in an attempt to solicit love, as the two can only ever remain in direct opposition to one another.

> "**There is no fear in love;** but **perfect love casteth out fear:** because **fear hath torment.** He that feareth is not made perfect in love." (I John 4:18)

The act of inducing fear in individuals only serves to fortify their proclivity for rebellion. While some may temporarily express love or admiration, as observed in this soldier's case, it primarily stems from the dread of anticipated consequences. Such displays of reverence prove to be superficial and insincere, invariably giving rise to a resurgence of rebellion, often marked by heightened defiance.

The captain's actions in this instance were solely a response to the imminent threat of death. Judging from the context, his repentance lacks authenticity, appearing rather coerced by the looming prospect of being consumed by flames which, in the eyes of both him and Elijah, seem to emanate from the throne of heaven just as in the account of Job which we have already considered.

Yet, there arises the contention: "Is it not verifiable that Elijah held the esteemed mantle of a prophet of the Lord? Moreover, did not Elijah, himself, beseech the celestial fire to descend and consume these individuals? Hence, it stands to reason that this occurrence must have been in accordance with the divine will of the Lord." Certainly, it remains an undeniable fact that Elijah, anointed as a prophet of the Lord, invoked fire from heaven to consume these men. Nevertheless, following our succinct exploration of the surrounding circumstances, it becomes imperative to pose the pivotal inquiry: did Elijah's actions truly reflect the character of God's kingdom? To address this, we must examine a particularly intriguing aspect of the life of John the Baptist, who emerged in the same power and spirit of Elijah:

> "**Now when John had heard in the prison the works of Christ, he sent two of his disciples,** And said unto him, **Art thou he that should come, or do we look for another?**" (Matthew 11:2-3)

In this context, it appears that John, during his time in prison, may have begun to cultivate skepticism about the true nature of Christ's mission—even raising doubts regarding His status as the Messiah. It is worth noting that prior to dispatching two of his own disciples, John the Baptist had already received reports of the miraculous works attributed to Christ. Subsequently sending his followers to question Christ can be attributed to a perceived misalignment between Christ's actions and John's expectations for the Messianic figure. But how is it that John, the greatest of the prophets, had a crisis of faith?

> "**Like the Saviour's disciples, John the Baptist did not understand the nature of Christ's kingdom. He expected Jesus to take the throne of David; and as time passed, and the Saviour made no claim to kingly authority, John became perplexed and troubled.** He had declared to the people that in order for the way to be prepared before the Lord, the prophecy of Isaiah must be fulfilled; the mountains and hills must be brought low, the crooked made straight, and the rough places plain. He had looked for the high places of human pride and power to be cast down. He had pointed to the Messiah as the One whose fan was in His hand, and who would thoroughly purge His floor, who would gather the wheat into His garner, and burn up the chaff with unquenchable fire. **Like the prophet Elijah, in whose spirit and power he had come to Israel, he looked for the Lord to reveal Himself as a God that answereth by fire.**" (Ellen G. White, *The Desire of Ages,* pg. 215)

Neither John the Baptist, the disciples of Christ, nor Elijah understood the nature of God's kingdom. They imagined a deity destined for conquest through force and supremacy; a Messianic figure who would appear in the guise of a military leader; a celestial kingdom characterized by imperial dominion. At the outset, their capacity to perceive the true essence of the Father's disposition eluded them—their understanding was enshrouded by the lies and manipulations of the adversary. *But this would change...*

> "**To John was opened the same truth that had come to Elijah in the desert,** when 'a great and strong wind rent the mountains, and brake in pieces the rocks before the Lord; but the Lord was not in the wind: and after the wind an earthquake; but the Lord was not in the earthquake: **and after the earthquake a fire; but the Lord was not in the fire:**' and after the fire, God spoke to the prophet

by 'a still small voice.' I Kings 19:11, 12. **So Jesus was to do His work, not with the clash of arms and the overturning of thrones and kingdoms, but through speaking to the hearts of men by a life of mercy and self-sacrifice.**" (Ellen G. White, *The Desire of Ages*, pg. 217)

Christ Himself made it clear that Elijah, too, misunderstood the true nature of the kingdom of God. In contemplating the ninth chapter of Luke, we discern Christ's subtle allusion to the prophet's misrepresentation of the divine methodology, particularly in the instance where fire from heaven was invoked to consume King Ahaziah's soldiers:

"And when his disciples James and John saw this, they said, **Lord, wilt thou that we command fire to come down from heaven, and consume them, even as Elias did? But he turned, and rebuked them, and said, Ye know not what manner of spirit ye are of. For the Son of man is not come to destroy men's lives, but to save them.** And they went to another village." (Luke 9:54-56)

These words illuminate the core of Christ's mission and character, depicting Him not as a harbinger of destruction but as a harbinger of salvation. At the same time, it may be inferred that Christ issued a rebuke which was not only directed at his disciples but also aimed at the actions of the prophet Elijah. A mere superficial analysis of Elijah's confrontation with the captains of fifty will invariably prompt individuals to conceive of a contrast between the Father and Son: Christ's earthly mission aimed at preserving lives, while the God depicted in the Old Testament seemed predisposed to take life, even resorting to the use of fire to destroy those who defied divine authority. However, we must acknowledge that such an interpretation is implausible, for the character of the Godhead must remain consistent and free from any incongruity. To suggest otherwise would imply the presence of a fundamental contradiction between Christ and the Father, suggesting disparate divine intentions toward humanity.

By subscribing to Elijah's initial portrayal of God—one characterized by fire and fury—we inadvertently yield to misapprehension and folly. Christ's rebuke, then, assumes broader significance, extending its relevance to *all* individuals who harbor analogous misconceptions concerning the nature of the Father. As inspiration unequivocally declares, it is not by might nor by power that God's kingdom advances, but rather by the gentle movements of the Spirit upon the hearts of God's children:

> "...This is the word of the LORD unto Zerubbabel, saying, **Not by might, nor by power, but by my spirit,** saith the LORD of hosts." (Zechariah 4:6)

> "And he [God] said, Go forth, and stand upon the mount before the LORD. And, behold, the LORD passed by, and a great and strong wind rent the mountains, and brake in pieces the rocks before the LORD; but the LORD was not in the wind: and after the wind an earthquake; but the LORD was not in the earthquake: **And after the earthquake a fire;** but **the LORD was not in the fire: and after the fire a still small voice.**" (I Kings 19:11-12)

Though initially confounded, the essence of God's kingdom was at last comprehended by Elijah, John, and the disciples—yet it still eludes many today. Neither might nor power are employed to subdue the conscience. Fear, likewise, is incapable of being a mechanism to kindle love, nor can it ever fulfill such a role. While Elijah's intentions were to honor the true God, his methods were fraught with theological and ethical missteps. Similar to John the Baptist, Elijah experienced a crisis of faith because he did not possess a complete understanding of the authentic nature of God at the time of his encounter with the soldiers of King Ahaziah.

Through His revelation to Elijah atop Mount Horeb, God endeavored to communicate a profound truth to His prophet: He does not resort to the utilization of powerful elements like strong winds, earthquakes, or fire as instruments to compel obedience from humankind. Force does not find a place within the repertoire of our Lord. Rather, it is His "still small voice" (1 Kings 19:12) that works in the hearts of men to turn them towards the paths of righteousness.

In the particular case of Elijah's confrontation with the captains and their fifties, a fundamental contradiction emerges if one maintains the conviction that it was indeed God who was accountable for the fire summoned by Elijah. It seems incongruous for God to say He is "not in the fire" (1 Kings 19:12), only to then subsequently employ that very element to violently consume entire armies of men. And while it is true that God dispatched fire to consume the sacrifice upon the altar in the presence of the prophets of Baal atop Mount Carmel, it's crucial to note that this fire was not deployed with the intent of taking human life; on the contrary, its purpose was to save them. Neither did the fire consume and destroy the burning bush upon which Moses was fixated. However, when Elijah invoked fire from heaven to consume Ahaziah's men, he had already been shown that God's power was not manifest in a fire intended for the purposes of death and devastation. The slavish submission of the third captain, as previously considered, failed to correspond with the nature of submission sought by God—one achieved by love and truth rather than by fear and coercion. This observation alone is sufficient evidence to suggest that the fire summoned by Elijah in this particular context did not originate from God.

> "The disciples knew that it was the purpose of Christ to bless the Samaritans by His presence; and the coldness, jealousy, and disrespect shown to their Master filled them with surprise and indignation. James and John especially were aroused. **That He whom they so highly reverenced should be thus treated, seemed to them a wrong too great to be passed over without immediate punishment. In their zeal they said, 'Lord, wilt Thou that we command fire to come down from heaven, and consume them, even as Elias did?' referring to the destruction of the Samaritan captains and their companies sent out to take the prophet Elijah. They were surprised to see that Jesus was pained by their words, and still more surprised as His rebuke fell upon their ears:** 'Ye

know not what manner of spirit ye are of. For the Son of man is not come to destroy men's lives, but to save them.' Luke 9:54-56.

"**It is no part of Christ's mission to compel men to receive Him. It is Satan, and men actuated by his spirit, who seek to compel the conscience. Under a pretense of zeal for righteousness, men who are confederated with evil angels sometimes bring suffering upon their fellow men in order to convert them to their ideas of religion; but Christ is ever showing mercy, ever seeking to win by the revealing of His love.** He can admit no rival in the soul, nor accept of partial service; but **He desires only voluntary service, the willing surrender of the heart under the constraint of love.**" (Ellen G. White, *The Acts of the Apostles*, pg. 540-541)

How then, do we account for what happened? Upon consideration of the broader context, it becomes clear. The captains and their fifties were under the authority of the King of Israel who had sent for help from Baalzebub, the god of Ekron.

"And Ahaziah fell down through a lattice in his upper chamber that was in Samaria, and was sick: and he sent messengers, and said unto them, **Go, enquire of Baalzebub the god of Ekron whether I shall recover of this disease.**" (2 Kings 1:2)

The god of Ekron was a pagan deity—a counterfeit inspired by Satan. In seeking aid from this god, the King was exposing himself to the dominion of the adversary.

"Know ye not, that **to whom ye yield yourselves servants to obey, his servants ye are to whom ye obey;** whether of sin unto death, or of obedience unto righteousness?" (Romans 6:16)

As these individuals served the King of Israel, who had chosen to align himself with Baalzebub, the deity of Ekron, they found themselves without divine protection from the destroyer. They had forsaken the shielding presence of Jehovah and instead sought refuge in mere idols crafted by human hands. This is further evidenced in the third and fourth verses of the second book of Kings:

> "**...Is it not because there is not a God in Israel, that ye go to enquire of Baalzebub the god of Ekron?** Now therefore thus saith the LORD, Thou shalt not come down from that bed on which thou art gone up, but shalt surely die." (2 Kings 1:3-4)

Here we may infer that the presence of the Lord was not among those in allegiance with King Ahaziah. Because they had become steeped in idolatry and gone after other gods, the Father's protective agency was withdrawn. As a result, the Lord endeavored to warn the King through the mouth of Elijah that by his persistence in sin, death would become his inevitable portion—God could not shelter him from the dastardly whims of the adversary. The same was true for the captains and their fifties who found themselves in strict obeisance to the King. Thus, Satan had unobstructed access to these men.

As the adversary exerted his dominion over these individuals, he endeavored to orchestrate their demise in a manner that would insinuate divine culpability. Just as in the instance of Job, he sought to provoke a scenario where fire from heaven would be exercised, thereby perpetuating a deception that would reverberate through the chronicles of history. This action would contribute to establishing the groundwork for his ultimate deceit, as delineated in the book of Revelation:

> "**And he [the beast/Satan] doeth great wonders, so that he maketh fire come down from heaven on the earth in the sight of men, And deceiveth them that dwell on the earth by the means of those miracles** which he had power to do in the sight of the beast..." (Revelation 13:13-14)

Satan would endeavor to cultivate the notion that it was God who was accountable for the many instances of the fatal blaze; that His power was used to incite death and destruction instead of healing and restoration. And under what circumstances could such a strategy find more apt application than when a prophet of the Lord might inadvertently become an unwitting accomplice?

Certainly, the arch-deceiver would unquestionably derive considerable satisfaction from such a fortuitous opportunity.

In this particular instance, Elijah found himself unintentionally harnessing the influence of Satan, primarily owing to his misinterpretation of the character of God and the essence of His kingdom. The disciples, too, were fostering a similar devilish disposition when they sought to call forth fire from the heavens to consume the Samaritans. Is it surprising, then, that Christ admonished their ambition? It is Satan that bears the responsibility for the fire that engulfed the captains and their men, much like his involvement in every other occurrence where fire is employed to instigate death and devastation. It comes as no astonishment, therefore, that Satan is frequently referred to as the dragon in numerous instances throughout scripture—a creature often associated with the ability to emit destructive flames.

> "**And the great dragon was cast out, that old serpent, called the Devil, and Satan,** which deceiveth the whole world..." (Revelation 12:9)

For a deeper understanding of what has been considered thus far in the current subsection, the author recommends the illuminating work by Adrian Ebens titled, *Agape; A Revelation of the Father's Character of Love*. Specifically chapter 6, which expounds upon the notion that God is not accountable for the catastrophic and lethal events entailing the invocation of celestial fire.

In summary, we have now outlined the accurate sequence of events in the narratives of Job and Elijah, specifically that God bore no responsibility in either instance for the outbreak of celestial fire that prompted death and devastation. Our assertion aligns with His well-established attributes of love and nonviolence and serves to reconcile these biblical stories with the character that Christ demonstrated in His life and ministry.

But what about Sodom and Gomorrah? Owing to the spatial constraints that confine us from conducting an exhaustive analysis of the destruction of these cities of the plain, we shall, therefore, offer only a brief overview of this matter.

> "Then the LORD rained upon Sodom and upon Gomorrah **brimstone and fire from the LORD out of heaven...**" (Genesis 19:24)

In light of our recognition that God does not employ celestial fire for the purposes of devastation, one might contemplate whether the account of Sodom and Gomorrah presents yet another instance in which an action has been erroneously ascribed to God, when it could be more accurately regarded as a consequence of His permissive will. We see this evidenced in the words of Isaiah, where the prophet alludes to the fact that, by their own willful transgression, Sodom and Gomorrah had stored up the natural consequences of sin for themselves:

> "The shew of their countenance doth witness against them; and **they declare their sin as Sodom, they hide it not.** Woe unto their soul! for **they have rewarded evil unto themselves.**" (Isaiah 3:9)

The prolonged embrace of sin ultimately begets the intrinsic destruction that is inherent to its very nature.

In this context, if it can be posited that the Lord did not directly instigate the shower of fire and brimstone upon Sodom and Gomorrah, one must inquire about the alternative occurrences that took place.

One theory suggests that the calamity visited upon the cities of the plain was executed by Satan. As a consequence of the peoples' severe and enduring entrenchment in sin, God's presence was compelled to withdraw from Sodom and Gomorrah, thereby subjecting them to the desolation wrought by the adversary.

Another possibility, to which the author subscribes, is that nature itself may have helped inspire the story. The earth, due to the onset of sin, has become prone to adversity and woe. The imprints of sin have left a stain upon the elements of creation, rendering the entire planet susceptible to swift and absolute devastation, were it not for the sustaining benevolence of God's grace upholding its very foundations.

> "**For we know that [because of sin] the whole creation groaneth and travaileth in pain** together until now." (Romans 8:22)

Similar to the birth pangs experienced by a woman during labor as she progresses towards giving birth, the earth is experiencing contractions in the form of natural disasters and is poised to yield to the ultimate and impending consequences of sin.

> "You will hear of wars and rumors of wars. Make sure that you are not alarmed, for this must happen, but the end is still to come. For nation will rise up in arms against nation, and kingdom against kingdom. **And there will be famines and earthquakes in various places. All these things are the beginning of birth pains.**" (Matthew 24:6-8, *NET*)

This is the reason why the saints must inherit a new earth—one which has been restored to perfection by God at the conclusion of the millennium.

> "For, behold, **I create new heavens and a new earth...**" (Isaiah 65:17)

In both scenarios, the transgressions of the populace caused God's safeguarding proximity to be abrogated, thereby exposing the cities to potential disaster and ruin—either by the influence of Satan or through natural cataclysm. And in both cases, God stands vindicated, absolved of the destruction erroneously attributed to His divine intervention—and rightfully so! Owing to the veracity of His loving and nonviolent nature, God cannot be held accountable for the events which we have considered thus far. In each instance, if a cursory examination of the text leads to the interpretation that God is the agent of destruction, it necessitates a rigorous process of reinterpretation. We must contemplate the notion that a deeper, more nuanced understanding lies beneath the surface—because “God is love” (1 John 4:8) and He does not contradict Himself.

Noah's Flood and the Destruction of the Earth

The narrative of the flood is frequently cited as proof that God exercises His divine power and authority to bring about the punitive death of all who persist in sin. After all, the sixth chapter of Genesis clearly states:

> "And GOD saw that the wickedness of man was great in the earth, and that every imagination of the thoughts of his heart was only evil continually. And it repented the LORD that he had made man on the earth, and **it grieved him at his heart. And the LORD said, I will destroy man whom I have created from the face of the earth...**" (Genesis 6:5-7)

At this point, the reader ought to have acquired a discerning acumen for the interpretation of verses that seemingly imply—or even directly suggest—God's powerful intervention in scenarios which serve to contradict His well-established attributes of selfless love and nonviolence. In every instance, owing to the employment of an ordinary Hebraism, God is said to actively initiate those circumstances which He merely allows.

The arrival of the worldwide deluge cannot be attributed to God's supposed dissatisfaction or antipathy with the antediluvians, as so many boldly suggest; rather, it stemmed from mankind's unceasing and flagrant allegiance with sin, ultimately precipitating their own cataclysmic demise.

> "**Satan is the destroyer.** God cannot bless those who refuse to be faithful stewards. All He can do is to permit Satan to accomplish his destroying work. **We see calamities of every kind and in every degree coming upon the earth, and why? The Lord's restraining power is not exercised.** The world has disregarded the word of God. They live as though there were no God. **Like the inhabitants of the Noachic world, they refuse to have any thought of God. Wickedness prevails to an alarming extent, and the earth is ripe for the harvest [of Satan].**" (Ellen G. White, *Testimonies for the Church,* vol. 6, pg. 388)

We can see that God only *permitted* the flood when we look more closely at how the Bible describes the state of the world prior to that great calamity:

> "**The earth also was corrupt before God, and the earth was filled with violence.** And **God looked upon the earth, and, behold, it was corrupt;** for all flesh had corrupted his way upon the earth." (Genesis 6:11-12)

Observe that in verse 11, the entirety of the earth was saturated with the violence committed by mankind. Inspiration tells us that, in the days of Noah, "the wickedness of man was great in the earth, and that every imagination of the thoughts of his heart was only evil continually." (Genesis 6:5). Due to humanity's sinister influence, the earth stood on the precipice of devastation.

The Hebrew word used for "corrupt" in each of the aforementioned verses [Genesis 6:11-12] is שָׁחַת (šāḥaṯ)—which literally means "to bring to ruin; to decay; to corrupt; to mar, perish, spoil; *to destroy*" (Strong's H7843). Owing to the profligate nature of the antediluvians, the earth itself was becoming more violent—more susceptible to disaster. Notice how verses 11 and 12 are translated in the New English Translation:

> "**The earth was ruined in the sight of God; the earth was filled with violence. God saw the earth, and indeed it was ruined,** for all living creatures on the earth were sinful." (Genesis 6:11-12, *NET*)

Prior to the onset of the cascading deluge, the earth had already suffered significant ruin and degradation. As a result of the wretched influence of sin, the earth began to experience a gradual process of deterioration, inexorably advancing towards a state of complete destruction. It was not then permitted to be wholly destroyed, however, because of God's Spirit—His enduring and safeguarding presence which, for so long, had been "upholding all things by the word of his power" (Hebrews 1:3). However, in Genesis 6:3 He warned:

> "And the LORD said, **My spirit shall not always strive with man,** for that he also is flesh: yet **his days shall be an hundred and twenty years.**" (Genesis 6:3)

The Noachic world was exhibiting a growing detachment from the divine, and given God's commitment to preserving human free will, in His Providence, He foresaw that, at this pace, the earth would expel its inhabitants within 120 years. Their resistance to the divine safeguarding of the Almighty, leading to the withdrawal of His protective agency, initiated a process whereby the very foundations of the earth were beginning to disintegrate.[2]

> "**Then the earth shook and trembled;** the foundations of heaven moved and shook, **because he [God] was wroth [sorely grieved].**" (2 Samuel 22:8)

> "**And the channels of the sea appeared, the foundations of the world were discovered,** at the rebuking of the LORD, **at the blast of the breath of his nostrils [in grief].**" (2 Samuel 22:16)

The idea that the earth is directly impacted by humanity's sin is clearly delineated in the scriptures. After Adam and Eve

---

[2] Certainly, we do not introduce a novel idea when proposing that the natural world responds to its Creator. In fact, this idea is entirely and fundamentally biblical, for He upholds "all things by the word of his power" (Hebrews 1:3). Moreover, "by the word of the LORD were the heavens made; and all the host of them by the breath of his mouth" (Psalm 33:6). We have abundant evidence to suggest that the natural world bears witness to the sentiments of its Author. In the book of Mark, Christ compelled the wind and the sea to be still (Mark 4:39). And in the book of Luke, it is recorded that the rocks themselves would have cried out if the people had held their peace (Luke 19:40). Therefore, as the thoughts of the antediluvians were only evil continually, and the Spirit of the Lord was forced to be entirely withdrawn, the reader can only imagine the clamoring response which the natural world might've produced.

sinned, the ground became cursed and began to produce thorns and weeds:

> "And unto Adam he [God] said, Because thou hast hearkened unto the voice of thy wife, and hast eaten of the tree, of which I commanded thee, saying, Thou shalt not eat of it: **cursed is the ground for thy sake;** in sorrow shalt thou eat of it all the days of thy life; **Thorns also and thistles shall it bring forth to thee;** and thou shalt eat the herb of the field..." (Genesis 3:17-18)

The curse inflicted upon the elements of the earth was not an act of God, but rather an immediate consequence of sin. In this context, God is not arbitrarily placing a curse on the land; rather, He is merely articulating the natural outcome that would arise as a result of Adam and Eve's transgression. Notice what the prophet Isaiah writes about the affect sin has upon the earth:

> "**The earth mourneth and fadeth away, the world languisheth and fadeth away,** the haughty people of the earth do languish. **The earth also is defiled under the inhabitants thereof; because they have transgressed the laws,** changed the ordinance, broken the everlasting covenant. **Therefore hath the curse devoured the earth...**" (Isaiah 24:4-6)

In Leviticus, we see that, since the earth itself is defiled, it too yields violent behavior akin to its sinful inhabitants:

> "**And the land is defiled:** therefore I do visit the iniquity thereof upon it, and **the land itself vomiteth out her inhabitants.** Ye shall therefore keep my statutes and my judgments, and shall not commit any of these abominations; neither any of your own nation, nor any stranger that sojourneth among you: (For all these abominations have the men of the land done, which were before you, and the land is defiled;) **That the land spue not you out also, when ye defile it, as it spued out the nations that were before you.**" (Leviticus 18:25-28)

Thus, when we encounter the statement, within the narrative of the flood, that "all the fountains of the great deep" were "broken up" (Genesis 7:11), it becomes apparent that this event did not stem from God's direct intervention, but rather it emerged as a natural consequence of humankind's sinful affections influencing the condition of the earth.

> "In the six hundredth year of Noah's life, in the second month, the seventeenth day of the month, **the same day were all the fountains of the great deep broken up, and the windows of heaven [the sky] were opened.**" (Genesis 7:11)

God's warning to the antediluvians was one of mercy, for His intent was to forestall the earth from vomiting out its inhabitants. Regrettably, the people chose to distance themselves from God. As their rebellion persisted, the earth grew increasingly vulnerable to the ravages of natural disasters and calamities. In the end, God had no choice but to withdraw Himself and allow the earth to purge its occupants who were slaves to sin and vice.

> "Men cannot with impunity reject the warning which God in mercy sends them. **A message was sent from heaven to the world in Noah's day,** and their salvation depended upon the manner in which they treated that message. **Because they rejected the warning, the Spirit of God was withdrawn from the sinful race, and they perished in the waters of the Flood...**" (Ellen G. White, *The Great Controversy*, pg. 431)

Had the contemporaries of Noah chosen to repent and seek the face of their Creator, both the earth and the seas would have found tranquility. The waters of the earth would have heard Christ's solemn command, "Peace, be still" (Mark 4:39), just as they did on that stormy evening while Jesus and His disciples were out at sea. Nevertheless, the people of Noah's time adamantly refrained from manifesting contrition. By entreating God to depart from their midst, they effectively beckoned the fatal waters of the flood. God's ability to aid them was rendered impotent, as they stubbornly refused His counsel.

> "**Hast thou marked the old way which wicked men have trodden?** Which were cut down out of time, **whose foundation was**

> **overflown with a flood: Which said unto God, Depart from us: and what can the Almighty do for them?**" (Job 22:15-17)

Scripture tells us that God's commandment—His word—holds the waters in their designated positions:

> "**When he [God] gave to the sea his decree, that the waters should not pass his commandment:** when he appointed the foundations of the earth..." (Proverbs 8:29)

Should our own actions compel His presence to recede from our midst, His word will find itself obliged to release its grasp, thereby allowing us to bear the inherent consequences of our own wayward choices. This causes our Father profound sorrow—He mourns for every one of His children who are lost to Satan's devices. For this reason, God forewarned the ancient nation of Israel that they stood on the precipice of repeating this same process, as did the antediluvians, of causing His presence to be withdrawn:

> "Be thou instructed, O Jerusalem, **lest my soul depart from thee; lest I make thee desolate, a land not inhabited.**" (Jeremiah 6:8)

Owing to the adversities wrought by mankind as a consequence of their own malevolent actions, nature is directly impacted, and it too bears the testimony of agony and strife.

> "The vine is dried up, and the fig tree languisheth; the pomegranate tree, the palm tree also, and the apple tree, even all the trees of the field, are withered: **because joy is withered away from the sons of men.**" (Joel 1:12)

It is no wonder, then, that at the time Christ was being nailed to the cross, nature itself bore witness to the sufferings of her Creator and Sustainer:

> "And they stripped him, and put on him a scarlet robe. And when they had platted a crown of thorns, they put it upon his head, and a reed in his right hand: and they bowed the knee before him, and mocked him, saying, Hail, King of the Jews! And they spit upon him, and took the reed, and smote him on the head. And after

that they had mocked him, they took the robe off from him, and put his own raiment on him, and led him away to crucify him... **Now from the sixth hour there was darkness over all the land unto the ninth hour...** And, behold, the veil of the temple was rent in twain from the top to the bottom; and **the earth did quake, and the rocks rent...**" (Matthew 27:28-31,45,51)

Inspiration clearly conveys a correlation between human actions and the adverse effects on the natural world, emphasizing the idea that nature reflects the consequences of human behavior. The transgressions of mankind exert a direct influence on their surroundings due to the necessary withdrawal of God's protective agency, which sustains the very foundations of the earth. The thorn emerges and stings man for his deliberate transgression. The thistle sprouts and pierces him for the sins which he has committed. The cascading torrents of water surge forth from their appointed locations and, in tumultuous chaos, envelop the entire earth in response to man's stubborn rebellion.

The natural realm, due to the onset of sin, and without the sustaining influence of Jehovah, pursues its inexorable course of desolation. This is why, in the context of the flood, scripture indicates that God was compelled to permit the antediluvians to be destroyed with, *or by*, the earth itself:

"And God said unto Noah, **The end of all flesh is come before me;** for the earth is filled with violence through them; and, **behold, I will destroy them with the earth.**" (Genesis 6:13)

Satan exalted in his victory over the souls of the pre-flood era. Through the enticement toward malevolence and rebellion, he orchestrated their ultimate demise. In like manner, he finds gratification in his proficient endeavor to instill in contemporary consciousness the notion that it was indeed God who bore responsibility for the violent destruction of multitudes in a world-wide deluge. However, the author believes that the discourse of this subsection provides sufficient evidence to the contrary: God cannot be held accountable for the flood in Noah's age. Nor can

He be convicted of any action that results in death, destruction, or decay. In every instance, sin is the ultimate culprit—and Satan its progeny. We must steadfastly guard against the adversary's attempts to obscure our perception of God's righteousness and benevolence through his cunning deceptions and insinuations. Upon a thorough investigation, God stands vindicated every time, and His character of selfless love and nonviolence may be readily discerned.

The Conquest of Canaan

"And we took all his cities at that time, and ***utterly destroyed the men, and the women, and the little ones,*** *of every city,* ***we left none to remain...*** *" (Deuteronomy 2:34)*

In the context of the theological issue which we have endeavored to reconcile in the current section, a pressing question emerges when we juxtapose the extensive evidence affirming the nonviolent nature of God with the scriptural injunction for the Israelites to carry out the wholesale annihilation of entire nations, ostensibly at the behest of the Almighty. This dilemma compels us to engage in a rigorous examination, as it raises profound ethical and theological paradoxes, particularly in the context of envisioning the people of God employing lethal force against defenseless women and children, all under the guise of God's explicit directive.

> "...we will go up and fight, **according to all that the LORD our God commanded us.** And when ye had girded on every man his weapons of war, ye were ready to go up into the hill." (Deuteronomy 1:41)

This command seems to stand in stark contrast to the guidance given by Christ, who zealously opposed the use of coercion and violence, explicitly rebuking the use of weapons.

> "Then said Jesus unto him, **Put up again thy sword into his place: for all they that take the sword shall perish with the sword.**" (Matthew 26:52)

As previously articulated by the author, the reconciliation of the Father's character with the divine attributes exemplified by Christ remains an imperative endeavor. If Christ staunchly refrains from endorsing the use of violence, then it becomes incumbent that the Father's disposition concurs accordingly.

With a more comprehensive analysis of the Israelites' conquest of Canaan, it becomes apparent that God's divine intent for the Promised Land did not involve its acquisition through warfare and bloodshed. The early Hebrews deviated from God's prescribed methods for claiming the land, instead pursuing their own bloodthirsty ambitions, and resorting to coercive means contrary to God's will.

> "**And I will send hornets before thee,** which shall drive out the Hivite, the Canaanite, and the Hittite, from before thee." (Exodus 23:28)

> "**And I sent the hornet before you, which drave them out from before you,** even the two kings of the Amorites; **but not with thy sword, nor with thy bow.**" (Joshua 24:12)

The Lord intended to displace the inhabitants of Canaan by means of troublesome hornets. This approach was nonlethal, causing only moderate irritation and inconvenience, thus compelling the current occupants to depart voluntarily in due course. God had made a solemn promise to grant the Israelites the Promised Land, and His capability to fulfill His promises will never waver. Nevertheless, the Israelites lacked faith in His ability to deliver the land to them. Faced with unbelief, weariness, and desperation, they ultimately sought to seize the land through their own efforts.

> "God had made it their privilege and their duty to enter the land at the time of His appointment, but through their willful neglect that permission had been withdrawn. **Satan had gained his object in preventing them from entering Canaan; and now he urged them on to do the very thing, in the face of the divine prohibition, which they had refused to do when God required it. Thus the great deceiver gained the victory by leading them to rebellion... They had distrusted the power of God to work with their efforts in gaining possession of Canaan; yet now they presumed upon their own strength to accomplish the work independent of divine aid...** 'we will go up and fight, according to all that the Lord our God commanded us.' Deuteronomy 1:41. So terribly blinded had

> they become by transgression. **The Lord had never commanded them to 'go up and fight.' It was not His purpose that they should gain the land by warfare,** but by strict obedience to His commands..." (Ellen G. White, *Patriarchs and Prophets,* pg. 392)

In pursuit of this objective, they embarked upon a mission to scout the land, dispatching capable individuals for this task. Notice how they attribute the command to do so directly to Jehovah:

> "**And the LORD spake unto Moses, saying, Send thou men, that they may search the land of Canaan,** which I give unto the children of Israel: of every tribe of their fathers shall ye send a man, every one a ruler among them." (Numbers 13:1-2)

But did God really issue such an instruction? Owing to the language of this verse, are we to infer that God, in His divine commitment to grant the land of Canaan to His people, required the use of spies? Did He not already possess omniscient awareness of the land's layout, the positioning of its cities, the means to displace its residents, and the method by which His people would inherit it without the need for conflict? If His promise was to bestow the land upon the Israelites, why would the employment of spies be necessary, especially in light of the earlier elucidation of His original intent to dispossess the current inhabitants through the instrumentality of hornets?

A careful reading of the biblical narrative reveals that the directive to dispatch spies stemmed primarily from the Israelites' own inclination:

> "And ye came near unto me [Moses] every one of you, and said, **We will send men before us, and they shall search us out the land,** and bring us word again by what way we must go up, and into what cities we shall come." (Deuteronomy 1:22)

The early Hebrews exhibited a marked lack of confidence in God's capacity to expel the existing occupants of the land, casting doubt upon His ability to fulfill His covenant with them.

Notwithstanding His proclamation that He had “set the land before” them and equipped them with the means to “go up and possess it,” urging them to have unwavering trust in Him, entreating them that they should “fear not, neither be discouraged” (Deuteronomy 1:21) because His promises were true and their fulfillment certain, they nevertheless persisted in harboring trepidation, skepticism, and despondency. Therefore, they independently elected to send scouts to assess the feasibility of taking the land, determining whether it might be seized with relative ease and identifying the cities that should be prioritized for conquest. In this particular instance, we observe yet another illustration where a command is seemingly ascribed to God's explicit instruction, whereas, in truth, He is merely affording His children the autonomy to act in accordance with their own innate inclinations and aspirations.

God did not direct the Israelites to spy out the land, nor did He command them to take Canaan by siege. The Promised Land was to be theirs by faith and faith alone, for it is a type of heaven—and we certainly do not gain heaven by our own works, but by faith only. When the Israelites faltered in their trust and obedience and resorted to seizing the land through violence and bloodshed, their actions significantly diverged from the divine will of God. The early Hebrews, in their acquiescence of the land of Canaan, deviated from the character which God endeavors for His children to exhibit. By suggesting that God instructed them to execute the ruthless massacre of men, women, and children—thereby escalating conflicts wherever possible—we inevitably contradict the clear declarations of scripture and undermine the nonviolent nature of the Father as exemplified by Christ. In each and every case, it is unequivocally manifest that Christ fervently renounces the application of violence, and this doctrinal stance extends harmoniously to the Father as well.

The Smiting of the Firstborns of Egypt

*"**For I will pass through the land of Egypt this night, and will smite all the firstborn in the land of Egypt, both man and beast;** and against all the gods of Egypt I will execute judgment: I am the LORD." (Exodus 12:12)*

Owing to the conclusion of our prior discourse concerning the early Hebrews' incursion into Canaan, wherein we firmly established the foundational premise that divine mandates do not encompass instructions that would condone the infliction of harm upon men, women, and children, it is therefore reasonable to postulate that God does not actively engage in such endeavors Himself. We do not venerate a god of violence, but indeed a God of boundless love, and it is inconceivable that a Being of such love would ever endorse violence or engage in it Himself.

In light of this consideration, would it be rational for one to then make the suggestion that, in a manner reminiscent of Satan's sinister influence upon King Herod to order the massacre of the babes of Bethlehem during the period of Christ's birth, God would actively work to slaughter the innocent firstborns of Egypt?

> "He [Satan] looked upon Christ from His birth as his rival. **He stirred the envy and jealousy of Herod to destroy Christ** by insinuating to him that his power and his kingdom were to be given to this new King. **Satan imbued Herod with the very feelings and fears that disturbed his own mind. He inspired the corrupt mind of Herod to slay all the children in Bethlehem who were two years old and under, which plan he thought would succeed in ridding the earth of the infant King.**" (Ellen G. White, *Confrontation*, pg. 27)

Undoubtedly, such a claim lacks logical coherence, and, as we shall demonstrate, may be readily and entirely refuted.

Given the literary convention wherein God is frequently ascribed actions which He merely permits, it prompts us to question who or what should bear culpability for the demise of Egypt's firstborns. This enigmatic figure becomes increasingly apparent in a later section of the Exodus narrative:

> "For the LORD will pass through to smite the Egyptians; and when he seeth the blood upon the lintel, and on the two side posts, the LORD will pass over the door, **and will not suffer the destroyer to come in unto your houses to smite you.**" (Exodus 12:23)

In this particular instance, the text unequivocally designates "the destroyer" as the entity held accountable for the death of the infants in Egypt. And as the author established earlier in chapter 5 of this volume, Satan may rightly be characterized as the destroyer. This concept is elucidated in numerous scriptural contexts, as we shall discern, including the book of Revelation:

> "And they had a king over them, which is the angel of the bottomless pit, **whose name in the Hebrew tongue is Abaddon, but in the Greek tongue hath his name Apollyon.**" (Revelation 9:11)

To briefly revisit our previous discourse from chapter 5: the utilization of the term "angel," in the context of Revelation 9:11, appears to denote the foremost among the malevolent angels, namely, Lucifer. The Hebrew name, אֲבַדּוֹן ('Ăḇaddōn), is an indication of "the angel who rules in hell,"—another allusion to Lucifer. This name, Abaddon, is literally translated "destruction." Its Greek equivalent—Ἀπολλύων (Apollyōn)—means "to destroy" (Strong's G0623). The name Apollyon accurately signifies "a destroyer" and is ascribed to this "angel of the bottomless pit" because it embodies his primary attribute. Therefore, in no way do we err in our designation of Satan as "the destroyer" within biblical interpretation.

This is further substantiated in 1 Corinthians, wherein the Apostle Paul refers to Numbers 21:4-6, affirming that the serpents troubling the Israelites in the wilderness were not sent by God, as is often assumed, but were, in fact, dispatched by "the destroyer,"—Satan himself.

> "Neither let us tempt Christ, as some of them also tempted, **and were destroyed of serpents.** Neither murmur ye, as some of them also murmured, **and were destroyed of the destroyer.**" (I Corinthians 10:9-10)

It is pertinent for the reader to apprehend the definition of the Greek word for "destroyer" in this particular instance, as it invokes a peculiar and underlying symbolism which applies to our current dialogue. The term, ὀλοθρευτής (olothreutēs), in verse 10, may be translated as "a ruiner that is (specifically) a *venomous serpent*; a destroyer" (Strong's G3644). In this context, the destroyer is intricately associated with a venomous or deadly serpent. Who else but Satan could embody such a depiction?—for we find in Revelation chapter 12:

> "And the great dragon was cast out, **that old serpent, called the Devil, and Satan,** which deceiveth the whole world: he was cast out into the earth, and his angels were cast out with him." (Revelation 12:9)

Arguably the most notorious of his disguises, our adversary adopted the form of a serpent within the confines of the Garden of Eden, employing this artifice as a means to deceive Adam and Eve. Furthermore, upon a thorough scrutiny of the passages in Numbers to which Paul was alluding, we unveil further profound symbolism that contributes to the recognition of the destroyer as synonymous with Satan, our adversary.

> "And they journeyed from mount Hor by the way of the Red sea, to compass the land of Edom: and the soul of the people was much discouraged because of the way. **And the people spake against God, and against Moses, Wherefore have ye brought us up out of Egypt to die in the wilderness?** for there is no bread, neither is there any water; and our soul loatheth this light bread. **And the LORD sent fiery serpents among the people, and they**

bit the people; and much people of Israel died." (Numbers 21:4-6)

Take note of the deliberate use of the term "fiery" to characterize the serpents sent to afflict the Israelites. This particular linguistic choice often carries connotations of infernal torment, potentially signifying a link to the origin of these slithering foes. In essence, it may imply that the source of these serpents can be attributed to the progenitor of suffering and misery, namely, Satan himself. As has already been articulated, and substantiated through the inspired writings of Paul, it may be convincingly demonstrated that these serpents were deployed by "the destroyer," and not by God.

The discerning reader will observe that in verse 6, the text incorporates Hebrew idiomatic expressions, attributing to God the agency of sending forth serpents to afflict the Israelites. A more accurate comprehension of the passage would suggest that, given the people's direct antagonism towards God and Moses as described in verse 5, God's Spirit was compelled to withdraw, consequently granting the adversary access to his prey and enabling him to plague the Israelites with venomous serpents. It is evident throughout the biblical narrative that those who place their trust in God are afforded protection; the perpetual presence of the Almighty functions as a bulwark—a hedge—against the malevolent intentions of the fallen foe.

"**Hast not thou made an hedge [of protection] about him,** and about his house, and about all that he hath on every side?" (Job 1:10)

"**The angel of the LORD encampeth round about them that fear [revere] him,** and delivereth them." (Psalms 34:7)

Therefore, in this instance, we must acknowledge the fact that God's divine hedge of protection, which for so long had shielded the Israelites during their trying time in the wilderness, was finally breached. Their profound lack of faith in God's ability to sustain them, coupled with their continued resistance to the leadership of His chosen servant Moses, served as the catalyst for their subsequent suffering and eventual demise.

> "He that diggeth a pit shall fall into it; and **whoso breaketh an hedge [of protection], a serpent shall bite him.**" (Ecclesiastes 10:8)

Nevertheless, upon bridging this concept back to our main focus of the firstborns of Egypt, we may know that God is not to blame—God is *not* the destroyer.

> "Sickness, suffering, and death are work of an antagonistic power. **Satan is the destroyer; God is the restorer.**" (Ellen G. White, *Counsels on Health*, pg. 168)

This is even more evident by the words of His Son, who is "the express image of" the Father's "person" (Hebrews 1:3).

> "For **the Son of man is not come to destroy** men's lives, but to save them. And they went to another village." (Luke 9:56)

> "For **the Son of man is come to save** that which was lost." (Matthew 18:11)

> "Even so **it is not the will of your Father which is in heaven, that one of these little ones should perish.**" (Matthew 18:14)

The divine character does not permit the concurrent embodiment of God as both a destroyer and a Savior. He cannot, simultaneously, fulfill the roles of Creator and destroyer, or serve as the Provider and Sustainer of all life while, at the same time, inciting death. Such dualities only serve to introduce incongruities and paradoxes into the essential coherence that constitutes the divine nature, for God's essence must be fundamentally devoid of self-contradiction.

In every discernible scenario within the Old Testament where it attributes malevolent circumstances to divine intervention, one may employ a Christological perspective as a means to elucidate the genuine affairs of the Father. By this method, it becomes evident that God is absolved of all responsibility for the phenomena of death, decay, and destruction. In each instance, if a mere surface-reading of the text begets an interpretation wherein God is posited as a Being of evil and hostility, then we, as believers in Christ, are required to reexamine and reinterpret. Every divine action must coincide and harmonize with the selfless love and nonviolent nature demonstrated in the life of Christ. We must contemplate the notion that a deeper, more nuanced interpretation lies beyond our immediate understanding—because "God is love" (1 John 4:8) and He does not contradict Himself.

> "To the pure, **You [God] show Yourself pure,** and to the morally corrupt, **You appear to be perverse…"** (Psalm 18:26, *ISV*)
>
> **"A study of the Bible shows us that God is only said to destroy when He removes His protective presence from the recipient of destruction** (Psalm 145:20; Isa 64:6-7; 43:25-28; 2 Kings 13:22-23; Prov 1:24-28; Hosea 5:6). **He is said to destroy when He 'gives people up' and allows their enemies to destroy them** (Isa 34:2; 2 Chron 12:5-7; Hosea 11:8-9; Eze 21:31). Therefore, when reading any Bible passage, especially in the Old Testament, that appears to teach that God personally engaged in destructive behavior, **it is best to interpret it in the permissive rather than in the causative.**
>
> "Thankfully some Bible translators recognize this truth and render certain passages to reflect it. For example, in Isa 64:7 we read, '…. for thou hast hid thy face from us, and hast consumed us, because of our iniquities.' Isaiah complained that God had consumed them. However, Isaiah also complained that God 'hid His face.' **The 'hiding' of God's face is defined in Scripture as the removal of His divine protection, thus allowing whatever forces of evil already poised to destroy to have their way** (Num 6:24-27; Deut 31:16-18; Isa 59:1-2). Therefore, the New Century Version is correct in rendering Isa 64:7 as, '…. That is because you have turned away from us and have let our sins destroy us.'
>
> "Many Bible students believe that gaining knowledge of the original Greek language is sufficient for interpreting and understanding the New Testament. **Yet, though the New**

Testament is written in the Greek rather than the Hebrew, it was still written from a Hebraic perspective. Thus, cultural idioms found in the Old Testament carry over into the New. Ignorance of this truth has led to grave misunderstandings of God's character and actions. One of several scholars have noted that '…. the idiom of the New Testament not unfrequently departs from classical Greek, and follows the Hebrew. **An interpreter who neglects this will fall into great difficulties, and commit many surprising and almost ridiculous mistakes.'** (Stuart, Moses, 1827, *Elements of Biblical Criticism and Interpretation*, London: B. J. Holdsworth, pg. 99)

"I would add to the above statement that **such surprising and difficult mistakes often lead one to mischaracterize God and paint a false picture of Him.** In order to avoid misrepresenting God as a harsh destroyer, one needs to recognize that the permissive idiom (or 'idiom of permission' as others refer to it) is frequent in the New Testament as well as in the Old… This same pattern by which God is said to destroy, which is by the loss of His protection over the sinning one rather than to directly inflict, continues into the New Testament… **Therefore, with all such passages, always keep in mind that God's primary method of destruction is 'permissive' and not 'causative' in the sense that He will no longer protect a person and will allow them to suffer the inevitable consequences of their sin.**" (Troy Edwards, *God Destroys Those Who Destroy His Temple*, vindicatinggod.org)

Having considered all that the author has presented thus far, our focus now turns to the pivotal event at Calvary. In the light that streams forth from the cross, we are afforded the profound revelation of God's boundless love for humanity, and the truth of His nonviolent and altruistic nature becomes beautifully magnified for all who rightly gleam its sacred radiance.

"The mystery of the cross explains all other mysteries. **In the light that streams from Calvary the attributes of God which had filled us with fear and awe appear beautiful and attractive…**" (Ellen G. White, *The Great Controversy*, pg. 652)

Section 4

The Cross of Calvary Reexamined

Chapter 10

Resurrecting the Truth: The Chronicles of Calvary Revisited

*"**The atonement,** made by the stupendous sacrifice of Jesus Christ, **will be seen by you in an altogether different light.**" (Ellen G. White, Signs of the Times, November 13, 1893)*

*"**By a correct understanding of God's actions in the Old Testament, we are assured that he does not destroy—regardless of circumstances.** However, the most compelling evidence that God does not come near the sinner to destroy him is found in the New Testament.*

*"The belief that Jesus died for us on the cross is nearly universal among Bible students, although there are differing views as to how the death of Jesus saves us. **Nevertheless, most believe that when Jesus died on the cross, he experienced what we are destined to experience without his self-sacrificing intervention on our behalf.***

*"If this is true, then we would expect to find that Jesus died the same way we would have to die in relation to what God 'does' to bring about death. **If we believe it is God who destroys the sinner, then we would also expect that God the Father came near to Jesus to kill him. Is this what we find? The gospel of Matthew gives a detailed account of the crucifixion of Christ. What were Jesus's last words just moments before his death? 'My God, my God, why hast thou forsaken me?' (Matt. 27:46, emphasis added).***

*"**This verse reveals how Jesus died. God the Father allowed his Son to experience what every person who rejects his love will experience in the end—separation from him, the Life-Giver. God the Father did not kill Jesus—our sin did:** 'The wages of sin is death' (Rom. 6:23). **Sin is perfectly capable of causing death all by itself, without any help from God. All life is from God with***

> ***no exceptions. All death is the consequence of sin with no exceptions. To imagine that God is the source of death is illogical—with no exceptions.*** *" (Jay A. Schulberg, Acts of Our Gentle God, pg. 70)*

Dear reader, we have now arrived at the crux of the issue. The entirety of this volume has been meticulously assembled, culminating in the paramount inquiry: did the Almighty take the life of His own Son? Having established the fact that God's character is defined by the attributes of selfless love and nonviolence, how do we then interpret the circumstances surrounding the cross?

In an effort to engage in a proper exploration of the prevailing view within Christendom regarding the cross, it is instructive to examine the interpretation of Christ's sacrifice as elucidated by the well-known Pastor, John MacArthur:

> "The reality of Christ's vicarious, substitutionary death on our behalf is the heart of the gospel according to God—the central theme of Isaiah 53. We must remember, however, that **sin did not kill Jesus; God did. The suffering servant's death was nothing less than a punishment administered by God for sins others had committed. That is what we mean when we speak of penal substitutionary atonement… He [God] fully satisfied justice and put away our sin forever through the death of his Son.** There's no way to sidestep the fact that the doctrine of penal substitution is unequivocally affirmed in the plain message of Isaiah 53." (John MacArthur, *The Gospel According to God,* crossway.org)

In this particular discourse, Pastor MacArthur explicitly asserts that the doctrine of penal substitutionary atonement, despite the current author's extensive efforts to refute it, constitutes the core of the gospel. This assertion is supported, according to MacArthur (and countless Christian denominations), by the discernible language of Isaiah 53. He contends that sin bore no responsibility for the death of Christ, instead positing that the Father, in His wrath, penalized His Son and brought about His demise to uphold divine justice. Yet, upon a more thorough analysis of the chapter in question, a distinctive and compelling counterargument to the Pastor's assured remarks emerges:

> "He is despised and rejected of men; a man of sorrows, and acquainted with grief: and we hid as it were our faces from him; he was despised, and we esteemed him not. Surely he hath borne our griefs, and carried our sorrows: **yet we did esteem him stricken, smitten of God, and afflicted.**" (Isaiah 53:3-4)

Notice the latter half of verse 4: "we [humanity] did esteem him [Christ] stricken, smitten of God, and afflicted." The prophetic words of Isaiah 53, scribed seven centuries prior to Christ's advent, unmistakably anticipate the profound misapprehension that would envelop humanity's understanding of the sacrifice at Calvary. In our flawed perception, we erroneously considered Christ as stricken and punished by God, though such was not the case. In fact, such an understanding is fundamentally at odds with reality.

As previously emphasized by the author, we maintain the position that God refrains from punitive actions, as the inherently morbid consequences of sin eliminate the necessity for penal retribution. As expounded upon in the supplied excerpt from Jay A. Schulberg's literary work, *Acts of Our Gentle God*, it is evident that sin possesses the innate capability to induce death and destruction autonomously, devoid of any divine intervention. Due to Christendom's misunderstanding of this matter, the authentic gospel message has become misconstrued. Lamentably, many individuals in the present day persist in adhering to such erroneous doctrines as penal substitutionary atonement—perhaps even unwittingly.

In the historical context of Christ's era, it was customary among the Jewish community to perceive prosperity and the accumulation of wealth as divine blessings, while conversely, suffering and affliction were attributed to grave moral transgressions and considered acts of divine retribution—God punishing the sinner for his or her wrongdoings. This Hebraic custom may be plainly seen among Christ's disciples when they asked:

> "And his disciples asked him, saying, Master, who did sin, this man, or his parents, that he was born blind? **Jesus answered, Neither hath this man sinned, nor his parents...**" (John 9:2-3)

In light of this constrained doctrinal perspective, it may be inferred that Jesus, during the immense suffering that ultimately culminated in His crucifixion, would have been regarded (*esteemed*) as both stricken and afflicted by God—condemned to death by divine decree on account of some egregious sin. The stark reality of Christ's crucifixion left a lasting impression upon numerous onlookers, reinforcing their conviction that His proclamation as the Messiah was untrue. In their understanding, the idea that God would subject their Deliverer to such a degrading mode of death seemed inconceivable.

> "He saved others; himself he cannot save. **If he be the King of Israel, let him now come down from the cross, and we will believe him.**" (Matthew 27:42)

The Jews, mirroring a sentiment that persists to this day, maintained the belief that God was the direct agent responsible for the demise and affliction of transgressors. To them, instances of disease, malady, or terminal illness were perceived as divinely ordained instruments of punishment for sins.

> "**It was generally believed by the Jews that sin is punished in this life. Every affliction was regarded as the penalty of some wrongdoing,** either of the sufferer himself or of his parents. **It is true that all suffering results from the transgression of God's law, but this truth had become perverted. Satan, the author of sin and all its results,** had led men to look upon disease and death as proceeding from God,-as punishment arbitrarily inflicted on account of sin. **Hence one upon whom some great affliction or**

> **calamity had fallen had the additional burden of being regarded as a great sinner.**" (Ellen G. White, *The Desire of Ages,* pg. 471)

For this reason, we esteemed Christ "stricken, smitten of God, and afflicted" (Isaiah 53:4). To a significant number of professing Christians, the cross symbolizes a doctrinal concept wherein the Son, through a legalistic framework, offers payment to the Father as a means of securing eternal benefits for humanity; of appeasing God's wrath and reconciling Him to the world. Sin necessitated punishment, and rather than carrying with it inherent consequences, sin was considered wrong solely by arbitrary decree. Consequently, it is believed that God is the One who must administer punishment for sin. In the pursuit of averting the complete annihilation of the human race under the weight of God's wrath, Christ willingly shouldered the burden of divine retribution imposed by the Father. This is penal substitutionary atonement.

Dear reader, this school of theology carries with it hazardous and heretical errors. Not only does this perspective lack a solid biblical foundation, but it also engenders a schism between the Father and the Son, resulting in a pronounced differentiation of their attributes, dispositions, and overall objectives. The Father seeks to destroy while the Son endeavors to save. With the Son's acquiescence, the Father would inevitably pursue the utter annihilation of humanity due to its unwavering entrenchment in sin. This contemplation, in turn, imparts to the Father certain unfavorable attributes—notably those of vengeance, anger, and retributive tendencies, thereby defacing His loving and nonviolent character which the author has undergone great lengths to defend. On the other hand, Christ preserves His loving and compassionate disposition by selflessly bearing the full weight of the Father's wrath upon Himself. Nevertheless, in doing so, He assumes a character that stands in stark contrast to the God which He espoused to the world. As a result, He becomes a liar and a deceiver, for, in that moment, it is revealed that He is altogether *dissimilar* from the Father: they are not one in nature, character, or purpose (John 10:30); He does not seek to do everything the Father does (John 5:19); we may have known Christ but the Father is nothing like Him (John 8:19; John 14:9)—the obligatory compatibility between the Father and Son becomes ambiguous, even wholly lost. The words of Augustine do well to succinctly summarize this idea:

> "**Does this mean then that the Son was already so reconciled to us that he was even prepared to die for us, while the Father was still so angry with us that unless the Son died for us he would not be reconciled to us?** ... The Father loved us not merely before the Son died for us, but before he founded the world." (Augustine, *Trinity*, 13.4.15)

The incarnation of Christ, assuming the likeness of sinful flesh, was not undertaken as a means of placating God through bribery, but rather to provide mankind with an exemplary model of what humanity might be when brought into union with divinity. Christ's sacrifice serves as a demonstration of the Father's love, not a manifestation of His wrath. The notion that the Father chastised His Son on the cross as an expiation for our sins requires reevaluation. In theological terms, the Father is not characterized by a punitive disposition towards sin. Consequently, there is no warrant for approaching the Father with trepidation. Rather, it should be understood that *both* the Father and Christ share the common purpose of mitigating the human condition of sin, seeking to provide spiritual healing and redemption.

> "**For God so loved the world, that he gave his only begotten Son,** that whosoever believeth in him should not perish, but have everlasting life." (John 3:16)

> "At that day ye shall ask in my name: and **I say not unto you, that I will pray the Father for you: For the Father himself loveth you,** because ye have loved me, and have believed that I came out from God." (John 16:26-27)

> **"There is no fear in love; but perfect love casteth out fear: because fear hath torment.** He that feareth is not made perfect in love." (I John 4:18)

If the claim were true that God drew near to Jesus to effectuate His prolonged and brutal execution, then one would anticipate encountering substantial biblical evidence to corroborate such a position. However, the empirical findings we encounter demonstrate quite the opposite. The scriptural narrative of the cross is consistent with what we have observed across numerous other instances where an individual succumbed to the culmination of sin's wicked and morbid influence. What we find is that God separates Himself from the individual—in this case, Christ—thereby allowing the natural and inexorable consequences of sin to manifest.

> "And about the ninth hour Jesus cried with a loud voice, saying, Eli, Eli, lama sabachthani? that is to say, **My God, my God, why hast thou forsaken me?**" (Matthew 27:46)

> "My God, my God, **why hast thou forsaken me? why art thou so far from helping me,** and from the words of my roaring?" (Psalm 22:1)

Here we observe that, rather than drawing near to Christ for the purpose of physically and forcefully overpowering Him, the Father abstained from proximate engagement, and it appeared to Christ that He had completely withdrawn Himself from the scene. Christ could not discern His Father's presence through the thick barrier which sin had erected between them. And it was this heart wrenching feeling—the feeling of being fully separated from His Father, the very Source of life—that relinquished Christ to the despair of death.

This assertion notwithstanding, it is imperative to clarify that Christ was entirely *without* sin, for the sins which He bore were not His own, but ours. The New Testament narrative is emphatically clear that, despite being tempted with every temptation which man himself might face, Christ yet remained free from the condition of sin and was made perfect in love.

> "**Who did no sin,** neither was guile found in his mouth..." (I Peter 2:22)

> "And ye know that he was manifested to take away our sins; and **in him is no sin.**" (I John 3:5)

> "For we have not an high priest which cannot be touched with the feeling of our infirmities; **but was in all points tempted like as we are, yet without sin.**" (Hebrews 4:15)

> "**And being made perfect,** he became the author of eternal salvation unto all them that obey him..." (Hebrews 5:9)

Although He bore no traces of sin, Christ experienced death in a manner analogous to the impending fate of every transgressor.

> "[Christ takes] upon Himself our nature (Heb. 2:16-17); and on Him was laid 'the iniquity of us all' (Isa. 53:6). **In order to save us, He had to come where we were, or, in other words, He had to take the position of a lost sinner.**" (E. J. Waggoner, *Signs of the Times,* July 3, 1884, pg. 409)

The sinner's destruction will not result from God's powerful intervention or punitive wrath; rather, death is merely the natural state of all things which find themselves separated from God's life-sustaining presence. Through the conscious and deliberate agency of the transgressor, there shall ensue an unavoidable confrontation with the deleterious ramifications of absolute estrangement from the benevolent and life-giving God, culminating in their eternal demise.

Christ took upon Himself the death which every unrepentant sinner must inevitably face, not to mollify an offended deity, but for the purpose of illustrating the authentic nature of sin and its adverse consequences. Simultaneously, in offering up His life for the sake of others, He perfected a righteous and other-centered character within His own humanity, thereby triumphing over the death which sin seeks to enforce upon every member of the human family. He now endeavors to impart this selfsame character—a character which is in harmony with God's principles for life—to all who receive Him.

> "**No man taketh it [my life] from me, but I lay it down of myself.** I have power to lay it down, and I have power to take it again. This commandment have I received of my Father." (John 10:18)

> "Greater love hath no man than this, **that a man lay down his life for his friends.**" (John 15:13)

> "Forasmuch then as the children are partakers of flesh and blood, he also himself likewise took part of the same; **that through death he might destroy him that had the power of death, that is, the devil...**" (Hebrews 2:14)

As a counterstatement to Pastor MacArthur's earlier assertion, the author firmly believes that *God did not kill Jesus; our sin did.* Again, this is not to say that Christ was sinful; rather, He willfully shouldered the burden of humanity's sins, with the explicit aim of effecting their remission and bestowing upon us the same righteous and quickening character which He perfected. This is what the Bible authors mean by the words, "Jesus Christ our *Saviour*" (Titus 1:4). Christ did not come to save us from the wrath of His Father; He came to save us from the condition of sin.

> "For then must he often have suffered since the foundation of the world: but now once in the end of the world hath **he appeared to put away sin by the sacrifice of himself.**" (Hebrews 9:26)

> "**For he [God] hath made [allowed] him [Jesus] to be sin for us,** who knew no sin; **that we might be made the righteousness of God in him.**" (2 Corinthians 5:21)

Just as we wrongly esteemed Him "stricken, smitten of God, and afflicted," the lost in the end will wrongly believe they, too, are "stricken, smitten of God, and afflicted" when, in fact, it is only the disease of sin running its deadly and inexorable course.

For the first time, Christ felt separated from His Father, and it was this apparent detachment from the Father's vitalizing presence, coupled with the weighty burden of every sin borne by humanity, which ultimately caused the death of the Son of God.

> "Few give thought to the suffering that sin has caused our Creator. All heaven suffered in Christ's agony; but **that suffering did not begin or end with His manifestation in humanity. The cross is a revelation to our dull senses of the pain that, from its very inception, sin has brought to the heart of God... When there came upon Israel the calamities that were the sure result of separation from God,—subjugation by their enemies, cruelty, and death,**—it is said that 'His soul was grieved for the misery of Israel.' 'In all their affliction He was afflicted: ... and He bare them, and carried them all the days of old.' Judges 10:16; Isaiah 63:9..." (Ellen G. White, *Education,* pg. 263)

An objection no doubt will be raised, rooted in yet another citation from Isaiah 53, specifically in the initial portion of verse 10...

> "**Yet it pleased the LORD to bruise him;** he hath put him to grief: when thou shalt make his soul an offering for sin, he shall see his seed, he shall prolong his days, and the pleasure of the LORD shall prosper in his hand." (Isaiah 53:10)

In alignment with our analysis of previous instances of scripture, it is incumbent upon the reader to interpret God's actions in this verse under the rubric of permissiveness. George Whitehead wrote:

> "**There are still those that reject and disesteem Christ, and that esteem him smitten or plagued of God, and even to have undergone the wrath and vengeance of his Father in their stead...** Whereas, first, God had never any such wrath nor revenge, against his innocent Son, to execute upon him... **It pleasing the Lord to bruise him, was neither in wrath, nor to take vengeance on him, nor yet actually or immediately by himself to bruise him, but permissively.**" (George Whitehead, *The Nature of Christianity, in the True Light Asserted: in Opposition to Anti-Christianism,*

Darkness, Confusion and Sin-pleasing Doctrines, pg. 25, published in 1833)

And Samuel Whitman further explains, in his work titled, *A Key to the Bible Doctrine of Atonement and Justification*:

> "'He had done no violence, neither was any deceit in his mouth. Yet it pleased the Lord to bruise him; he hath put him to grief.' [Isaiah 53:9-10]. **It is asserted, you say, by the prophet, that it pleased the Lord to bruise his well beloved Son.** Answer; **and it is equally true, that God said, that the serpent [Satan] should bruise him [Genesis 3:15; Revelation 12:9].** From this, it is evident, that **in whatever sense the hand of God might be concerned in the event, it was not from his immediate hand, but by the power of Satan through divine permission.**" (Samuel Whitman, *A Key to the Bible Doctrine of Atonement and Justification*, pg. 298-299, published in 1814)

All attempts to present the cross in a manner that implicates the Father in the death of His Son should be wholly disregarded. Amongst every one of these efforts, the adherent exhibits a conspicuous inability to accurately harmonize their interpretation with the biblical text, particularly in relation to its message regarding reconciliation. Numerous false doctrines, among them penal substitutionary atonement, strive to propagate the idea that it was God who required reconciliation to mankind, as opposed to mankind who required it. In the context of God's word, the clarity regarding this matter is beyond all dispute:

> "And all things are of God, **who hath reconciled us to himself by Jesus Christ,** and hath given to us the ministry of reconciliation; To wit, that **God was in Christ, reconciling the world unto himself,** not imputing their trespasses unto them; and hath committed unto us the word of reconciliation." (2 Corinthians 5:18-19)

> "For if, **when we were enemies, we were reconciled to God by the death of his Son,** much more, being reconciled, we shall be saved by his life." (Romans 5:10)

In the first edition (1957) of the *Seventh-Day Adventist Bible Commentary*, the entry for Romans 5:10 states:

> "**The Bible nowhere speaks of God being reconciled to man.** It is true that the death of Christ made it possible for God to do for man what He otherwise could not have done (see on Rom. 3:25, 26)... But this does not mean that God needed to be reconciled. **The alienation was entirely on man's part (see Col 1:21).**"

And the commentary on 2 Corinthians 5:18, from the same source, has this to say regarding reconciliation:

> "Reconciliation involves no change on God's part for God never changes. **It is not God who needs to be reconciled to man but man who needs to be reconciled to God.** There has never been enmity on God's part."

However, prior to a comprehensive exploration of the scriptural theme of reconciliation, it is imperative for the author to first explain the origin of humanity's enmity toward God and the ensuing fear that enveloped. In doing so, the reader will come to understand why reconciliation was needed, as well as where the doctrine of penal substitutionary atonement—or the idea that God demanded the death of His Son so as to not kill us—originated.

> "The Lord says, 'I will put enmity between thee [Satan] and the woman.' [Genesis 3:15]. **The enmity does not exist as a natural fact. As soon as Adam sinned, he was in harmony with the first great apostate, and at war with God; and if God had not interfered in man's behalf, Satan and man would have formed a confederacy against heaven,** and carried on united opposition against the God of hosts." (Ellen G. White, *Signs of the Times*, July 11, 1895)

Where did fear come from? Was there ever such a thing as fear before there was sin? Prior to the onset of sin, did mankind ever harbor feelings of animosity or distrust toward God? In order to provide insight into these piercing inquiries, we must revisit the Genesis account and the narrative of Adam and Eve. In doing so, we will discover that prior to the introduction of sin, the notion of fear was entirely non-existent; Adam and Eve saw God only as a benevolent Father. But by the serpent's cunning and persuasive rhetoric, Adam and Eve began to perceive God as threatening, unforgiving, and dangerous. As a result, enmity (*fear and hatred*) became deeply embedded into the hearts of our earliest ancestors, catalyzing a rift between humanity and God. The transformative impact of sin upon human nature disrupted our communion with the Divine. Consequently, our ability to accurately discern God's loving nature was impaired, giving rise to the penal legal view and appeasement-based theology.

The penal legal view—otherwise known throughout the discourse of this treatise as imperialism—emphasizes that sin, in and of itself, does not intrinsically inflict harm upon the transgressor. Instead, the key proposition is that the ultimate source of harm emanates from the retributive actions of God Himself—the Lawgiver. This theological perspective posits that God employs His authoritative and sovereign power to institute arbitrary punishments, which serve as a deterrent and corrective force against wrongdoing and sin. Because they are arbitrary, it is therefore implied that without such measures, transgressors could persist in a perpetual state of sin, as sin, independent of external consequences, lacks inherent deleterious qualities. In essence, proponents of the penal legal view suggest, whether they realize it or not, that the crux of the matter lies *not in the nature of sin but rather in God's attitude toward the sinner*. Even though there exists a divine love for the transgressor, this theological doctrine maintains that God remains bound by the necessity of satisfying punitive justice, which may encompass severe consequences such as death or torment, as a response to the sinner's transgressions. Thus, the doctrine of penal substitutionary atonement advances the lie that Christ's mission and sacrificial death aimed to modify God's disposition towards humanity, underscoring the idea that it was God who needed to be reconciled to man, rather than the other way around. Here's how Wikipedia defines it:

> "The penal substitution theory teaches that **Jesus suffered the penalty for mankind's sins. Penal substitution derives from the idea that divine forgiveness must satisfy divine justice,** that is, that **God is not willing or able to simply forgive sin without first requiring a satisfaction** for it."

However, as elucidated in previous sections of this work, the immutability of God's character encompasses His gracious capacity to freely forgive sin (Isaiah 55:7). Nevertheless, Satan's stratagem was aimed at obscuring this truth, thus shrouding the nature of the Father and the concept of sin in ambiguity. Reflecting upon the book of Genesis, we encounter the Father's words addressed to Adam and Eve:

> "But of the tree of the knowledge of good and evil, thou shalt not eat of it: **for in the day that thou eatest thereof thou shalt surely die.**" (Genesis 2:17)

Now, does this constitute a divine threat, or does it carry the weight of a solemn warning? How one perceives the context of God's words here has profound implications.

> "**In love he had said, Ye must not eat of it,** even as the father says to the child, You must not eat of these berries, my son, they are poison." (George Fifield, *God is Love,* pg. 22)

Employing an instructive analogy from Kevin J. Mullins' literary work, *Did God Kill Jesus Instead of Killing Us?*, envision a scenario where you and I find ourselves in mid-flight aboard an aircraft at an altitude of 35,000 feet. In this hypothetical scenario, if you were to admonish me with the statement, "By leaping from this plane without a parachute, you will surely die," should I then interpret this remark as a direct and personal threat to my life, or does it serve as a means to highlight the inexorable consequences associated with such an action? Certainly, the statement would signify a sincere warning from a loving friend. Yet, let us contemplate a circumstance where an individual deceived me, leading me to ardently believe that I would "*not* surely die" from the fall. Instead, due to my disobedience to your directives, they convince me that it would be you who, upon my landing, would be the agent of my demise. In such a situation, it is undeniable that I would harbor a profound fear not so much for the impending fall as for the perceived actions you would then take against me. It would also be difficult to still imagine you as my friend, given that the perceived endangerment to my life, via your own intervention, would elicit opposition (*enmity*) toward you within my heart.

Put simply, when the laws of God—or the fundamental principles upon which life operates—are violated, inevitable and inherent repercussions are sure to ensue. However, in the Garden of Eden, Satan successfully manipulated mankind's perception of these principles, leading Adam and Eve to a misconstrued understanding. By distorting God's utterances, the arch-deceiver cunningly beguiled our first parents, convincing them that God's instructions posed a threat, and that eating of the tree held no intrinsic consequence of its own, but by doing so, such defiance would oblige God to impose arbitrary punishments—even death. For the first time, the fear of God found its refuge in the minds of mankind, and this fear begat enmity. Observe how Adam and Eve reacted to God's entreaties following their transgression:

> "And when the woman saw that the tree was good for food, and that it was pleasant to the eyes, and a tree to be desired to make one wise, she took of the fruit thereof, and did eat, and gave also unto her husband with her; and he did eat. And the eyes of them both were opened, and they knew that they were naked; and they sewed fig leaves together, and made themselves aprons. **And they heard the voice of the LORD God walking in the garden in the cool of the day: and Adam and his wife hid themselves from the presence of the LORD God** amongst the trees of the garden. **And the LORD God called unto Adam, and said unto him, Where art thou? And he said, I heard thy voice in the garden, and I was afraid,** because I was naked; and I hid myself." (Genesis 3:6-10)

Upon tasting of the fruit, they saw that it did not immediately cause them death, though, unbeknownst to the couple, their very nature had already suffered drastic disfigurement and God had at once intervened to obstruct the inexorable consequences of sin from taking their toll—namely, eternal nonexistence. Discerning no sudden effects, their initial thought was that the serpent must have been right after all, in that they would "not surely die" (Genesis 3:4) from eating of the tree itself. In due course, the two of them arrived at the deduction that it must, by extension, be God Himself who would exact the consequences upon them—that He would be the agent to actualize His own declaration: "in the day that thou eatest thereof thou shalt surely die" (Genesis 2:17).

Believing the serpent's falsehoods, they began to distrust God, even to the point of entertaining the notion that He would personally bring about their swift and utter destruction. These deceitful notions prevented Adam and Eve from perceiving God as He truly is. In their corrupted perception, the transgression itself was not the primary concern—God was! Their altered understanding of God's nature, spurred by Satan's deceit, transformed the Father's earnest warning into a grave threat. They no longer trusted their Maker. Sin had induced Adam and Eve to question the veracity of reality, irrespective of its manifest clarity; and what remains for the intellect to contemplate in the absence of truth but lies and falsehoods? It is these lies and misrepresentations of God that foster our inherent distrust of Him.

> "When we speak of unbelief, we do not mean that a person believes nothing. **The mind must rest upon something; and when it does not grasp truth, it lays hold of error.** All men in one sense believe, and the effect produced upon the heart and character is according to the things believed. **Eve believed the words of Satan, and the belief of that falsehood in regard to God's character, changed the condition and character of both herself and husband.**" (Ellen G. White, *Review and Herald*, January 5, 1886)

Such were the events that transpired with our earliest predecessors, and they bequeathed these selfsame fears and misconceptions about God to the entirety of the human race, courtesy of their now-fallen nature which sin and the ensuing falsehoods engendered.

In the wake of Adam and Eve's susceptibility to the serpent's artful sophistry in leading them to sin, coupled with their newfound apprehension regarding God's intentions, a substantial alteration transpired within the very fabric of their being. This transformation, in turn, defaced the fundamental character of humanity, ushering in the state of fallen man.

In the context of Adam and Eve's experience, the extent of degradation that permeated their hearts and minds serves as a testament to the profound impact of sin. This perspective challenges the popular notion that sin is solely a judicial determination of guilt, instead highlighting it as a substantial change in the core nature of the individual. Adam and Eve's nature underwent a fundamental shift as an unavoidable consequence of their allegiance to sin. In stark contrast, the nature of God and Christ remained unaltered, as they were without sin. This fact serves as a witness to their changeless qualities of boundless love and inexhaustible forgiveness. Given that it was humanity's nature that had changed and not God's, it was therefore humanity that necessitated reconcilement—and scripture corroborates this idea.

> "And all things are of God, **who hath reconciled us to himself by Jesus Christ,** and hath given to us the ministry of reconciliation; To wit, that **God was in Christ, reconciling the world unto himself, not imputing their trespasses unto them;** and hath committed unto us the word of reconciliation." (2 Corinthians 5:18-19)

God, in His love for us, took it upon Himself to initiate the process of reuniting humanity with Himself. Such efforts as only love and wisdom could devise were made to convince man of his error and to reconcile him back to God.

In the divine endeavor to reunify humanity with heaven, it becomes imperative to recognize that this harmonious reunion may only be accomplished through God's employment of selfless love and nonviolence, thereby eliciting our renewed trust in Him so that He may effectuate the healing of our sinful condition. The juxtaposition of such benevolent intentions with the notion of humanity's *perceived* obligation to appease God's wrath through sacrifices and offerings underscores the profound contrast between the divine pursuit of reconciliation and the misguided concept of appeasement-based theology. Heaven required no appeasement, for alienation was entirely on man's part, therefore it was humanity that needed to be appeased—or convinced of their error. Sacrifice was not a demand placed by God; instead, it was a requirement *perceived* by humanity.

> "**Sacrifice and offering thou didst not desire;** mine ears hast thou opened: **burnt offering and sin offering hast thou not required.**" (Psalm 40:6)

While this statement may pose a challenge for some, let us persist in pursuing this line of thought to its logical conclusion.

Following the transgression in Eden, the penal legal view (the false conclusion that God administers arbitrary punishment for sin) was conceived in the hearts and minds of mankind—and with it, appeasement-based theology. This theology centered around the idea that God's punitive retribution could be nullified through sacrificial offerings. Having partaken of the forbidden fruit and mistakenly attributing their forthcoming downfall to divine intervention, Adam and Eve found themselves grappling with the nascent apprehension of mortality. In a time when the concept of death was hitherto unknown, this notion became the couple's dreaded nightmare. The fear of death, or more accurately, *the fear of God*, emerged as a natural consequence of the sin condition in man.

> "And deliver them who **through fear of death** were all their lifetime **subject to bondage.**" (Hebrews 2:15)

In accordance with the doctrinal tenet that no man comes to the Father except through the Son, it transpired that the Son of God visited Adam within the precincts of the garden. Inquisitively probing into Adam's deeds, though already aware of what had taken place, He proffered an opportunity for repentance. Believing that this was the time when divine punishment would occur, and desperately seeking to avert eternal death, Adam engaged in a final endeavor to absolve himself. He pondered the possibility of shifting the blame onto another, allowing them to bear the divine punishment and its ultimate consequences, thus securing his liberation. Considering this to be his sole recourse, Adam shifted responsibility onto Eve, even going so far as to implicate the Lord for providing him the woman. In other words, by deflecting blame onto Eve, Adam had inadvertently placed Christ at fault for his transgression, as it was Christ who had facilitated Adam's association with Eve by providing "an help meet for him" (Genesis 2:18).

> "And he [Christ] said, Who told thee that thou wast naked? Hast thou eaten of the tree, whereof I commanded thee that thou shouldest not eat? And the man [Adam] said, **The woman whom thou gavest to be with me,** she gave me of the tree, and I did eat." (Genesis 3:11-12)

> "An expression of sadness came over the face of Adam. He appeared astonished and alarmed. To the words of Eve he replied that this must be the foe against whom they had been warned; and **by the divine sentence she must die.** In answer she urged him to eat, repeating the words of the serpent, that they should not surely die. **She reasoned that this must be true, for she felt no evidence of God's displeasure...**" (Ellen G. White, *Daughters of God,* pg. 24)

> **"Adam cast the blame upon his wife, and thus upon God Himself: 'The woman whom thou gavest to be with me, she gave me of the tree, and I did eat.'** From love to Eve, he had deliberately chosen to forfeit the approval of God and an eternal life of joy; **now he endeavored to make his companion, and even the Creator**

Himself, responsible for the transgression." (Ellen G. White, *From Eternity Past*, pg. 27)

Oblivious to the profound implications of his actions, Adam had just rendered judgment upon Christ as the rightful bearer of the penalty for sin, thereby condemning Him to death—an outcome which he perceived as a solemn requirement from God but was, in reality, what he himself required, believing it was the only way for him to be exonerated. Adam's fear of God had instigated an unacknowledged enmity, deep within himself, towards all of heaven. This manifested in his attempt to (indirectly) assign blame onto Christ, effectively condemning Him to die in his place. Here we have the origin of penal substitutionary atonement (the flawed idea that God demands the death of Christ in order to extend forgiveness to the sinner), the pinnacle of appeasement-based theology. This concealed enmity (*hatred*) harbored within the human heart towards the Son of God is precisely the heritage of the carnal mind—or fallen nature—bequeathed to us by Adam, destined to remain undisclosed to our dull senses until fully manifested.

"If I covered my transgressions as Adam, by **hiding mine iniquity in my bosom...**" (Job 31:33)

"And you, that were sometime **alienated and enemies in your mind by wicked works...**" (Colossians 1:21)

"Because **the carnal mind is enmity against God:** for it is not subject to the law of God, neither indeed can be." (Romans 8:7)

Strong's definition for the word "enmity," in the Hebrew: אֵיבָה ('êybâh), and in the Greek: ἔχθρα (échthra), is "hostility; by implication a reason for opposition: enmity, hatred" (Strong's H0342; Strong's G2189). Deep within Adam's psyche, fueled by a mistaken belief that God intended him harm, there existed an unacknowledged hatred—a seed of rebellion. This profound hatred, once provoked, led to Adam's implicit inclination for Christ to be the one put to death, rather than himself.

"**Whosoever hateth his brother is a murderer:** and ye know that no murderer hath eternal life abiding in him." (I John 3:15)

In an effort to shield himself from confronting his murderous disposition, Adam shifted his internal feelings of wrath and condemnation onto God and made it seem as if God demanded the death of Christ. This is a medically recognized process known as psychological projection, where an individual copes with trauma by deflecting and repressing unwanted thoughts and feelings. It involves attributing one's own unconscious emotions, impulses, or qualities onto another person. To Adam, it seemed as though God required the shedding of blood in order to be appeased, yet in reality, the inverse held true—Adam required it. As a result of his profound, yet unwarranted, fear of divine punishment, Adam had adopted a "kill or be killed" mindset, and this was reflected in his condemnation of Christ.

"In its malignant forms, **it is a defense mechanism in which the ego [carnal mind] defends itself against disowned and highly negative parts of the self by denying their existence in themselves and attributing them to others,** breeding misunderstanding and causing untold interpersonal damage." (https://en.m.wikipedia.org/wiki/Psychological_projection)

The Pharisees demonstrated the same impulse when they, in many instances, publicly showcased their contempt for the Son of God. Unbeknownst to them, concealed within the recesses of their hearts, lay an unconscious hatred for God the Father; a hidden enmity towards heaven; a murderous seed of rebellion.

"Did not Moses give you the law, and yet none of you keepeth the law? **Why go ye about to kill me? The people answered and said, Thou hast a devil: who goeth about to kill thee?**" (John 7:19-20)

The climax of humanity's deep-seated enmity manifested unequivocally during the crucifixion, wherein the leaders of Israel orchestrated the execution of the Son of God.

> "**Ye are of your father the devil, and the lusts of your father ye will do. He was a murderer from the beginning,** and abode not in the truth, because there is no truth in him. When he speaketh a lie, he speaketh of his own: for he is a liar, and the father of it." (John 8:44)

A careful study of this process reveals that the doctrine of penal substitutionary atonement is a result of mankind projecting its internal inclination to kill the Son onto the Father. Consequently, the events at the cross are misinterpreted as a demonstration of the Father's condemnation and wrath instead of our own. Correctly understood, the crucifixion of the Son of God was a manifestation of mankind's own enmity rather than a true reflection of God's punitive anger. Stated another way, the tumultuous expressions of brutality, rage, and torment that transpired at Calvary were, fundamentally, reflections of humanity's fallen nature, rather than being indicative of divine attributes.

> "Wherein in time past ye walked according to the course of this world, according to the prince of the power of the air, **the spirit that now worketh in the children of disobedience:** Among whom also we all had our conversation in times past in the lusts of our flesh, fulfilling the desires of the flesh and of the mind; **and were by nature the children of wrath,** even as others." (Ephesians 2:2-3)

For so long, humanity has projected their own profound sentiments of hatred onto God, casting a veil of darkness and misunderstanding over the significance of the cross. Historically, there has been a prevailing belief that the events at Calvary showcased manifestations of God's wrath, condemnation, and blood-thirst—culminating in Christ's demise. Contrary to this perception, it is imperative to recognize that these occurrences were, in fact, a consequence of human agency and a revelation of human characteristics. Unable to face the depravity of our fallen nature, we merely project our own faults onto the Creator.

"These things hast thou done, and I kept silence; **thou thoughtest that I was altogether such an one as thyself:** but I will reprove thee, and set them in order before thine eyes." (Psalm 50:21)

The Almighty harbors no sentiments of wrath or condemnation towards either His Son or humanity. Conversely, empirical evidence illustrates that it is humanity which harbors these very sentiments towards the Almighty. The time has come when we must face our fallen nature and repent. We must accept the notion that "God so loved the world, that he gave his only begotten Son, that whosoever believeth in him should not perish, but have everlasting life." (John 3:16). The purpose underlying Christ's sacrifice was not the appeasement of an offended deity, but rather the revelation of inherent enmity within human hearts. This revelation serves as a catalyst for repentance, marking the commencement of a curative process. The cross was not only a demonstration of the love that God held for man, but it also served to exhibit the hatred which man held for God.

"In the death of Christ 2,000 years ago, **the seed of enmity in Adam was fully manifested and humanity saw the full results of what was laying in the heart of Adam undeveloped and uncomprehended.**" (Adrian Ebens, *Cross Examined and Cross Encountered,* pg. 18)

Before the bloody events that transpired at Calvary, however, God sought to disclose to humanity, including Adam, their deep hostility towards heaven. To illustrate the gravity of Adam's betrayal and the true implications of his enmity, God *permitted* the sacrifice of one of His cherished animals. The animal skins which God used to clothe our first parents were a bounty of the first sacrificial service performed by Adam.

"Unto Adam also and to his wife did the LORD God make coats of skins, and clothed them." (Genesis 3:21)

"To Adam, the offering of the first sacrifice was a most painful ceremony. His hand must be raised to take life, which only God could give… **As he slew the innocent victim, he trembled at the**

> **thought that his sin must shed the blood of the spotless Lamb of God. This scene gave him a deeper and more vivid sense of the greatness of his transgression...**" (Ellen G. White, *Patriarchs and Prophets,* pg. 68)

As articulated by the author, concealed within the profound recesses of Adam's heart was an unacknowledged inclination to kill the Son of God. In order that this impulse might be unveiled to Adam, and the entire human race, God *allowed* the sacrifice of an innocent animal.

As established in previous segments of this treatise, the manifestation of God's wrath or anger, biblically characterized as an intense expression of grief or sorrow, transpires when, with reluctance, He withdraws His divine presence, thereby allowing individuals to pursue the inclinations of their own hearts. In congruence with Adam's desire to deflect the repercussions of sin, perceiving them merely as arbitrary punishments from God, and transferring them onto another—an act he believed would spare him from said punishment but was, in truth, simply a manifestation of his murderous intentions toward Christ—God permitted him to perform the very act upon an innocent animal. This was designed to prompt Adam's confrontation with his innate carnal nature so that he would seek the Lord for forgiveness. With the purpose of revealing to Adam his own proclivity to inflict harm upon the Son of God, in His allowance, God sanctioned Adam to carry out the sacrifice of the animal, symbolically emblematic of Christ.

Respecting the free will of His creatures, God permitted Adam to act in accordance with the desire already present in his heart. God, however, did not wish that any one of His creatures should ever suffer death. It saddened His countenance to witness what had become of Adam through sin. He longed for His child to understand that He did not demand punishment for transgression. Adam's state had not yet reached an irreparable juncture; he could still be healed of his sinful condition. If only he would entreat the Father for mercy, he would see that nobody had to die—that sacrifice was not required to obtain God's forgiveness. Devoid of the necessity for appeasement, the blood of His beloved creatures was expended in vain. The sacrificial service was not a service required by God, nor was it esteemed by Him; instead, it was a requirement perceived by humanity in order that they could believe they were eligible to be forgiven. God merely *provides* the sacrifice; it is humanity who demands it and carries out the bloody ordeal, believing it to be what God demands. It was only used by God as a diagnostic tool, to make sin abound, that grace might much more abound.

> "For I **spake not unto your fathers, nor commanded them in the day that I brought them out of the land of Egypt, concerning burnt offerings or sacrifices:** But this thing commanded I them, saying, Obey my voice, and I will be your God, and ye shall be my people: and walk ye in all the ways that I have commanded you, that it may be well unto you." (Jeremiah 7:22-23)

The clarity of inspiration on this matter is evident. Rather than favoring sacrifice, God earnestly desires transformative shifts in the hearts and minds of His people. His preference is to see His children return to harmony with Him, rather than persisting in a cycle of death and bloodshed. And yet, how is it that so many do not understand this fact? How is it that so many can ignore such plain statements as these?

> "To do justice and judgment is **more acceptable to the LORD than sacrifice.**" (Proverbs 21:3)

> "**For I desired mercy, and not sacrifice;** and the knowledge of God more than burnt offerings." (Hosea 6:6)

> "And Samuel said, Hath the LORD as great delight in burnt offerings and sacrifices, as in obeying the voice of the LORD? Behold, **to obey is better than sacrifice,** and to hearken than the fat of rams." (I Samuel 15:22)

> "But to do good and to communicate forget not: for with such sacrifices God is well pleased." (Hebrews 13:16)

"In burnt offerings and sacrifices for sin **thou hast had no pleasure.**" (Hebrews 10:6)

"Will the LORD be pleased with thousands of rams, or with ten thousands of rivers of oil? shall I give my firstborn for my transgression, the fruit of my body for the sin of my soul? **He hath shewed thee, O man, what is good; and what doth the LORD require of thee, but to do justly, and to love mercy, and to walk humbly with thy God?**" (Micah 6:7-8)

"**For thou desirest not sacrifice;** else would I give it: **thou delightest not in burnt offering.** The sacrifices of God are a broken spirit: a broken and a contrite heart, O God, thou wilt not despise." (Psalm 51:16-17)

"But if ye had known what this meaneth, **I will have mercy, and not sacrifice, ye would not have condemned the guiltless.**" (Matthew 12:7)[3]

"**To what purpose is the multitude of your sacrifices unto me? saith the LORD:** I am full of the burnt offerings of rams, and the fat of fed beasts; and **I delight not in the blood of bullocks, or of lambs, or of he goats. When ye come to appear before me, who hath required this at your hand, to tread my courts?**" (Isaiah 1:11-12)

"And the scribe said unto him, Well, Master, thou hast said the truth: for there is one God; and there is none other but he: And to love him with all the heart, and with all the understanding, and with all the soul, and with all the strength, and to love his neighbour as himself, **is more than all whole burnt offerings and sacrifices.**" (Mark 12:32-33)

---

[3] In contemplating Christ's words in this passage, one can envision a parallel scenario wherein He engages with Adam amidst the environs of the garden, endeavoring to illuminate the inner workings of Adam's unconscious thoughts and emotions as he assigns responsibility to Eve for his transgression, thereby implicating Christ, who stands blameless. If Adam had believed God to be merciful, instead of believing Him to require sacrifice for transgression, then Adam would merely have asked for forgiveness and would not have condemned Christ to death.

The evidence is clear and convincing. To suggest that the Father requires pacification through elaborate offerings or sacrifices, as a means to secure divine forgiveness, constitutes the epitome of absurdity. The inherent absurdity of this claim is even more compounded by its fabulous origination in paganism. Nonetheless, this belief persists among contemporary Christian discourse.

> "While God has desired to teach men that from His own love comes the Gift which reconciles them to Himself, the archenemy of mankind has endeavored to represent God as one who delights in their destruction. **Thus the sacrifices and the ordinances designed of Heaven to reveal divine love have been perverted to serve as means whereby sinners have vainly hoped to propitiate, with gifts and good works, the wrath of an offended God...**" (Ellen G. White, *Prophets and Kings*, pg. 685)

> "A propitiation is a sacrifice. The statement then is simply that Christ is set forth to be a sacrifice for the remission of our sins. 'Once in the end of the world hath He appeared to put away sin by the sacrifice of Himself.' Hebrews 9:26. **Of course the idea of a propitiation or sacrifice is that there is wrath to be appeased. But take particular notice that it is we who require the sacrifice, and not God. He provides the sacrifice. The idea that God's wrath has to be propitiated in order that we may have forgiveness finds no warrant in the Bible. It is the height of absurdity to say that God is so angry with men that He will not forgive them unless something is provided to appease His wrath, and that therefore He Himself offers the gift to Himself, by which He is appeased... The heathen idea, which is too often held by professed Christians, is that men must provide a sacrifice to appease the wrath of their god.** All heathen worship is simply a bribe to their gods to be favorable to them. If they thought that their gods were very angry with them, they would provide a greater sacrifice, and so human sacrifices were offered in extreme cases [Micah 6:6-8]. They thought, as the worshipers of Siva in India do today, that their god was gratified by the sight of blood." (E. J. Waggoner, *Signs of the Times*, January 23, 1896)

The adoption of an appeasement-based theology stands as a consequential byproduct of adhering to the penal legal view. The propagated notion suggests that, in order to avert divine retribution, one must mollify God through the ritualistic bestowal of gifts and offerings—the ultimate and final offering being His own Son. This entrenched belief, premised upon the brutal act of slaying the beloved Son to secure divine favor, invites logical scrutiny. It seems inherently *illogical* to posit that such a malevolent action would evoke any compassion from the Father. And are we also to believe that God Himself offers the gift to Himself, by which He is appeased? Such a provision by God on behalf of humanity implies love, not wrath.

> "**For God so loved the world, that he gave his only begotten Son,** that whosoever believeth in him should not perish, but have everlasting life." (John 3:16)

Within the paradigm of appeasement-based theology, the circumstances of the cross are construed as a fulfillment of heaven's desires; by crucifying the Son of God, it is incorrectly assumed that humanity was actually doing *what God wanted*. The impression many receive is that God aspired for this to happen—needed it even—in order for His anger to be appeased and His justice satisfied. This conceptualization of the cross markedly distorts the entire narrative of salvation and the character of the God we worship! It presents God as the One who demands death, and the One who carries out its execution. Simultaneously, it serves to conceal from humanity the reality of our innate hostility (*enmity*) towards God and His Son inherited from the events in Eden.

> "Sometimes this idea of propitiating the wrath of God has taken an easier form,-that is, easier for the worshippers. Instead of sacrificing themselves, they have sacrificed others. **Human sacrifices have always been to a greater or lesser extent connected with heathenism.** Men shudder as they read of the human sacrifices offered by the ancient inhabitants of Mexico and Peru, and by the Druids; but professed (not real) Christianity has its

awful list. Even so-called Christian England has made hundreds of burnt offerings of men, for the purpose of turning away the wrath of God from the country. **Wherever there is religious persecution to any degree, it springs from the mistaken idea that God demands a victim.** This is shown by the words of Christ to His disciples: 'The time cometh, that whosoever killeth you will think that he doeth God service.' John 16:2. **All such worship has been devil worship, and not worship of the true God...**" (E. J. Waggoner, *The Present Truth*, vol. 9, September 21, 1893, pg. 387)

"**We said, God is doing all this; God is killing him, punishing him, to satisfy his wrath, in order to let us off. That is the pagan conception of sacrifice.** The Christian idea of sacrifice is this. Let us note the contrast. 'God so loved the world, that he gave his only begotten Son, that whosoever believes in him should not perish, but have everlasting life.' That is the Christian idea. Yes, sir. Indifference keeps, hatred keeps, selfishness keeps... But love, and love only, sacrifices, gives freely, gives itself, gives without counting the cost; gives because it is love. That is sacrifice, whether it is the sacrifice of bulls and goats, or of him who is the Lamb of God. It is the sacrifice that is revealed throughout the entire Bible. **But the pagan idea of sacrifice is just the opposite. It is that some god is always offended, always angry, and his wrath must be propitiated in some way.**" (George Fifield, *1897 General Conference Daily Bulletin Sermon Series number 1*)

Before proceeding, let us briefly review the sequence of events as they've unfolded thus far...

In the very beginning, God gave clear instructions to our first parents regarding the tree of knowledge, ensuring they were well aware of Satan's fall and the peril associated with heeding his temptations. God did not strip them of the ability to consume the forbidden fruit, however. Instead, He left them as free moral agents, with the choice to believe His word, accept His love, remain in harmony with His creation, and live; or to heed the tempter, reject His love, separate themselves from Him, and perish. Our earliest ancestors opted to trust the words, misguided as they were, of a serpent; and yet, he had given them no tokens of his love. The serpent had contributed nothing to their well-being, unlike God who had provided them with all that was nourishing and delightful to behold.

In the midst of opulence and aesthetic splendor, Adam and Eve, ensnared by the serpent's deception, fell prey to the belief that a concealed wisdom, comparable to that of God, was being deliberately withheld from them. Rather than embracing the love which God had shown them and entrusting themselves to Him, Adam and Eve regrettably cultivated a base distrust in His benevolence, opting instead to adopt the deceptive rhetoric articulated by Satan. In choosing such a course, Adam and Eve were actively severing their connection to the very Source of life. In choosing to disregard God's love and care, and instead pursue the selfish appetites of their own hearts, our first parents placed themselves on a path towards self-destruction and spiritual separation.

Their rebellion compounded, however, for after having succumbed to the serpent's deception and tasting of the forbidden fruit, Adam and Eve adopted the unfounded belief that, rather than sin carrying with it inherent consequences, it was God who meted out punishment for sin. Their understanding was that they must die for their transgression—that God's justice demanded the death of the sinner and that every sin must be severely punished. Just like their progeny, Cain, they did not believe that God was able to forgive forthright.

> "And Cain said to the Lord God, **My crime [is] too great for me to be forgiven.**" (Genesis 4:13, *LXX*)

As a result, Adam and Eve cultivated a profound fear of God, viewing Him as the ultimate cause of their impending and eternal demise. Adam, perceiving that absolution from punishment hinged upon someone being put to death, pronounced this morbid decree upon his wife, thereby indirectly implicating the Son of God as the one to be held responsible—effectively condemning

Him to death in an effort to secure the preservation of his own life. This occurrence lays bare the unpalatable attribute of selfishness within the heart of the sinner.

Given our understanding that God is not the instigator of sin's punishment, it is crucial for the reader to bear in mind that these emerging impulses and misconceptions originate solely within the heart and mind of Adam as a direct consequence of his character and judgement being tarnished by sin. Spurred by his newfound fear of God, Adam unwittingly adopted a "kill or be killed" frame of mind. In order to avoid confrontation with his deeply entrenched desire to kill Christ, Adam projected his murderous inclinations onto the character of God, casting God as the bearer of animosity and wrath rather than acknowledging these attributes within himself.

Inheriting the same nature as Adam, we, too, tend to share his belief that reconciliation hinges upon God's requirement for sacrificial bloodshed, when, in reality, it is humanity that seeks appeasement through sacrifice; it is man who is convinced of his eligibility for divine forgiveness only after he has shed the blood of the innocent; it is humankind that clamors for the necessity of the death of Christ. As Adrian Ebens once put it, in those words, "the woman whom thou gavest to be with me" (Genesis 3:12) are contained the seeds of the cry "crucify him" (Luke 23:21) that would erupt 4,000 years later.

The seed of enmity took root within Adam's heart, and the genuine implications of his actions remained hidden, even from his own recognizance. If confronted with the charge that he in fact had a deep-seated desire to bring about the death of the Son of God, Adam would have answered in a manner reminiscent of his descendants:

> "...**Why go ye about to kill me?** The people answered and said, **Thou hast a devil: who goeth about to kill thee?**" (John 7:19-20)

Adam would have categorically rejected the Son of God's diagnosis. The sole remedy for this entrenched animosity necessitated its explicit manifestation, thereby compelling humankind to repent for their inherent proclivity toward violence against the Son of God. For this purpose, the sacrificial service was permitted.

Through the sacrificial system, God was able to illustrate His unwavering love and mercy for the sinner, illuminating these truths against the backdrop of humanity's imperfect concepts of atonement. In the pursuit of mankind's acceptance of forgiveness, a sacrificial figure had to assume the burden of punishment for sin, in accordance with their perception of God's demands. Lacking this element, humanity would never have been able to envision the feasibility of divine forgiveness, clinging to the conviction that it was God who required appeasement in order to be reconciled, rather than recognizing that the opposite was true. Therefore, the sacrificial system emerged as a tangible representation of human contemplation, rather than being an accurate reflection of God's requirements for forgiveness.

> "To open their eyes, and to turn them from darkness to light, and from the power of Satan unto God, **that they may receive forgiveness of sins,** and inheritance among them which are sanctified by faith that is in me." (Acts 26:18)

As observed in the Old Testament narratives explored in the previous section, where God, in His anger (*grief*), allowed people to follow their own inclinations, thereby creating an appearance as if He was directly responsible for commanding said actions, we understand that these were, in fact, merely demonstrations of His permissive will. So it is with the sacrificial system. He undertakes this approach for a twofold purpose: firstly, to safeguard free will, and secondly, in anticipation that individuals will comprehend the malevolence of sin and its ruinous consequences. This, in turn, is envisaged to serve as a catalyst for their penitent return, beseeching Him for mercy and healing. His longing is for His children to acknowledge their need of Him and realign themselves with the principles that sustain life. Regarding the sacrificial service, He only instructed mankind in accordance with the inclinations of their own heart, so that, by doing this, He might amplify the prevalence of sin, with the ultimate purpose of magnifying the abundance of grace which He is ever ready to impart.

> "Moreover the law entered, **that the offence might abound. But where sin abounded, grace did much more abound...**" (Romans 5:20)

> **"Wherefore I gave them also [allowed them to follow] statutes that were not good, and judgments whereby they should not live...** to the end that they might know that I am the LORD [and seek me in the day of their trouble]." (Ezekiel 20:25-26)

> "I [the Lord] will go and return to my place, till they acknowledge their offence, and seek my face: **in their affliction they will seek me early.**" (Hosea 5:15)

Upon the presence of sin in one's heart, God's primary response is to convict and unveil the nature of that transgression. The human heart, susceptible to self-deception, frequently blinds itself to its own sinful nature, resorting to falsehood as a means to evade confronting its inherent carnality (Jeremiah 17:9). When we deviate from the divine will, it is within the Providence of God to permit the unfettered pursuit of human aspirations, allowing them to mature. His commands, as a result, often fall prey to misinterpretation, as individuals may wrongly attribute their own selfish and sinful desires to divine intent. In response, He must permit these human inclinations to unfold, in order to lay bare their corrupt and unfruitful consequences. Through this very same process, the sacrificial system came into being.

The doctrinal insistence upon the idea that "without the shedding of blood, there is no forgiveness" (Hebrews 9:22, *NLT*)—whether in the pre-Christian or post-Christian era—does not originate from a divine decree; rather, it is a tenet prescribed and embraced by humanity. Within this paradigm, mankind grapples with the conviction that God's forgiveness is contingent upon the presentation of a sacrificial offering. In a previous section of this volume, it was established that the allusion to blood, in the context of Hebrews 9:22, is decidedly spiritual in application. It is a metaphor signifying the embodiment of the life and character of Christ. Under no circumstance does it denote a literal necessity for God to witness blood flow in order to assuage His divine displeasure, such as the pagan gods require.

> "As Jesus came into the temple, He took in the whole scene. He saw the unfair transactions. He saw the distress of the poor, **who thought that without shedding of blood there would be no forgiveness for their sins.**" (Ellen G. White, *The Desire of Ages,* pg. 157)

On the other hand, inherent within our own fallen nature is the deep-seated longing to seek the spectacle of bloodshed; and this inclination is then projected onto the divine. In accordance with His permissive will, God affords us the liberty to engage in this sacrilegious observance, recognizing it as the singular avenue through which He could impart to us instructive revelations about His love and mercy. The symbolic act of sacrificing the animal, emblematic of the crucifixion of Christ, serves as a manifestation of the underlying enmity concealed within our hearts towards God.

All of this, that we might come to realize that He is not characterized by wrath—*we are* (Ephesians 2:3). The sacrificial system's sole purpose was to unveil the seed of enmity within our hearts, providing an opportunity for its open acknowledgment and confession. Through this process, a transformative realization emerges, prompting a repentance from the longstanding misapprehensions we harbored about God and afterward seeking to be healed of our sinful condition.

> "Every pagan religion has its sacrifice, and this sacrifice is derived from the true Sacrifice by which the world is to be redeemed, through a degeneracy from the true type of that sacrifice which

God gave to man at the gate of forfeited Eden. But Satan has brought it around so that the pagan sacrifice means just the opposite of the true. **The meaning of the true sacrifice is this: 'God so loved the world, that he gave his only begotten Son.' Every sacrifice truly offered was a revelation, an expression of that great sacrifice by which God was to give the pledge to all his intelligent creatures of all worlds that he so loved them that, if need be, he would give his life to redeem them. But the pagan sacrifice speaks of a god of wrath and anger, whose wrath must in some way be appeased, perchance by the blood of a lamb, or it may be only by the blood of a fair maid, or innocent child, or some other human victim.** When he smells the freshly flowing blood, they believe his vengeance will be satisfied, he will be propitiated.

"**What shall we say of the false idea of the atonement, held even by many in the popular Protestant churches of today, and expressed in a late confession of faith in these words, 'Christ died to reconcile the Father unto us'?** This is not the place to enter into a discussion of that theme; **suffice it to say that it is the pagan idea of sacrifice applied to Christianity.**" (George Fifield, *God is Love*, pg. 23)

If all of this seems just a little too farfetched, or off the mark, the reader would do well to ponder the following questions: who's fundamental nature was changed as a result of sin—God's or man's? Therefore, who was it that necessitated reconciliation (*restoration to unity*), and to whom? And in the conventional framework of the sacrificial system, which perspective is more prominently conveyed?—That it was God who needed to be reconciled, or man? The primary *implication* of the sacrificial system, by its mainstream interpretation, is that, before He could be reconciled to man, God needed to be appeased through sacrifices and bloodshed. Contrary to this notion, the scriptures unequivocally state that it was not God, but man who needed to be reconciled. Therefore, the traditional interpretation of the sacrificial system begs reevaluation, as it must conform to our newly acquired understanding of God's nonviolent character in order to align with the gospel message. For it to be understood in any other way, it would be a contradiction of the preceding quotations, as well as of the plain testimony of scripture; but understood thus, all is in harmony.

> "Since the announcement to the serpent in Eden, 'I will put enmity between thee and the woman, and between thy seed and her seed' (Genesis 3:15), Satan had known that he did not hold absolute sway over the world. There was seen in men the working of a power that withstood his dominion. With intense interest he watched the sacrifices offered by Adam and his sons. **In these ceremonies he discerned a symbol of communion between earth and heaven. He set himself to intercept this communion. He misrepresented God, and misinterpreted the rites that pointed to the Saviour. Men were led to fear God as one who delighted in their destruction. The sacrifices that should have revealed His love were offered only to appease His wrath.** Satan excited the evil passions of men, in order to fasten his rule upon them." (Ellen G. White, *The Desire of Ages*, pg. 115)

With this truth in mind, we now resume our exploration of the scriptural theme of reconciliation. But first, if the reader would like a more comprehensive insight into the subjects we have just discussed, the author suggests consulting the following literary works:

• *Cross Examined and Cross Encountered*, by Adrian Ebens

• *At-One-Ment; the Pathway to Complete Restoration with God*, by Adrian Ebens

• *Did God Kill Jesus Instead of Killing Us?*, by Kevin J. Mullins

> "The Lord never came to deliver men from the consequences of their sins while those sins yet remained ... Yet, feeling nothing of the dread hatefulness of their sin, **men have constantly taken this word that the Lord came to deliver us from our sins to mean that he came to save them from the punishment of their sins.**

"This idea has terribly corrupted the preaching of the Gospel. The message of the Good News has not been truly communicated... Unable to believe in the forgiveness of the Father in heaven, imagining him not at liberty to forgive, or incapable of forgiving forthright; not really believing him God who is fully our Savior, but a God bound — either in his own nature or by a law above him and compulsory upon him — to exact some recompense or satisfaction for sin, **a multitude of religious teachers have taught their fellow men that Jesus came to bear our punishment and save us from hell. But in that they have misrepresented his true mission."** (George MacDonald, *Discovering the Character of God,* Minneapolis: Bethany House, 1989, pg. 39)

"Many will object that until the demands of a broken law are satisfied, fellowship is impossible to be restored. But we must realize that God's laws are not arbitrary but are creation principles that operate on cause and effect, not by rewards and punishments imposed artificially. When this correction is installed in our logic we can begin to see more clearly how salvation and **the cross of Christ are intended to reconcile us to God, not appease an offended deity angry over broken rules...** By letting us unleash all the venom of our world's animosity against God on Jesus, He knew that the lies behind all that animosity would inevitably be exposed and would at last be discredited. **This is what was pleasing about all the evil that happened to Jesus from God's perspective, not that it would placate some pagan notion that God was furious at sinners but that sinners would come to see the lies that kept them angry and hostile towards God...** Jesus came to reveal the trustworthiness of God's heart, and because He did so in such a spectacular way He exposed all the deceptions of the enemy. He has proven that He can be trusted to represent God truthfully and consistently and that all of Satan's allegations are groundless, false and sinister. **This is the method by which God achieves victory over evil – by making Himself vulnerable instead of using His infinite power to overwhelm His enemies. By making His own soul a sacrifice to allow sin to be exposed, He defeats the power of evil and the true power of love is finally seen."**

(Floyd Phillips, *It Pleased God,* biblicalconcepts.blogspot.com, August 12, 2018)

In theological terms, the concept of reconciliation is often misunderstood. As the author has already gone through such lengths to convey, for so long mankind has committed gross error in their understanding of God's character. Imagining Him not at liberty to forgive forthright, we incorrectly cast Him as One whose attitude is spiteful towards our fallen race; that instead of seeking to heal and restore, He endeavors to punish and destroy. Consequently, our fear of Him incites our inclination to, in an effort to escape divine punishment, appease Him in some way—whether by gifts and offerings or good works. All of these are merely vain attempts at reconciling God to ourselves; fruitless efforts of persuasion to encourage a shift in His attitude toward us, as if a God of boundless love needed convincing in order to harbor sentiments of compassion for His children.

In its proper biblical context, the concept of reconciliation emphasizes that it is humanity that needs to be reconciled to God, rather than the other way around. This perspective underscores the idea that humans, due to their sinful condition, are separated from a divine and perfect God. Biblical reconciliation implies a restoration to harmony with heaven through spiritual healing and transformation. It emphasizes the role of human response in seeking a renewed connection with the divine, reflecting a proactive approach in the pursuit of spiritual unity. And God endeavors to facilitate all of this, and more, through the demonstration of His loving and nonviolent nature in the person of His Son.

> "**God does not need to be reconciled to man, for, like the mother's love, His love ever follows us, even when we are in the downward way, seeking to bring us back to Him. But man needs to be reconciled to God.** In some way there must be an atonement made. **Not that God's wrath must be satisfied, so that He will look with favor upon offending man, but that God's love must be so manifest, in spite of the existence of suffering and sin, that men**

will turn their hearts toward Him, as the flower toward the sun... **The word 'atonement' means at-one-ment. Sin had brought misery, and misery had brought a misunderstanding of God's character. Thus men had come to hate God instead of loving Him... There must be an atonement. An atonement can be made only by God so revealing his love, in spite of sin and sorrow, that men's hearts will be touched to tenderness; and they, being delivered from Satan's delusions, may see how fully and terribly they have misunderstood the divine One,** and so have done despite to the Spirit of his grace. Thus they may be led, as returning brethren, to come back to the Father's house in blissful unity. **The atonement is not to appease God's wrath so that man dare come to Him but it is to reveal His love so that they WILL come to Him. It was not Christ reconciling God unto the world, but God in Christ reconciling the world unto himself.** It is nowhere said that God needed to be reconciled unto us; he says, 'I have not forsaken you, but you have forsaken me.'" (George Fifield, *God Is Love*, pg. 66, 69-70)

Delving into the profound concept of reconciliation between God and humanity, the author defers to the instructive words of E. J. Waggoner—a prominent American Adventist evangelist, physician, and theologian. Known for his theological contributions in the early years of the Church's development, especially regarding the 1888 message of righteousness by faith, Waggoner's work serves to illuminate the intricate threads of reconciliation woven into the theological fabric, providing a lens through which we may perceive the ever-present love that God has for His children. His insights invite profound contemplation, and the author provides them here, not merely for explanatory purposes, but also to bring about a decisive conclusion to the matter of biblical reconciliation. The reader would do well to take solemn notice of his words. In his illuminating 1893 discourse, Waggoner advances the following thoughts:

"Let us now sum up the case of the relation between the natural man and God. (1) All have sinned. (2) Sin is enmity against God; it is rebellion. (3) Sin is alienation from God; men are alienated and enemies in their minds by wicked works. Colossians 1:21. (4) Sinners are 'alienated from the life of God.' Ephesians 4:18. But **God in Christ is the only source of life for the universe, and therefore all who are thus alienated from His righteous life are by the very nature of things doomed to death.** 'He that hath the Son hath life; and he that hath not the Son of God hath not life.' I John 5:12.

"**From all that has preceded it is very evident that the only object that Christ could have in coming to earth and dying for men, was the reconciliation of man to God, so that he might have life.** 'I am come that they might have life.' John 10:10. 'God was in Christ reconciling the world unto Himself.' 2 Corinthians 5:19. 'And you, that were sometime alienated and enemies in your mind by wicked works, yet now hath He reconciled in the body of His flesh through death, to present you holy and unblameable and unreproveable in His sight.' Colossians 1:21, 22. Christ suffered for sins, the just for the unjust, 'that He might bring us to God.' I Peter 3:18. 'If when we were enemies, we were reconciled to God by the death of His Son, much more, being reconciled, we shall be saved by His life.' Romans 5:10.

"'But,' someone will say, 'You have made the reconciliation all on the part of men; I have always been taught that the death of Christ reconciled God to man; that Christ died to satisfy God's justice, and to appease Him.' **Well, we have left the matter of reconciliation just where the Scriptures have put it; and while they have much to say about the necessity for man to be reconciled to God, they never once hint of such a thing as the necessity for God to be reconciled to man. To intimate the necessity for such a thing is to bring a grave charge against the character of God. The idea has come into the Christian Church from the Papacy, which in turn brought it from Paganism, in which the only idea of God was of a being whose wrath must be appeased by a sacrifice.**" (E. J. Waggoner, *The Present Truth*, vol. 9, September 21, 1893, pg. 386)

Waggoner continues…

"**Stop a moment, and think what reconciliation means. The existence of enmity is the only necessity for reconciliation. Where**

there is no enmity, there is no necessity for reconciliation. Man is by nature alienated from God; he is a rebel, full of enmity. Therefore man needs to be reconciled-to have his enmity taken away. **But God has no enmity in His being. 'God is love.' Consequently there is no necessity for Him to be reconciled; there is no possibility of such a thing, for there can be no reconciliation where there has been no enmity.**

"Again: 'For God so loved the world, that He gave His only begotten Son, that whosoever believeth in Him should not perish, but have everlasting life.' John 3:16. **Surely, they who say that the death of Christ reconciled God to men, have forgotten this blessed text. They would separate the Father and the Son, making the former the enemy, and the latter the friend, of man.** But God's heart was so overflowing with love to fallen man, that He 'spared not His own Son, but delivered Him up for us all;' and in so doing He gave Himself, for 'God was in Christ reconciling the world unto Himself.' The Apostle Paul speaks of 'the church of God, which He hath purchased with His own blood.' Acts 20:28. This effectually disposes of the idea that there was any enmity toward man on the part of God, so that He needed to be reconciled. **The death of Christ was the expression of God's wonderful love for sinners.**" (E. J. Waggoner, *The Present Truth*, vol. 9, September 21, 1893, pg. 386)

"Why have we dwelt so long upon the fact that man must be reconciled to God, and not God to man?

"**Because in that alone is man's hope.** If God ever had any enmity in His heart against men, there would always arise the torturing thought, 'Perhaps He is not yet sufficiently appeased to accept Me; surely He cannot love so guilty a being as I am.' And the more one realised his guilt, the greater would be his doubt. But **when we know that God never had any enmity towards us, but that He has loved us with an everlasting love, and that He has loved us so much that He gave Himself for us, that we might be reconciled to Him, we can joyfully exclaim, 'If God be for us, who can be against us?'.**" (E. J. Waggoner, *The Present Truth*, vol. 9, September 21, 1893, pg. 387)

Waggoner concludes by saying:

> "The case, therefore, stands thus: All have sinned. Sin is enmity against God, because it is a condition of alienation from the life of God. Therefore sin is death. **The one thing, then, that man stood in need of was life, and this is the one thing that Christ came to give.** In Him was life that sin could not touch, and that could triumph over death. His life is the light of men… **Christ came to impart the life of God to man, for it is that which they lack.** The lives of all the angels in heaven could not have met the demands of the case; not because God was so inexorable, but because they could not have imparted any life to man. They had no life in themselves, but only the life that Christ imparted to them. But **God was in Christ, and in Him God's everlasting life could be given to everyone who would receive it. Remember that in giving His Son, God gave Himself, and you will see that a sacrifice was not demanded to satisfy God's outraged feelings, but that, on the contrary, God's inexpressible love led Him to sacrifice Himself, in order to break down man's enmity, and reconcile us to Himself…**" (E. J. Waggoner, *The Present Truth,* vol. 9, September 21, 1893, pg. 388)

What boundless love! What an immense display of divine affection! As Waggoner expressed: in giving His Son, God gave Himself. This statement rightly conveys that the sacrificial death of Christ could not have been for the purpose of satisfying the divine wrath of the Father, for this would, in turn, indicate that it was undertaken to effectuate the reconciliation of God to humanity—a notion that diverges significantly from the biblical narrative. Instead, the principal aim of Christ's death was the reconciliation of humanity to God, serving to address our unconscious need for appeasement and instilling in us the conviction that we could be forgiven.

> "**The true idea of the atonement makes God and Christ equal in their love, and one in their purpose of saving humanity.** 'God was in Christ, reconciling the world unto himself.' **The life of Christ was not the price paid to the Father for our pardon; but that life was the price which the Father paid to so manifest his loving**

> **power as to bring us to that repentant attitude of mind where he could pardon us freely.**" (George Fifield, *God is Love*, pg. 24)

And yet, this stands as just one of the reasons necessitating Christ's death. Although a significant motif of the cross pertains to reconciliation, this does not inherently equate to salvation, for reconciliation is merely the *beginning* of the work of atonement.

> "In the one sacrifice of Christ, all the daily sacrifices, and the sacrifices of all the yearly atonement days, found their complete fulfillment. Christ was offered 'once for all.' **But since in the figure the atonement was not made when the offering was slain, but was made with his blood [life] afterwards, so it must be in the reality. The death of the offered victim was only the preparation for the atonement; it furnished the means by which the atonement could be made...** We cannot here go into the particulars of the atonement, but can merely show that **the atonement was only begun and was not completed on the cross.**" (E. J. Waggoner, *Signs of the Times*, June 15, 1888)

For the object of atonement to be gained, the entrenched condition of sin necessitated overcoming, and humanity lacked the inherent capacity for such a feat without divine aid. Beyond an understanding of God's true character, what was required for mankind's salvation was a remedy for sin's morbid and inexorable influence. The world, lost in sin and separated from God, needed more than to have God revealed, and the right way to Him pointed out. This alone would have left man longing but impotent. This is why the moral influence theory of atonement fails at fully articulating the reason for Christ's sacrificial death. What we stood in need of, along with these things, was the power of God in us. That power, Christ imparts to everyone who has faith. This source of power must be revealed before the atonement could be made; for men, to be made one with God and one with each other, must be enabled, in spite of sin, to walk in the paths of righteousness.

Here is presented the twofold purpose of Christ's sacrifice and its redemptive effect upon the sinner: firstly, it sought to reestablish humanity's trust in God (*reconciliation*), thereby facilitating the sinner's willing acceptance of His restorative agency. This pursuit could only be realized through a dual imperative. (1) There existed a necessity for a conspicuous demonstration of God's selfless love and nonviolent character. This was achieved through Christ's life, ministry, and ultimate sacrifice, where He unveiled to fallen humanity the love and splendor of the Father in heaven.

> "**The knowledge of God as revealed in Christ is the knowledge that all who are saved must have. This is the knowledge that works transformation of character.** Received into the life, it will re-create the soul in the image of Christ. This is the knowledge that God invites His children to receive, beside which all else is vanity and nothingness." (Ellen G. White, *Acts of the Apostles,* pg. 475)

Simultaneously, (2) humanity required a revelation of their own intrinsic carnality and the enmity which they bore against their Creator, thus conceding to their need for a remedial endeavor. This revelation ultimately unfolded during Christ's crucifixion, laying bare mankind's profound propensity towards rebellion and exposing it for all of creation to comprehend. Recognizing their complicity in the murder of the Son of God, coupled with an acknowledgement of the dichotomy that exists between their nature and the Father's, the sinner is induced to repent of the enmity harbored within their heart and turn to God for healing, *where they are at once reconciled.*

> "For if, **when we were enemies, we were reconciled to God by the death of his Son,** much more, **being reconciled, we shall be saved by his life.**" (Romans 5:10)

This brings us to the second purpose of Christ's death: life. Due to humanity's legacy from Adam, our sinful state was inherently terminal in nature, for we "were dead in trespasses and sins" (Ephesians 2:1). Destined for the eternal embrace of death by way of sin, what man stood in need of was life by way of righteousness. Eternal life, the only remedy for eternal death, was what Christ came to impart to all who have faith. He assumed, *as the substitute for humanity*, our sin, enabling us to freely share in His righteousness. It is in this sense that He suffered death, that we "might have life" (John 10:10).

> "That as **sin hath reigned unto death,** even so might **grace reign through righteousness unto eternal life** by Jesus Christ our Lord." (Romans 5:21)

> "**...Himself took our infirmities,** and bare our sicknesses." (Matthew 8:17)

> "'For as the Father hath life in himself; so hath he given to the Son to have life in himself.' [John 5:26]. **Christ, then, being the only begotten Son of God, partakes of his attributes, and has life in himself. That is, he is able to impart life to others.**" (Ellen G. White, *Signs of the Times,* September 4, 1884, pg. 538)

In Christ alone is the remedy for our sinful condition. From the throne of grace comes the most precious gift of salvation, and this gift is ours to keep. "Christ hath redeemed us from the curse of the law" (Galatians 3:13)—from sin and death. This He did by "being made a curse for us" (Galatians 3:13), and so we are freed from all necessity of sinning. If anyone has not this blessing, it is because he has not recognized the gift, or has deliberately thrown it away. Sin can have no dominion over us if we accept Christ in truth and without reserve. "For we which have believed do enter into rest," because the "works were finished from the foundation of the world" (Hebrews 4:3). It is a full and complete salvation that God has provided. It awaits us as we come into the world. And we do not relieve God of any burden by rejecting it, nor do we add to His labor by accepting it. Those who accept Christ's glorious deliverance from the curse of the law—deliverance not from obedience to the law, for obedience is not a curse, but from *disobedience* to the law—have in the Spirit a taste of the power and the blessing of the world to come. All this power is given into His hands, that He may dispense the blessed gift unto men, imparting His own righteousness to the helpless human agent. As He said to the storm-tossed sea, so to the passion-tossed soul

Jesus waits, and waits in love, to say, "Peace, be still." The merits of Christ's own character are bestowed upon His people by faith, and faith alone. *This* is righteousness by faith.

> "The Bible does not say that God punished the human race for one man's sin, but that the nature of sin, namely, my claim to my right to myself, entered into the human race through one man. But it also says that another Man took upon Himself the sin of the human race and put it away — an infinitely more profound revelation... **Sin is something I am born with and cannot touch—only God touches sin through redemption. It is through the Cross of Christ that God redeemed the entire human race from the possibility of damnation through the heredity of sin. God nowhere holds a person responsible for having the heredity of sin, and does not condemn anyone because of it. Condemnation comes when I realize that Jesus Christ came to deliver me from this heredity of sin, and yet I refuse to let Him do so.** From that moment I begin to get the seal of damnation. 'This is the condemnation [and the critical moment], that the light has come into the world, and men loved darkness rather than light...' (John 3:19)." (Oswald Chambers, *My Utmost for His Highest*, http://utmost.org)

> "When your condition was terminal, when selfishness reigned unchecked in your minds, and when your hearts were tied to the destructive cravings and practices of the world, God intervened and brought you the life-giving Remedy—Jesus Christ. He reclaimed you from your terminal condition, nullifying the pathology report that certified you as dead in sin; he made it clear that the written code [the law], with its regulations, was only a diagnostic instrument designed to expose our terminal state and teach us the need for a true cure... Through his death, he revealed the truth about God and—in his humanity—eradicated selfishness, thus he completely destroyed Satan's weapons of lies and selfishness, and triumphed over Satan at the cross." (Colossians 3:13-15, *The Remedy Bible*)

While the author fervently contests the heretical doctrine of penal substitutionary atonement, the biblical legitimacy and credibility of Christ's substitutionary role nonetheless endures, albeit in a markedly distinct sense from the implications of the penal legal perspective. In his 1978 book, *The Death of Christ*, Fisher Humphreys conceded that there could be a more proper understanding of substitutionary atonement, but he emphatically denied that the Father punished the Son for our sins on the cross. In his words:

> "Men punished him for alleged crimes, probably blasphemy and revolution, but God, who knew he was righteous, did not disapprove of him at all; he approved of him. To put it another way, **Jesus experienced the pain which a man might feel if he were being punished by God for great sins, but he was not punished by God.**" (http://www.albertmohler.com/2013/08/12/the-wrath-of-god-was-satisfied-substitutionar-atonement-and-the-conservative-resurgence-in-the-southern-baptist-convention/)

Although Humphreys rightly states that God did *not* initiate punishment upon Christ, he neglects to address the nuances of *how* precisely Christ functions as our substitute. The context of His substitutionary death departs from the prevalent notions of penal substitution, instead finding closer resonance with what the author refers to as *transplant substitutionary atonement*. This theory of atonement suggests a spiritual transplantation where Christ substitutes our spiritual condition with His own, akin to the idea of a transplant replacing one organ with another. Within this framework, the focus would be on Christ's substitution leading to a profound change or renewal in our spiritual state. He prompts this transformation, and takes upon Himself our burdens, permeating our very being and identifying Himself so fully with us that it is "not I, but Christ" that "liveth in me" (Galatians 2:20). In doing so, He effectively and progressively restores us to an authentic state of righteousness, as opposed to a mere superficial or forensic proclamation of "righteousness so-called" that is typically striven for by those who adhere to a penal legal view.

> "All true obedience comes from the heart. It was heart work with Christ. **And if we consent, He will so identify Himself with our**

thoughts and aims, so blend our hearts and minds into conformity to His will, that when obeying Him we shall be but carrying out our own impulses. The will, refined and sanctified, will find its highest delight in doing His service. When we know God as it is our privilege to know Him, our life will be a life of continual obedience. Through an appreciation of the character of Christ, through communion with God, sin will become hateful to us." (Ellen G. White, *The Desire of Ages,* pg. 668)

Undoubtedly, it becomes apparent that Christ's role as our substitute diverges from an elementary understanding wherein the Father inflicts arbitrary punishment upon Him in our stead. Indeed, the nature of Christ's substitutionary death must be recognized as something much more profound. What is more accurate, is that *He became sin for us, in order that we might be made the righteousness of God in Him.*

"**For he hath made him to be sin for us,** who knew no sin; **that we might be made the righteousness of God in him.**" (2 Corinthians 5:21)

He shouldered our wretched condition, imputing to us the essence of His own righteousness and supplying fallen humanity with the remedial agency of His character. It is in this transcendent capacity that Christ functions as our consummate substitute and Savior.

"Being born of a woman, Christ was necessarily born under the law, for such is the condition of all mankind, and 'in all things it behooved Him to be made like unto His brethren, that He might be a merciful and faithful High Priest in things pertaining to God, to make reconciliation for the sins of the people.' Hebrews 2:17. He takes everything on Himself. 'He hath borne our griefs, and carried our sorrows.' 'Himself took our infirmities, and bare our disease.' Matthew 8:17, R.V. 'All we like sheep have gone astray; we have turned every one to his own way; and the Lord hath laid on Him the iniquity of us all.' **He redeems us by coming into our place literally, and taking our load off our shoulders. 'Him who knew no sin He made to be sin on our behalf; that we might become the righteousness of God in Him.' 2 Corinthians 5:21,**

R.V. In the fullest sense of the word, and to a degree that is seldom thought of when the expression is used, He became man's substitute. That is, He permeates our being, identifying Himself so fully with us that everything that touches or affects us touches and affects Him. He is not our substitute in the sense that one man is a substitute for another, in the army, for instance, the substitute being in one place, while the one for whom he is substitute is somewhere else, engaged in some other service. No; Christ's substitution is far different. **He is our substitute in that He substitutes Himself for us, and we appear no more. We drop out entirely, so that it is 'not I, but Christ.' Thus we cast our cares on Him, not by picking them up and with an effort throwing them on Him, but by humbling ourselves into the nothingness that we are, so that we leave the burden resting on Him alone...**" (E. J. Waggoner, *The Present Truth,* vol. 13, March 31, 1897, pg. 197)

Final Remarks

In concluding these chapters, the author would express his overpowering sense of the weakness and incapacity of the human mind to comprehend, and of human language to reveal, the wisdom which is unsearchable, and the love "which passeth knowledge" (Ephesians 3:19). There are many who are troubled with constant doubts of God's love for them, and of their acceptance with Him. They fail to see Love's hand in God's dealings with the world, and, worse still, they fail to see this hand in His dealings with them in their own lives. The conclusions drawn in this work have sought to reveal much of God's love, even among instances in scripture where His love could not be readily discerned without careful study. Regrettably, instead of embracing beautiful truths such as these that have been expressed by certain pioneers of our faith, contemporary Adventists have steadfastly rejected them—even working to undermine them by haughty criticism and censure. In denying truth, one naturally adopts falsehoods; the light that shines forth from Calvary becomes impeded, shunned, and eventually undiscerned entirely. A penal legal interpretation of the atonement is preferred among the ranks of God's workmen, as it soothes us in one of two directions: (1) it allows a covering of righteousness for those who perceive the standard of true righteousness to be overbearing and loathsome, or (2) it allows us to depend upon our own works, decide how *we* want to serve God, and justify ourselves—two sides of the same coin.

> "**What they desire is a method of forgetting God which shall pass as a method of remembering Him. The papacy is well adapted to meet the wants of all these.** It is prepared for two classes of mankind, embracing nearly the whole world—**those who would be saved by their merits, and those who would be saved in their sins.** Here is a secret of its power." (Ellen G. White, *The Great Controversy*, pg. 572)

The way in which the Lord led the Advent pioneers who came before us away from penal substitution and appeasement-based theology has been lost and forgotten. The Church has decided to interpret its own history in a manner where our preconceived ideas aren't challenged. A new path has been forged, wayward as it might be, and the contemporary Church has adopted certain doctrines which commit gross injustices against the character of God.

> "We have nothing to fear for the future, except as we shall forget the way the Lord has led us, and His teaching in our past history..." (Ellen G. White, *Christian Experience and Teachings*, pg. 204)

Contained within recent publications, a discernible departure from the plain statements of scripture regarding who necessitated reconciliation is evident, signaling a noteworthy shift in the Church's perspective. Among these literary compositions is enshrined the doctrine of penal substitutionary atonement as a fundamental tenet of Adventist belief. In the book, *Seventh-day Adventists Believe; A Biblical Exposition of 27 Fundamental Doctrines*, published in 1988, the following ideas are expressed:

> "**For a loving God to maintain His justice and righteousness, the atoning death of Jesus Christ became a moral and legal necessity.** God's justice requires that sin be carried to judgment. **God must therefore execute judgment on sin and thus on the sinner. In this execution the Son of God took our place, the sinner's place, according to God's will.**" (*Seventh-day Adventists Believe*, pg. 111)

> "**Persons unwilling to accept the atoning blood of Christ receive no forgiveness of sin, and are still subject to God's wrath...** Christ's self-sacrifice is pleasing to God because **this sacrificial offering took away the barrier between God and sinful man in that Christ fully bore God's wrath** on man's sin. **Through Christ, God's wrath is not turned into love but is turned away from man and borne by Himself.**" (*Seventh-day Adventists Believe*, pg. 111)

This account of the circumstances surrounding Christ's sacrificial death dismisses the sentiments expressed by some of the founding figures of our faith. The plain teachings of scripture on this matter, dutifully embraced and upheld by many of our pioneers, become distorted by a framework of punitive justice and legality. The love of God is misconstrued as being contingent upon the actions and performance of the individual—ultimately reduced to a mere conditional reward that hinges solely upon what an individual does or achieves. This characterization deviates from the intrinsic nature of love itself. Divine love, being so much more abundant and profound than what mortal man himself can fathom, may only be rightly represented as an unrestricted and perpetual affection, regardless of man's state or condition.

Moreover, such expressions as articulated in the aforementioned work erroneously posit that it is God's wrath, *not the condition of sin*, which forms the insurmountable obstacle separating humanity from the sublime expanse of heaven. This exposition of doctrine is not only in conflict with the teachings of the Bible, but also at variance with the foundational principles espoused by the forerunners of the Advent movement.

> "**To break down the barrier that Satan had erected between God and man, Christ made a full and complete sacrifice,** revealing unexampled self-denial. He revealed to the world the amazing spectacle of God living in human flesh, and sacrificing Himself to save fallen men. **What wonderful love!**" (Ellen G. White, *Signs of the Times,* September 24, 1902)

Now is the time for the people of God to dispel the falsehoods and misconceptions that only serve to intensify the divide between heaven and earth—the penal legal view standing out as the foremost among them. Before concluding this treatise, it is necessary to succinctly underscore the notable disparities between the penal legal view and the framework termed "natural law" which has been tediously delineated throughout the pages of this volume.

• Within the paradigm of penal legal theory, God is constrained by a legal obligation to mete out punishment for transgressions, thereby satisfying divine justice. In contrast, in the author's doctrinal stance, it is posited that God is duty-bound to affect the salvation of sinners as an imperative for upholding true divine justice.

• In the context of penal legal theory, Jesus' death is construed as the payment of a legal penalty—bearing the sins of humanity, enduring the punishment, and facing the Father's wrath; a "ransom" if you will.[4] In contrast, according to the view presented herein, Jesus' death serves as the remedy for humanity, effectively addressing and resolving the issue of sin in man.

• Under the penal legal view, God killed Jesus in our place in order for His wrath to be appeased (*paganism*); God needed to be reconciled to man. Under natural law, "God so loved the world that He gave His only begotten Son" to be mankind's Savior (John 3:16); man needed to be reconciled to God (Romans 5:10; 2 Corinthians 5:18-19; Colossians 1:21).

• Within the framework of penal legalism, salvation is characterized as the claiming of a legal pardon through the literal blood of Jesus, aimed at averting the Father's wrath and rectifying one's celestial records. In accordance with natural law, salvation

---

[4] As a response to sentiments surrounding the text in Matthew 20:28, wherein it states that "the Son of man came... to give his life [as] a ransom for many"—it is suggested, by numerous individuals, that this is evidence of penal substitution, and that Christ paid the ransom to the Father in order to free us from the punishment for transgression. The ransom, under this framework, would be Christ's blood. But the author would pose the question: is it the Father whose children have been kidnapped that requires a ransom in order to receive them back?—Or does the kidnapper require the ransom? To take this illustration even further; what if the children develop Stockholm syndrome, and they believe the words of their kidnapper over the words of their Father? Would the children, then, also require the ransom be paid before they could believe that their actual Father indeed loved them and wanted to effectuate their return to Him?

involves acknowledging the truth revealed by Jesus about God, entrusting one's heart to Him, and consequently receiving a new heart and a righteous spirit that He graciously imparts to the believer. This transformative process results in a rebirth—a regeneration into godliness. Within this framework, righteousness is obtained by faith.

• Within the context of penal legalism, the atonement is reduced to a legal transaction, whereby one is pronounced righteous despite an inherent lack of righteousness. Within the paradigm of natural law, the journey of atonement commences with reconciliation and finds its culmination in the individual being restored to perfect harmony with God, orchestrated by the transformative agency of Christ within the innermost facets of the sinner's heart and mind; "at-one-ment."

• Under the penal legal view, the essence of the gospel lies in Jesus' death to appease God's wrath and expiate our sins. Nevertheless, under this framework, the Father remains obligated to inflict death upon us should we neglect to transfer all our sins, whether known or unknown, onto Christ. Within the scope of natural law, the gospel heralds that God diverges significantly from the misrepresentations and distortions propagated by Satan, and asserts that His law lacks tyrannical imposition. Punishment is not arbitrarily inflicted by God, as sin carries with it inherent consequences. God, in His love for humanity, does not condemn us for the sinful nature which we inherited from Adam, opting instead for a redemptive stance, actively engaging in our salvation. As a token of the Father's love, Jesus was appointed as the remedy, entrusted with the restoration of our primordial condition and our deliverance from the profound and perilous repercussions of sin.

• Within the paradigm of penal legalism, the gospel message undergoes distortion, being relegated to a legalistic realm focused on meticulous adherence to rules, sectarian distinctions, and the precise applications of blood, etc. In the context of natural law, the final message of mercy is centered upon God's character of love and nonviolence, captivating our trust and establishing His law and character in their rightful place: within the hearts and minds of humanity (Jeremiah 31:33; Hebrews 8:10). This doctrinal understanding of Jesus, the Father, and the plan of redemption is present truth for every generation.

To suppose that any amount of credibility may be attached to penal legalism and the doctrine of penal substitutionary atonement constitutes a weighty indictment against the character of God. By adhering to such theories, the people of God persist in a juvenile comprehension of their Creator, exhibiting a preference for spiritual infancy—a favor of milk over meat. The appointed laborers in God's service must now mature and advance toward the pinnacle of Christ's complete stature, attaining an understanding of the loving and nonviolent disposition of the Father in heaven, and dismissing any influence which aims to perpetuate a distorted image of God.

> "**This will continue until we all come to such unity in our faith and knowledge of God's Son that we will be mature in the Lord, measuring up to the full and complete standard of Christ.** Then we will no longer be immature like children. We won't be tossed and blown about by every wind of new teaching. **We will not be influenced when people try to trick us with lies so clever they sound like the truth.**" (Ephesians 4:13-14, *NLT*)

And if we err by the conclusions drawn in this treatise, and the author has taught that God is more loving than He really is, then I beg of you to show me my error, for "God is love" (1 John 4:8), and I cannot get around the wonderful truth of this verse in letting it dictate all that I conceive of the Almighty God.

Dear reader, this is the work which we now face. Let us pray for one another, that the work may be done diligently, according to the Lord's standards, and that His character of selfless love and nonviolence may be plainly seen, and His glory manifested, in the words and deeds of those who go about to share this final message of mercy with the world. Just as the Father sent His Son, so too does He send you and me, not to condemn the world, but that it might be saved through the demonstration of what He Himself has wrought in each of us.

Even so, come, Lord Jesus. Amen.

> "The last rays of merciful light, **the last message of mercy to be given to the world, is a revelation of His character of love.** The children of God are to manifest His glory. **In their own life and character they are to reveal what the grace of God has done for them.**" (Ellen G. White, *Christ's Object Lessons,* pg. 415)

"Weary soul, why not come to him and confess your sin, and accept the comfort and the consolation of his love? Why stay away because of fear? Why fancy longer that he loves you only when you may chance to feel yourself that you have done well and nobly? Why think that days of penance and weeping are necessary after you have sinned before he will receive you?

"Even now his arms are open for you. Even now the Saviour knocks at the door of your heart. Does the mother love the boy only when he is good, and forget and hate him when he is wayward? Does not her love cling to him ever, tenderer still in the darkest hour of his sin? Is it not the cord to draw him back to virtue and to joy?

"So does not the goodness of God lead thee even now to repentance [Romans 2:4]? Dost not thou hear him say to thee, 'The mother may forget the child, but I will not forget thee' [Isaiah 49:15]? O that we might ever realize that we are his children, and that he made us for the joy of loving us and of having us love him; and that, while self-exiled, feeding on the swine's husks of earthly hopes and pleasures, he mourns us as his children still, though lost, ever holding himself ready to run and meet us a long way off on our return, and greet us with kisses of joy?

"To realize this is to know God, and to know him is to love him, and this is life eternal."

(George Fifield, God is Love, pg. 29-30)

Figure 2

Figure 2 shows a steel-plate engraving titled, "The Way of Life," by Thomas Moran, one of America's foremost landscape artists. The engraving was commissioned by James White in 1880 and completed in 1883 following James' death. The illustration marks a progression from previous iterations—specifically the 1873 and 1876 designs—and reflected a change in James White's emphasis on his gospel interpretation; namely, that Christ, not the law, is the center of the plan of salvation.

The Three Angels' Messages

"And I saw another angel fly in the midst of heaven, having the everlasting gospel to preach unto them that dwell on the earth, and to every nation, and kindred, and tongue, and people, Saying with a loud voice, Fear God, and give glory to him; for the hour of his judgment is come: and worship him that made heaven, and earth, and the sea, and the fountains of waters. And there followed another angel, saying, Babylon is fallen, is fallen, that great city, because she made all nations drink of the wine of the wrath of her fornication. And the third angel followed them, saying with a loud voice, If any man worship the beast and his image, and receive his mark in his forehead, or in his hand, The same shall drink of the wine of the wrath of God, which is poured out without mixture into the cup of his indignation; and he shall be tormented with fire and brimstone in the presence of the holy angels, and in the presence of the Lamb: And the smoke of their torment ascendeth up for ever and ever: and they have no rest day nor night, who worship the beast and his image, and whosoever receiveth the mark of his name. Here is the patience of the saints: here are they that keep the commandments of God, and the faith of Jesus."

(Revelation 14:6-12)

www.ingramcontent.com/pod-product-compliance
Lightning Source LLC
LaVergne TN
LVHW041314080426
835513LV00008B/452

9798218385446